LOVED AND UNLOVED
The Girl Child in the Family

कन्याप्येवं पालनीया शिक्षणीयातियत्नतः

— *मनुसम्हिता*

(And even the girl child should be nurtured
and educated with care)

— *Manusamhita*

LOVED AND UNLOVED
The Girl Child in the Family

Jasodhara Bagchi, Jaba Guha
and Piyali Sengupta
School of Women's Studies, Jadavpur University

Loved and Unloved: The Girl Child in the Family
was first published in September 1997 by
Stree, 16 Southern Avenue, Calcutta 700 026

© 1997 by Stree
ISBN 81-85604-20-7

Distributed by
Bhatkal Books International
Mumbai, Calcutta, Delhi, Pune

Typesetting and design by
LOGS, 6 Ram Hari Mistri Lane, Calcutta 700 013
and printed by Webimpressions (India) Pvt Ltd,
34/2 Beadon Street, Calcutta 700 006

Published by Mandira Sen for STREE, an imprint of
Bhatkal and Sen, 16 Southern Avenue, Calcutta 700 026

To the girl child of the future

CONTENTS

PREFACE

Our purpose is to focus on the precarious existence of the girl child in the family. She remains a drudge, is kept illiterate, fed inadequately and married off early in order to maintain the family's status as well as to provide for its future. Fifty years of independence have not been enough to guarantee the natural claim to childhood for most of our girl children. The girl child is caught in a complex social process which, in a sense, 'naturalizes' her deprivation. The book attempts to study her situation within her family and is published with the hope that she will cease to be the endangered sex and that her future will become secure.

Traditionally, the family has been viewed as a supportive and protective institution, especially for girls. We have critically examined such a deeply entrenched but grievously mistaken view. Questions of gender-based discrimination within the family have been addressed, and possible areas requiring intervention have been discussed, revealing the retrogressive forces that operate, within and outside the family, in restricting the opportunities and choices available to the girl child (and hence to the woman). We find that very little is known about these matters.

The first time the girl child received a special focus was the decision by the SAARC countries to declare 1990 as the Year of the Girl Child, thus drawing attention to the particular problems she faced in this part of the world. In response to this declaration, the Department of Women and Child Development, Ministry of Human Resource Development, Government of India, sponsored a national project on the Girl Child and the Family. The study was carried out simultaneously by twenty-two of the UGC sponsored centres of women's studies located in different regions of India. It was co-ordinated by a central co-ordination committee. The aim was to make it possible to observe not only the special characteristics of the situation and problems of the girl child in each separate area, but also to bring to our notice the common features that emerged from the study, so as to provide an overall picture of the condition of the girl child in our country. It was a survey-based, collaborative, research-cum-action project which aimed at generating comparative data on a set of parameters relevant to the condition of the girl child. At the same time, each individual centre remained free to investigate additional problems specific to the region concerned. We have used the data from the survey to illustrate our arguments in the book. It is interesting to note that because of the gravity of the crisis the girl child faced, the SAARC countries have extended the time-frame, declaring the period up to 2000 to be the Decade of the Girl Child.

The study of the girl child in her family environment was expected to help to reduce the gaps in our understanding of the situation, and hence improve our planning and execution of related programmes. Since the problems call out for intervention, academic research and action programmes must necessarily go hand-in-hand if the exercise was to be at all meaningful. This was the rationale and background of the national project titled 'The Girl Child and the Family'.

In West Bengal, the School of Women's Studies, Jadavpur University, was entrusted with this work. A primary survey of 600 sample households was carried out in selected areas of the state. The target group consisted of girls in the age group of 7-18 years. The sampling methodology and questionnaire were formulated by the Central Co-ordination Committee and used by all the twenty-two centres involved in the project. Information was collected not only about the girl herself, but also about the household she lived in, her family background and the perceptions of her mother.

Jasodhara Bagchi has written the short survey of relevant literature as well as a historical analysis of the evolution of the problematic of the girl child in Bengal (Chapters 1 and 2). Chapter 1,'The Bengali Girl Child', places her in the historical setting, tracing the social construction of the girl child through the processes of social change that characterized the colonial period in Bengal. Working our way through the maze of debates, discussions and representations that feature the girl child in this historical phase, we see the anxieties of the newly emerging elite class (popularly known as the *bhadralok*). The social deprivation of the girl child was articulated mostly along the lines of her legal and marital status, negotiating several religious orthodoxies to make room for a school-going, game-playing girl child. So much has the dominant class taken the girl child for granted that we thought it would be salutary to remind ourselves of the prolonged struggle that went into the appearance of the 'girl child', as distinct from 'woman' on the Bengal social scene. Our epigraph (pii) is from the *Manusamhita* that exhorts that the girl child be nurtured and educated. Vidyasagar had these words carved on the carriages that ferried girls to Bethune School.

The second chapter analyses, not exhaustively, but through select examples, the treatment of the girl child after independence. The secondary material covered dates from 1974, when, due to the appearance of the Status Committee Report and the UN Decade of Women, there is a leap in the quantum of writing on women. The writings that we have surveyed, mediated as they are with the developmental perspective, show a distinct shift in the class component. The girl child of the dominant class no longer occupies the centre stage. The discussions and debates now focus on the poorer deprived sections of society. What is emphasized is the threat that society poses against itself in putting severe constraints on the resources of survival that remain accessible to the majority of the girl children among the rural and urban poor. Ironically, both among the elite in its formative years and the labouring poor today, it is the family that colludes with the various ideological and economic apparatuses to deprive the girl of her legitimate childhood.

A preliminary analysis of the survey results prepared by Jaba Guha and Piyali Sengupta follows (Chapters 3-7). Chapter 3 gives the particulars of the sample chosen for this study. The first part of this chapter describes in detail the sampling technique, the sample size, and the selection of households for survey. The second part provides information about the six areas that were chosen for investigation. These area profiles describe the physical features of the regions, their demographic characteristics and the facilities available to the people living in these areas. Because we wished to investigate and observe the status and condition of the girl child within the family, information about the household and the family was therefore considered to be vitally important. The family environment is of tremendous significance in the life of a child—whether a girl or a boy. The living conditions within the households, the socioeconomic status of the families, the cultural background of the communities, parental attitudes, and so on, are all determinants of her/his physical and emotional well-being as well as of the opportunities available. These also play an important role in shaping a child's ideas and perceptions. Chapter 4 discusses the condition, the attitude and the perception of the mother of the girl child who plays such a crucial role in her nurturing. This chapter, too, has been divided into two parts. The first part describes the kind of household that the girl child comes from. It gives details about the physical environment that she lives in, the family's economic standing and its members, including the father of the girl child, who is usually the head of the household.

The second part of Chapter 4 provides information about various aspects of the life of the mother (widely acknowledged as the primary influence on her daughter), her perceptions about her children in general and of her daughters in particular. Chapter 5 is about the girl child herself. Four aspects of her life have been studied in detail, and data about her health, her educational status, her work and her socialization process are presented.

Statistical data often fail to reveal the subtle nuances of the lives of the girl children observed during the survey. Individual case studies may yield more effective and meaningful insight in such matters and may help to bring into sharper focus some of the problems and possibilities of the girl child. Chapter 6 presents individual profiles of selected girl children. These profiles contain details about the lives of the girl children, their daily activities, their perceptions, hopes, ambitions and prospects. Not only do these case studies give information about the girl children themselves, but these also highlight the ideas and opinions of their mothers and other family members. This shows the extent to which the personality and views of the girl child, as also the opportunities she gets, are influenced by the attitudes and status of her mother, and also indicates whether attitudes have changed perceptibly from one generation to another.

Chapter 7 describes briefly the action programmes organized by the investigators in two of the areas surveyed. The first was a teaching-cum-learning experience in Kustia village of South 24-Parganas, and the other was an awareness-generation programme in Phulmalancha village of the same district. The findings are discussed in the Conclusion.

As the Conclusion suggests, because of the constraints of time and resources, we have not been able to carry out a satisfactorily structured and detailed analysis of the data collected through this survey. The discussion presented is based on aggregative simple averages and is, therefore, limited in scope and content. We can perceive the emergence of certain broad features, and insight has been obtained about some areas of interest requiring more in-depth study, and we hope to use the survey material for further research.

It hardly needs mentioning that a work of this nature would not have been possible without initiative, cooperation and help from a number of sources. First, our sincere thanks to the Department of Women and Child Develpment, Ministry of Human Resource Development, Government of India, for sponsoring and funding the project. We also express our gratitude to S. K. Sen, the then vice-chancellor of Jadavpur University, who gave us active help and support while the work was in progress. We would like to thank the Central Co-ordination Committee, specially S. Anandalakshmy (convenor), Vina Mazumdar and Maithreyi Krishnaraj for monitoring the project through guidelines and workshops; Dr. Nijhawan of the ICSSR and Susheela Kaushik for their painstaking help in processing the data.

The research investigators and the coding and tabulation teams worked beyond their stipulated time to make the project a success. Chandreyee Niyogi took part in a pilot survey and translated into Bengali the original English questionnaries supplied by the Central Co-ordination Committee. The initial search for the locale from census data was conducted by Dr. Baby Das, Chandreyee Niyogi, Sarmistha Deb, Ishita Chakrabarty and Samita Chatterjee even before they formally joined the project.

Dr. Baby Das helped in choosing the locations in South 24-Parganas. In setting up the project, conducting the survey and coding, we had enoromous support and active help from our colleague Dr. Debesh Chakraborty, professor of economics.

The survey work was considerably facilitated by the help we received from the administration of two districts. In South 24-Parganas Deb Kumar Sanyal, the then additional district mgistrate, helped us with introductions and necessary information about local conditions. Sibdas Bhattacharya, the sabhadhipati of the district, introduced us to the BDOs of the two blocks where our villages were located, who, in turn, sent word to the respective panchayat offices. Considerable hospitality was extended to us on our initial visits and to our team of investigators when they went to the villages for survey work. The panchayat pradhan of Kustia arranged for the accommodation of our team of investigators. The panchayat pradhan of Phulmalancha and the other members of his office also made arrangements for accommodation, enabling our investigators to feel at home in this remote village. In Barddhaman, Mehboob Zahedi, who was then the sabhadhipati of the district, put the Guest House of the zilla parishad at our disposal and helped us with necessary introductions. We were grateful to have the hospitality of Mohit Bhattacharya, the former vice-chancellor of Burdwan University, in the University Guest House. The zilla parishad office contacted the BDOs who then guided us to the village panchayats. In Gunar, the pradhan and the upa-pradhan of the panchayat extended a warm welcome to us and arranged for the accommodation of our team. In Pichkuri, Samiran Banerjee contacted the panchayat office for us and with his team of two helped our investigators to conduct the survey in the village. To all of them our gratitude and thanks.

We thank Prasanta Chatterjee, the mayor of Calcutta, and several members of his office, specially the staff of the offices of the executive engineers, borough committees Nos. 9 and 10, for providing us with information and material for the survey in the urban wards. Dalsinghar Yadav, the councillor of Ward No.79 rendered invaluable help in guiding the survey teams to some of its difficult areas. We also wish to acknowledge the assistance of Kulendu Shome, the councillor of Ward No. 96.

A survey of this scope and magnitude naturally implied a vigorous search for material and information. Krishna Dutta, the former librarian of the Central Library of Jadavpur University, and Preeti Mitra were extremely helpful. Arun Ghosh, the then librarian of the Centre for Studies in Social Sciences, Calcutta, and his assistants were always ready to help us. Sukumar Sinha, deputy director, Census Office, was also very helpful. Dr Ashim Kumar Mukhopadhyay collected some secondary material from libraries and newspapers. Sarbani Goswami and Abhijit Sen located material, and the latter also helped with proofreading. Shivani Banerjee-Chakrabarty contributed three short stories on the girl child, selecting and translating them, for the collection brought out by Veena Poonacha of the S.N.D.T. Women's University, Mumbai. Karuna Chakrabarty and all members of the School of Women's Studies were always ready to lend a helping hand whenever necessary.

We thank the department of economics for lending us space for housing the schedules while the coding and the writing of the report was in progress. We thank A. Rahaman, Dibakar Karmakar and Kamal Chakraborty for their assistance in data handling and in typing out the manuscript. Anuradha Kapoor took a number of photographs on one of our trips to the village in Barddhaman. We also thank Dr. Baby Das for arranging an immunization camp while leading the survey work in Phulmalancha, and Dr. Arati Basu Sen Gupta for initiating the Action Programme in Health Awareness among the women of Phulmalancha.

We are grateful to the Humanist Institute for Co-operation with Developing Countries (HIVOS), The Netherlands, India Regional Office, Bangalore, for financial assistance that helped to publish this work.

1
THE GIRL CHILD AND
THE FAMILY IN BENGAL
THE HISTORICAL SETTING

Why do we speak of the girl child and not the child, whether a boy or a girl? This is a question that came up frequently as we set up the project at the instance of the Department of Women and Child Development, Ministry of Human Resource Development, Government of India. Was it just an empty bureaucratic category dished out by the United Nations for organizing the so-called 'development' funds? Looking at the half-fed, half-clad boys working in the innumerable tea stalls, canteens and small dingy kar-khanas that litter the slums of Calcutta, one cannot help feeling a little chilled by the singling out of 'girls' in situations of gruelling poverty and deprivation. Yet as we look closer into the evidence of history and literature, we can see the rationale behind studying this social category in its depth. The gender disparity that vitiated our developmental process had its origin at the most vulnerable point in a woman's life : as a girl child growing up in a family. Paradoxically this was the enclosed space in which the sapling was supposed to be nurtured as a flowering and fruit-bearing tree.

In the patrilineal, patrilocal family structure of caste Hindu Bengal, the sapling was transplanted very early to the marital home. Hence the Telugu proverb that the girl child was a tree that belonged to another courtyard applied equally to Bengal. Since child marriage was the order of the day, the girl child was captured in the psycho-social memory of Bengalis in, what Prabha Krishnan called in another context, 'an idiom of loss' (1990). In this memory, the Bengali girl child is perpetuated in the endless songs about Durga (alias Uma alias Parvati), visiting her natal home for the three days of her autumnal worship. As I have argued elsewhere, the familial mode with a distinct accent on maternal nurturing marks the predominant culture of Bengalis (Bagchi 1990: WS 65-66). It is within the family that the girl child finds her natural habitat (Ray 1993: 17ff). Her mental universe is constructed as one long preparation to be a good wife and a good mother. Her socialization process has to be deduced from the ritual practices that were supposed to regulate her everyday life. The quotidian proverbs of Bengal also capture the trials and tribulations of the Hindu Bengali girl child in her marital home. Her daily life was one long regulation to keep the Goddess Lakshmi appeased and to thwart the machinations of Alakshmi (the antonym of Lakshmi).[1] On the fragile shoulder of the girl child lay the burden of keeping the patriarchal structure of the caste Hindu family's gateway to bliss.

I

'Shishukanya'—'Girl Child'—has occupied a major space in the emerging middle class consciousness of Bengal. The social reform movement that characterized the first half of the nineteenth century addressed itself predominantly to the 'Woman Question'.

One of the primary tenets of the moral justification of British rule in India was the barbaric treatment meted out to their womenfolk by Indian men. If we look at the major items listed under such social practices we realize why the 'girl child' emerges as the chief victim. Female infanticide, child marriage, and the consequential suffering of the child widows and to cap it all, *sati*, or the immolation of young nubile widows on the husband's pyre, all emerge as crimes against the girl as the child as well as the bride. In the perception of the early colonial administrators, and, with a slight change of focus, in that of the indigenous elite reformers, an upper caste Hindu girl child was the 'endangered sex' (Miller 1982). Saving the girl child was the priority in the social agenda which was one of the key consitituent elements of the ideology that helped the new middle class to carve a place for itself in society.

Perhaps the earliest campaign in colonial Bengal for intervening in a brutal social practice against women was the campaign for banning *satidaha* or the immolation of widows led by Raja Rammohan Roy, culminating in the legislation against the practice in 1829. Although by and large, this practice affected older women and not the category of the girl child, the latter did not, however, remain entirely unaffected by it. From the records of one year in the district of 24-Parganas alone, out of thirty-five widows burnt, we find mention of two brahmin girls aged 16 and 17 who had committed sati, and one kayastha (*coyat* in the record) bride aged nineteen who had also died with her husband (Ghosh 1978 : 234). What is brought out in the arguments for and against the practice of widow immolation was the shastric injunction pointing to the necessity for the wives to preserve their chastity. Most of the arguments at the time of the legislation were culled by the British administrators from the pundits who quoted the Shastras. The British were keen to be seen to be right: they wanted their legislation to conform to the brahminic injunction of the Shastras. To cite a telling instance, Mrityunjay Vidyalankar, the chief pundit of the British administration, who was by no means a liberal reformer, gave his verdict against widow immolation, preferring the purity of life-long abstinence and penance on the part of the upper caste Hindu widows:

> I regard a woman's burning herself as an unworthy act, and a life of abstinence and chastity as highly excellent. In the Shastras appear many prohibitions of a woman's dying with her husband, but against a life of abstinence and chastity there is no prohibition (Ahmed 1976: 129).

Rammohan Roy was far from the licentious westernized infidel that his opponents claimed him to be. He argued from the Shastras, using Manu as his authority (Ahmed 1976; Mani 1989)

> Manu in plain terms enjoins a widow to continue till death forgiving all injuries, performing austere duties, avoiding every sensual pleasure, and cheerfully practising the incomparable rules of virtue which have been followed by such women as were devoted to only one husband (Roy 1993: 2-3; Mani 1989 : 103).

Thus in saving from death the widow, whom the official discourse described as the 'tender child' (Mani 1989 : 97), Rammohan gave the reformer's sanction to a set of practices that were a major source of oppression of the girl child. In Bengal, it resulted in the sorry plight of the child widow. Harrowing stories and articles abound in Bengali literature, often written by women writers, on the heart-rending deaths of child widows in brahminical households, as they were denied a drop of water on the *ekadashi* (the eleventh day of the lunar fortnight), a day of fasting without water (Mukhopadhyaya 1967; Jyotirmoyee Devi 1971).

It was in this terrain left open by Rammohan that the next great reformer of Bengal, Ishwarchandra Vidyasagar, mounted a three-pronged campaign to improve the lot of child widows. The first was a common lamentation on the condition of women:

> In a society in which the menfolk have no mercy, no religion, no sense of justice, no sense of good or bad, in which mere conventionality is considered the chief activity and the supreme religion, let no more women be born.

Alas, the powerless women! I do not know what sins
have compelled you to be born in such a society (cited in
Bagchi 1992:31).

In the decades to follow this lamentation was heard often from
Kailashbasini Devi's *Hindu Abalaganer Hinabastha* (The Wretched
Condition of Hindu Women) to Trailokyanath Mukhopadhyay's
Damarucharit (The Tales of Damaru). It was picked up in fiction
by such mainstream writers as Saratchandra Chattopadhyay (in
Bamuner Meye (The Brahmin's Daughter) and by powerful women
writers such as Jyotirmoyee Devi and Ashapurna Devi, whom
feminist researchers are bringing to the fore.[2]

The second prong of Vidyasagar's campaign was the movement
for widow remarriage. Vidyasagar faced the full blast of Hindu
orthodox counter attack, but also encomium from many quarters. If there were songs lampooning him there were others that
lauded him:

Long live Vidyasagar
For moving the Sadr
That widows be re-married (Bagchi 1992).

In rousing public opinion Vidyasagar did not deviate from the
main contours of the shastric injunction, as legislation in colonial
India regarding women's marital status invariably belonged to the
domain of the personal laws which were supposed to be modelled
on the Shastras and the Sharia. In order to influence British
legislative machinery it was necessary to argue in the terms used
by the pundits. For the benefit of the legislators Vidyasagar
located the *sloka* in the *Parasharsamhita* which he considered to
be the appropriate one for the present *kaliyuga*. But Vidyasagar's
secular argument against the dangers of child widows pointed to
the social dangers of unregulated female sexuality:

An adequate idea of the intolerable hardships of early
widowhood can be formed by only those whose daughters,
sisters, daughters-in-law, and other female relatives, have
been deprived of their husbands during their infancy.

How many hundreds of widows, unable to observe the
austerities of a *brahmacharya* life, betake themselves to
prostitution and foeticide, and thus bring disgrace upon the
families of their fathers, mothers and husbands. If the
marriage of widows be allowed, it will remove the insupport-

able torments of life-long widowhood, diminish the crimes of prostitution and foeticide and secure all families from disgrace and infamy. As long as this salutary practice will be deferred, so long will the crimes of prostitution, adultery, incest and foeticide flow on in an ever-increasing current; so long will family stains be multiplied, so long will a widow's agony blaze in fierce flame (Vidyasagar 1976: 16-7).

Vidyasagar shared with the Hindu orthodoxy the conviction that the purity of the social order is closely tied up with the right channelling of female sexuality through marriage. The social acceptance of widows that Rammohan pleaded for that would prevent satidaha could not be upheld because of the presence of large numbers of child widows, created by noxious social practices such as *kulin* polygamy among brahmins. Unmarried brahmin girls were considered *arakshaniya* ('unprotectable'), hence to be married off at any cost to bridegrooms of any age and marital status whatsoever.

This is where Vidyasagar infiltrates the third phalanx of his campaign. The marriage of the upper caste Hindu girls at a very early age meant that the world of 'new education', that is, Western-style colonial education, was closed to them. The upper caste society was also the socially upward mobile class in the British port and capital city of Calcutta. Since amelioration of the condition of the girl child was one of the main social agenda of this class, educating the girl child also became a major item of reform. The rich paradox of the personality of Vidyasagar comes into play here. If ever there was an intellectual who donned the robe of a traditional brahmin (cropknot and all) it was Vidyasagar, yet his educational programme partook of the Western bourgeois liberal ideology that aimed at a self-fashioning symptomatic of a hegemonic class. True to his propensity to sanctify all social acts through shastric injunctions, he invoked the authority of the most stringent of law givers on women, Manu, to sanction the education of the girl child. When he started one of the earliest non-religious schools for girls in Calcutta with the famous philanthropist John Drinkwater Bethune, he had a sloka from Manu inscribed on the carriages that ferried the girls from the 'respectable' Hindu families between the school and their homes. He was quite categorical about the need to nourish the girl child physically and intellectually and the counterproductivity of early marriage:

Hence the appropriate time when the girls needed to be nurtured physically with due attention to the improvement of their bodies, they were sacrified to another family through marriage. Being immersed in such a sea of suffering is, indeed, extremely unfair (cited in Bagchi 1992a : 31).

Being sent away to the unknown terrain of another family required a different kind of socialization. That was an ideal of unquestioning submissiveness to the marital patriarchal ideal and learning the elaborate art of cuisine and daily religious rituals. The identity of the girl child was constituted between two apparently contradictory pulls: one was that of the newly derived world of knowledge imparted in new-style schools; the other was that of domesticity and the so-called feminine rituals required for the religious festivals and the smooth running of an upper caste household. The historical emergence of the girl child in Bengal into fully fledged womanhood can only be understood through the intricate meshing of the two worlds. In Bengal, a great deal of thinking had gone into the making of the girl child that cannot be neatly polarized into the 'tradition-modernity' or 'inside-outside' dichotomy.

Even the Brahmo (reformed Hindu) upbringing of the girl child tended to rely on a strictly defined, cleaned up image of the Hindu scriptures, and a whole array of *desaja* (homegrown) ritual practices and proverbs regulated the life cycle of a Bengali girl child. The specificity of the Bengali girl child has to be gleaned out of these indirect records and practices, much of which have pre-colonial roots.

As many commentators have remarked, Bengali culture is permeated by the psychology of *vatsalya sneha* (the affection for one's offspring). The mother-child relationship takes precedence over all other familial mores that have found expression in Bengal (Bagchi 1990: WS 66; Roy 1993: 29-32). Even the two conflicting religions which have contested over the psycho-social imagination of a Bengali Hindu, Vaishnavism and the Shakta cult of Kali, have found a meeting point in the sentiment of the mother-child relationship. Songs about engaging escapades of the child Krishna are echoed almost homologously by the sad appeals to Mother Kali in the popular Shyamasangeet.

In this ambience the girl child is captured in an idiom of loss. A girl child is the cause of the mother's tears for all the hostility she has to suffer in her marital home. A very popular genre which has captured the suffering of the Bengali girl child are the songs of welcome (*agamani*) and the songs of parting (*bisarjan*) of the goddess Durga. Her autumnal worship is represented as the annual visit of the child bride to the natal home (Dube 1989: 168).

Much of the regulation of a girl child's life among the upper castes of Bengal captures this tension with the marital home. The main *rasa* that the girl child evokes in the vast body of proverbs, rituals, and so on, is that of sadness at the cruel treatment of the girl child in her marital home, where she is consigned from the age of eight or, at any rate, before the onset of puberty. This is part of the ritually pure status attained by the upper castes to ensure the patrilineal and patrilocal aspects of brahminical dispensations. The more the male elite of Bengal confronted the colonial state authority through social reforms, educational reforms and through religious reforms, the more the girl child came to be marked out as a 'reserved' zone for which a strong contestation emerged about the best way of 'empowering' her.

To begin with, she was sought to be left outside the purview of literate culture. For the Hindu girl child, there was a widely prevalent belief that education induced early widowhood. There were various counter-arguments offered against this, one of which was to cite the case of the Victorian women who had received the blessings of education but who had not been blighted by widowhood. By and large, however, the domestic arena was recognized as the most suitable school for girls.

Within the family little girls were socialized into growing up as model wives and the tools of this socialization came from the rituals accompanying the major *rites de passage* such as birth, death, puberty, marriage and childbirth as well as the ritual practices of everyday living. This was a world in which women were governed by oral culture rather than by print culture. Proverbs and the *bratakathas* (the instructional narratives accompanying the ritual penance known as the *bratas*[3]) were the major sources of the personality-formation of the girl child and should, therefore, be studied with some care to understand the emergence of the girl child.

Women remain the main vehicles of the ritual purity of the patrilineal transmission of brahminical patriarchy. We pay special attention to these practices, for these mark the social spaces occupied by women and may therefore be seen to lend a certain amount of autonomy to women's lives. But these rituals operate within the overarching governance of Brahminism with its need to maintain the purity of patrilineal descent. In the shastric cannon, it is the boy who satisfies the unfulfilled desires of the dead parents by performing the last rites known as the *shraddha*. The girls are merely to be brought up as the *sahadharmini* who follows the husband in performing the ritually pure dharma. Taking anthropological stock of the social function of the rituals and bratas, Leela Dube says:

> The structuring of women as gendered subjects through
> rituals and practices is fundamentally implicated in the
> constitution and reproduction of a social system charac-
> terized by the subordination of women. To state this, how-
> ever, is not to argue that women are passive, unquestioning
> victims of these practices. It is to suggest that Hindu rituals
> and practices set certain limits in terms of the dispositions
> they inculcate among women and the different kinship roles
> with varying status within the family. The ritual and prac-
> tices and the social systems are imbued with a certain
> givenness and appear as a part of the natural order of things
> (Dube 1988: 181).

Though Leela Dube is arguing for the whole of Hindu India, one
can say that in the case of Bengal it would seem reasonable to
claim that because of their 'givenness' and their 'appearance'
as 'natural order', the bratas and the attendant rituals have also
been perceived as the surest formulae for correct socialization of
Hindu girls (Roy 1993:36-38).

Interestingly, the bratas became part of the indigenous response to the challenge of Westernization that marked the
Swadeshi movement in Bengal. The proselytizing zeal of the
missionaries and the 'improving' zeal of the social reformers
tended to see these everyday practices as remnants of the pre-
modern barbaric practices to be finally terminated by the occiden-
tal rays, either of the Gospel or of the Enlightenment, spreading
their power through education. The four walls of the *antahpur* in
which women practised these rituals, like the 'purdah' practised
by the sharif Muslim women, were perceived as the enemy of light.
With the onset of Swadeshi nationalism from the last quarter of
the nineteenth century there was a clear attempt to glorify indigenous practices, emphasizing their 'difference' from the values and
milieu of the Western rulers. There was a resultant resurgence of
interest in the bratas and feminine rituals as signifying a cultural
superiority over the then rulers—the British—as well as the past
'alien' rulers, the Muslims. Hindu womanhood, with its propensity
towards penance, fasts and rituals became the hallmark of the
purity of our national identity, increasingly ethnicized to mean a
Hindu identity. There came out many collections of these feminine
bratas in order to highlight this aspect of our cultural heritage.
One such typical collection by Baboo Paramesh Prasanna Ray

provides a telling Preface:

> This literature contains the simple basic principles that
> permeate our rural life in different shapes and forms. If
> these get lost due to changing times, a major item of the
> antiquity of our Nation would be lost. None cared because
> of indifference to the fate of our own Nation. However, those
> sad days have ended. This book is an indication that a
> renewed interest has been born among us to know our own
> country first hand (Ray 1908: i).

By fasting and performing the bratas Hindu women practised
devotion towards gurus, faith in religion and domestic ideals and
control of the senses. Just as the West had adopted the Kinder-
garten method, Ray claimed similarly our girls have been taught
religious principles through the strategy of barbrata from time
immemorial. In defence of this argument he quoted a long passage
from an article by Sister Nivedita (mentioned as an American lady)
published in the Modern Review. The passage is an eloquent
example of her Swadeshi crusade to preserve the beauty and
perfection of the Hindu way of life.

> Nothing could be more perfect educationally than the
> bratas. Some of these bratas like that which teaches the
> service of the cows, or the sowing of the seeds, or some
> which seem to set out on the elements of geography,
> astronomy have an air of desiring to impart which we now
> distinguish as secular knowledge. They appear, in fact, like
> surviving fragments of an old educational scheme. But for
> the most part, they constitute a training in religious ideas
> and religious feelings. India has, in these, done on the
> religious and social plane that what Europe is trying in
> the Kindergarten, to do on the scientific (quoted in Ray
> 1908: v).

The School of Women's Studies, Jadavpur University, has
reprinted Raibari (The Ray Household), a novel by Giribala Devi
who was born in 1890 (see Bagchi 1990 : 14). The book brings out
the entire process of the socialization of girls. Like most girl
children born in a well-to-do brahmin family, Giribala had no
formal schooling because she had been married off at an early age
into the rich zamindar family of the Rays, in a neighbouring village
in East Bengal (which now constitutes Bangladesh). In Raibari,

which is an autobiographical novel, Giribala Devi depicts the painful socialization process whereby the girl child Binu, symbolically named 'Banalata' (wild creeper) is moulded by the multifarious demands of the elaborate religious and domestic rituals of her marital home (pp. 10-14). By a most skilful deployment of narrative strategy the initiation of the child bride is communicated through the brilliant 'reality-effect' produced by what Henry James has called the 'solidity of specification'. The elaborate culinary practices of this zamindar household formed the most elaborate ritual of all. Giribala Devi also chose an important ritual season of the autumnal religious festivals, when a number of major goddesses, namely, Durga, Lakshmi and Kali, are worshipped within the span of a lunar month. Along with the mainstream worship, festivals in which only the women of the household are allowed to cook the main offerings (*bhog*) for the mother goddess, the parallel 'little tradition' of feminine bratas goes on to initiate the girls into the ways of an upper class/upper caste pattern of domination. The main disseminator of these *meyeli* (pertaining to women) lore is the widowed grandmother-in-law. Once the power-centre of this household, characteristically called *Karta-ma* (not just the feminine of the master, but the mother figure who is acknowledged as the master) her only authority lies in the fact that she is the mother of the present head of the household, the centre of power in the household having shifted to her daughter-in-law.

The figure of the widowed grandmother is a brilliant *tour de force*. In the novel she stands as simultaneously marginalized and empowered. She is marginalized as her husband, who used to be the head of this prestigious household, is now dead. Her power arises from the fact that once she headed this huge patriarchal household. She is fully socialized in the ways of this house which is her marital home, and takes it on herself to educate the newcomer girl bride. The grandmother is one of the most convincing agents of the socialization of the child bride because she is no longer the direct disciplining agent, that role having been assumed by the mother-in-law, the wife of the present master of the household. Having lost her position to her daughter-in-law the grandma stands as the repository of the ritual practices and the acceptable commonplaces of socialization that makes a girl child fit into the patriarchy of the marital home. Characteristically, the most humorously narrated account of a ritual practice of a brata is that of *Garosi*, a brata that was much written about at that time. The brata takes place between the worship of Lakshmi, the goddess of prosperity, who is worshipped by the Bengalis on the full moon day after the Durga Puja, and that of Kali, the fearsome goddess who is worshipped in the darkness of the *amabasya* (new moon). In the middle comes the *Garosi* brata, when the malevolent force of alakshmi (the antonym of Lakshmi), bound with her in a binary relationship, is appeased. This is a genuinely women's ritual where no priests are needed. The purpose of the brata is to ensure the marriage of unmarried girls. In the case of married girls it ensures the birth of a son that preserves the lineage and hence provides the ritual fulfilment of a woman's life in the clan. It also helps to restore lost property. So the women of the household propitiate the goddess of un-prosperity, imploring her not to come back. The grandmother is the director of ceremonies who leads the troupe of women to the village pond. Women of other families and from other castes are also seen performing the same brata.

The grandmother is also the rich treasure house of popular wisdom captured in proverbs. Her portrayal in the novel has been hailed by folklorists as giving a rare demonstration of the live context in which the proverbs were used. Proverbs are specially important in capturing the lives of women, even though of the upper class, because their lives were caught in the mesh of oral culture, outside the purview of print culture. Since several collections were made to capture these nuggets of popular wisdom before they disappeared like bubbles in the sea of print culture, it is possible to try to gauge the social perception of these women's lives, particularly that of the life of a girl child.[4]

In the novel *Raibari*, we also see in operation, the other face of the process of 'recasting women' by remoulding a child bride. Parallel to the world of bratas and proverbs is the other vital process that links her to the 'modern' world of print culture. Among the upper class male elite who usually married girls who did not have a chance to go to school, the husbands often took on the role of educators. Since it had to be fitted into the strict codes of the much extolled Hindu joint family, it had to be done in secret, in the depths of the night, when husband and wife at last had the chance to come together in the intimacy of the bedroom.[5] In *Raibari* we see this process brought to life, with the young husband of Binu. The upright eldest son of the household takes on the formal education of his child bride late at night. Binu's socialization process can no longer remain confined to the kitchen, the domestic rituals and sewing. She also has to be initiated into the ways of a New Woman and the print culture, without which nationalism is incomplete (Anderson: 1983). Reading and writing provides an open sesame to the world outside. The young husband, Prasad, represents the newly educated male elite, studying in Presidency College, Calcutta, the oldest institution of Western learning. He visits his village home for the autumn holidays, prepares himself for the future task of heading the household, which includes education of the child wife.

As yet no tension emerges between the two modes of socialization to which Binu is subjected. Once, we leave the schematic structured world of *Raibari*, however, and enter the more turbulent mainstream fiction written by both male and female writers, the two modes do not remain so comfortably contained. Rabindranath Tagore's fiction openly brings out the conflicts. Many more variations of the theme follow from writers both male and female. The girl child's world of socialization becomes one of the most contested fields both in Bengali fiction and the vast body of periodical literature that formed a less celebrated, but nonetheless a potent alternative.[6] Women often wrote in these periodicals and even went on to edit their own journals.

The education of girls became a recurrent theme in these writings. Since the time of Vidyasagar there had been a steady growth of women's education (Bagal 1949: 105). It was a social space designated as status and empowering for women. It was also one of the ways of class consolidation, as it did not percolate down to the women toiling in the market place or the public area. But we must not think of the process as a smooth and steady march to progress. If Western education was a feature characterizing the men of the rising middle classes, a number of hurdles were posed for the girls. A resistance to school education in Bengal, fear of early widowhood was a frequently invoked threat to prevent the upper caste Hindu girls from being educated (Basu 1989: 66). It was also supposed to encourage women in becoming immodest, undisciplined and uncontrollable, specially when it became clear to the patriarchs that Western education and school as the recognized institution of learning had come to stay. Anticipating this, Vidyasagar took on the challenge of Hindu orthodoxy by throwing a sloka from Manu at them (Bagchi 1992: 31).

Apart from the vast body of writing contained in the periodicals which debated women's education endlessly, quite a number of independent studies have come up that have tried to evaluate the contribution of education to the general construction of gender (Murshid 1983; Borthwick 1984; Karlekar 1986,1989,1991; Bannerji 1992). These studies have brought home the complexity of the psychological situation and the social dynamics within which the selfhood of the modern Bengali woman was formed. They also bring out the varied pressures within which young middle class girls were initiated into the process of education. The basic fear was that of girls losing their submissiveness through education.[7] In a best-selling book called *Bharater Nari* (Indian Women), which was recommended way back in 1933 as a textbook for girls in middle and high schools, and which ran into many editions, we find an eloquent plea for differentiating women's education from that of men :

> It is not right to think that unless they are taught in schools and colleges, garbed with rich clothes, women's access to education is closed forever (Bhattacharya 1933 : 9).

Using the rhetoric of the Swadeshi 'self-help' the author argues that just as a trained engineer may not be considered illiterate for not being well versed in Shakespeare or Byron:

> Similarly, a noble lady, well experienced in the religion [lit. dharma] of domesticity, engaged in nuturing children, devoted to the care of her husband, may be unlettered but should not be considered illiterate (ibid).

By treating engineering skills and domestic skills homologically, domestic virtues were made into the Nationalist paradigm of an ideal Indian woman, who had been able to resist the allurements of a 'Western' education with its alleged foppery, which was placed on par with the use of a 'foreign' import. The purity of the Indian Nation was upheld by the purity of Indian womanhood unsullied by school education and novel reading (Sarkar 1987: 208). Reading books was the devil's snare, the 'primrose way to dalliance'. Under these circumstances the girl child going out to school and college often led to serious fights within the family.

It is such a fight that forms the centrepiece of the famous trilogy of Ashapurna Devi, specially the first volume, *Pratham Pratisruti*. In the novel Ashapurna quite justifiably puts the major blame on the early marriages of girls. This is a theme that was reiterated throughout the debate that went on around the Age of Consent Bill. In 1891 it was raised from eight to twelve after Phulmani, a ten-year-old girl, was killed by the experience of marital rape (Sarkar 1992). The orthodoxy in Bengal ganged up against the girl child and the need to keep her properly contained through early marriage (Mayo 1931: 64-67).

Early marriage, as the mothers and teachers (sometimes even male relatives) felt, meant depriving the girl not only of education, but of the pleasure of childhood itself. This was seen as a 'cause' around which many different types of writing were organized. A lot of writing is now found on the Bengali 'bhadramahila' as one of the archetypes of the newly rising middle class woman in India, but there seems to be a dearth of analysis of the material that accrued around the 'khukurani' or 'khukumani'—the endearing names given to middle class girls. If the construction of the feminine forms one of the crucial components in the reproduction of class in Bengal, the girl child must take a large share in this discussion. The girl child decade, therefore, should not only deal in policy matters in a superfical way but should generate indepth studies of the girl child being given a social space in the thinking of the class that emerged with hegemonic ambitions. The middle class construct of the girl child as 'khukumani' meant that she must be both liberated as a child and committed to the domestic virtues for which her life was a long preparation. Her games and the literature produced specially for her consumption thus reflected the double burden that she would have to take on as a 'bhadramahila'. She would have to be rooted in the family ideology and at the same time display signs of westernized freedom. It was for such a child that collections of nursery rhymes and fairly tales were produced in the colonial period. The effective reproduction of class within the constraints of colonialism in literature for children and adolescents, with its attendant gender construction, has been rendered brilliantly in a book written in Bengali (Bandyopadhyay 1991).

Side by side with the controversial figure of the girl child as the fitting icon of the authentic Indian tradition, childhood becomes a prized space, something that symbolizes the superiority of civilization. If the prized boy child of an upper class family is the 'khokababu' (the boy child), on whom rests the task of keeping the lamp of the family alight (*bangsher bati*), the girl child becomes the gem of the parent's eyes. It is not as if the khukumani is brought up on a principle of equality with the boy child. What is heightened is her world of femininity in her dress, in the games she plays and the docile sweetness of her mien (Roy 1993).

Opening the pages of the forgotten periodical literature of the late nineteenth century and the nine decades of this century, one sees the obsession with the body and mind of the girl child. A full survey of literature would run to several volumes. Only some are indicated in the present analysis. Health, education and imagination were also talked about. Children's literature, in trying to reproduce the innocence of childhood, endlessly repeated the socially accepted gender stereotypes (Bandyopadhyay 1991; Ray 1993). Her upbringing was that of a good, well-protected proto-bhadramahila, encouraged to play feminine games of doll's house, read books 'suitable' for girls, discouraged from physical action and the spirit of adventure. An elaborate code of socialization resulted in the khukumani 'becoming' (to borrow Simone de Beauvoir's word) a bhadramahila (Roy 1993; Kakar 1978; Borthwick 1984; Bandyopadhyay 1991; Bagchi 1992b).

NOTES

1: The Bengali expression for 'good girl': '*lakshmi meye*' (the girl who is like Lakshmi). The social implications of this harmless expression are far from being innocent. Some of these have been spelt out in the section on indigenous socialization (see also note 3).

2. I have paid a tribute to Jyotirmoyee Devi as a writer close to the active fighters for women's freedom. The edition of her writings published by the School of Women's Studies, Jadavpur University, brings out her indignation at women's oppression under the patriarchal social order.

    All the three stories on the girl child contributed by Shivani Banerjee-Chakravorty to the eloquent volume edited by Veena Poonacha show how sensitive women writers were to this issue. Ashapurna Devi's trilogy has been analysed to bring out the latent conflict between her selfhood and her socialization process within the family in Shivani Banerjee-Chakravorty, 'Carving a Self: Feminist Consciousness, the Family and Socialization Process in Asharpurna Devi's Trilogy' (Paper presented at the Fifth National Conference of the IAWS, Jadavpur University, February 1991).

3. In 1927, between April and October, there were as many as four articles on the practice of this particular brata. The articles on brata to be performed by girls alone will need a long appendix (courtesy: Abhijit Sen).

4. There were several well-known collections of Bengali proverbs in the nineteenth and the early twentieth century. A few choice translations follow to give a flavour of the proverbs:
    A girl child is a 'treasure possessed by strangers' and 'travels on another's boat'. A girl's 'fate' is that of a 'slave girl'. The blows of this miserable 'fate' are ironically, 'administered by the father'. The source of misery is the marital home: 'O what fun in the house of the 'in-laws'/Blows of the broomstick every

third day.' Or, 'The house of the in-laws is a bowl of honey/
Tied by the rope and kicks every other day.'

The child bride is clearly deprived of her 'entitlement' in nutritious
food, her secret love of fish is satirized: 'The wench cuts herself to
pieces in shame/ Doesn't mind eating fish under the veil.'

Another cruel insinuation about her hunger: 'Too shy to eat
rice/Daughter-in-law opens her mouth wide as a grapefruit.'

The ideal for the girl child is the sati or the constant wife:
'We call her sati/who is dedicated entirely to her husband's
feet.'

It is she who glorifies the patriarchal order:
'The husband of a constant wife/Is the spire of a Chariot/
That of the inconstant one/Is the debris of a broken boat.'

Yet faith and constancy work only one way. The husband is free
to marry many wives and the proverbs capture the fear of the
co-wife: 'I build the house by cutting down the Asath tree,/I
redden my feet by chopping off the co-wife.'

Even one's sister is not free from jealousy: 'Other co-wives displace
you/The co-wife sister burns you to death.'

The world of women that comes across through the proverbs or
sayings is a grim one: 'The girl will burn, ashes will fly/Only then
will her praise soar high.'

5. The particular genre of women's educational manual written by
    husband-teachers reflect the entire gamut of a girl's socialization
    process. The table of contents of two parts of a book belonging to
    this genre, 'Conversations with the Wife' follows:

PART I
Relationship between Husband and Wife/ Few Letters/
Relationship between Men and Women/ Reading and Writ-
ing/ Looking after Body and Mind/A Few Things to Know
Specially: Love; Music; Painting, and Embroidery; Customs;
Clothes and Apparel.

PART II
Religion of Women/Women's Diseases/Nursing/Treat-
ment/Domestic Skills/Cooking/Accounting/Relatives and

Guests/ Two Stories/Midwifery/Child-Rearing/ Educating the Child/Higher Education/God and Religion/Conclusion/Final Words.

6. The following list is selected from a compilation by Abhijit Sen from Bengali periodicals. Though far from exhaustive, it is cited to give an idea of the range of obsession with educated women.

    Kailashbasini Devi, 'Hindu Abalakuler Bidyabhyas O Tahar Samunnati' (The Learning of the Hindu Women and Their Thorough Improvement) 1787, Sakabda.

    Krishnabhabini Das, 'Shikshita Nari' (The Educated Woman) Sahitya, Asvin 1298 B.S.

    —, 'Karyamulak Shiksha O Jatiya Unnati' (Vocational Education and National Improvement), Pradip, Sravana 1308 B.S.

    Rokeya S. Hosain, 'Asha Jyoti' (The Ray of Hope), Nabanur, Jyaishtha 1313 B.S.

    Jnandanandini Devi, 'Stree Shiksha' (Women's Education), Bharati O Balak, Asvin 1288 B.S.

    Hemlata Sarkar, 'Stree Shiksha O Shikshita Mahila' (Women's Education and the Educated Women), Bharat Mahila, Baisakh 1313 B.S.

    —, 'Narijatir Shiksha' (The Education of Women), Bharat Mahila, Baisakh/Asad, 1314 B.S.

    Binodini Sengupta 'Asmaddeshiya Balika Jiban' (Girl Child's Life in Our Society), Antahpur, Asvin 1307 B.S.

    Swarnakumari Devi, 'Streeshiksha O Bethune School' (Bethune School and Women's Education) Bharati O Balak, Sravana 1294 B.S.

7. There are a few subversive images in Bengali literature. Hemendrakumar Ray's Minu insisted on accompanying the boys, Bimal and Kumar, on their adventures. On one occasion she sings of her possible reaction of indignation if an Inca king had tried to make her into an 'Incee' (the Bengali feminine derived from Inca!). In more recent times Nalini Das has created the detective team Gandalu, consisting of four girls who combine adventure with detection. They usually make their first appearance on the pages of the children's magazine Sandesh that Nalini Das once edited jointly with Satyajit Ray and Lila Majumder.

REFERENCES

Ahmed, A.F. Salahuddin (1976). *Social ideas and social changes in Bengal: 1818-1835*. Calcutta: Rddhi.

Bagal, Jogeshchandra (1940). History of the Bethune School and College. In *Bethune College and School centenary volume: 1849-1949*, edited by Kalidas Nag. Calcutta, 1-125.

Bagchi, Jasodhara (1989). *Naribadi dhrishtibhangite adhunik bangla kathasahitya: Du charti katha* (a few words concerning modern Bengali Fiction from a Feminist Perspective). In *Bharat ithihase nari* (Women in Indian History), edited by Ratnabali Chattopadhyay and Gautam Neogi, Calcutta: K.P.Bagchi.

—(1990a). Representing nationalism : Ideology of motherhood in colonial Bengal, *Economic and Political Weekly*, Review of Women Studies 25 (October):WS 65-71.

—(1990b). *Amader katha*. In *Raibari*, edited by Subir Roy Chowdhury and Abhijit Sen. Calcutta: Dey's Publishing and School of Women's Studies, Jadavpur University.

—(1992a). *Vidyasagar o kanyashishu* (Vidyasagar and the girl child). *Eksathe*, Vidyasagar Special Number (April 1992).

—(1992b). Becoming woman: Socialisation and gender in mass media. Presented at 'Feminisms: France, India, Russia'. Paris, Ecole des Etudes des Hommes, Paris, May.

Bandyopadhyay, Sivaji (1991). *Gopal-rakhal dwandwa samash: Oupanibeshbad o bangla shishusahitya* (Colonialism and Bengali children's literature). Calcutta: Papyrus.

Bannerji, Himani (1991). Women's education proposals in popular magazines in colonial Bengal, *Economic and Political Weekly* WS 43 (Oct): 50-62.

Basu, Aparna (1988). A century's journey : Women's education in Western India, 1820-1920. In *Socialization, education and women*, Explorations in gender identity, edited by Karuna Chanana. Delhi: Orient Longman.

Bhattacharya, Upendrachandra (1933). *Bharater nari* (Indian women), 19th ed, 1957. Calcutta: Modern Book Agency.

Borthwick, Meredith (1984). *Changing role of women in Bengal 1849-1905*. Princeton, N.J: Princeton.

Chattopadyay, Saratchandra (1920). *Bamuner meye* (The brahmin's daughter). Calcutta: Sisir Publishing House.

Devi, Ashapurna (1964). *Pratham pratisruti* (The first promise), 25th rpt, 1984. Calcutta: Mitra and Ghosh.

Devi, Giribala (1990). *Raibari* (The Ray household), edited by Subir Roy Choudhury and Abhijit Sen. Calcutta: Dey's Publishing and School of Women's Studies, Jadavpur University.

Devi, Kaliashbasini (1863). *Hindu mahilaganer hinabastha* (The wretched condition of Hindu women). Calcutta: Gupta Press.

Dube, Leela (1989). Socialization of Hindu Girls in patrilineal India. In *Socialization, education and women: Explorations in gender identity* edited by Karuna Chanana. New Delhi: Orient Longman.

Ghosh, Benoy (1978). *Selections from English periodicals of nineteenth century Bengal*, vol.1 (1815-1833). Calcutta: Papyrus.

Kakar, Sudhir (1978). *The inner world: A psychoanalytic study of childhood and society in India.* New Delhi: Oxford University Press.

Karlekar, Malabika (1986). Kadambini and the bhadralok : Early debates over women's education in Bengal, *Economic and Political Weekly*, 21, 17 (April).

--- (1988). Women's nature and the access to education. In *Socialization, education and women: Explorations in gender identity*, edited by Karuna Chanana. Delhi: Orient Longman.

Mani, Lata (1989). Contentious traditions : The debate on sati in colonial India. In *Recasting women : Essays in colonial history*, edited by Kumkum Sangavi and Sudesh Vaid. New Delhi : Kali for Women.

Mayo, Katherine (1931). *Mother India*, vol. 2. London : Cape.

Miller, Barbara (1981). *The endangered sex.* Ithaca : Cornell University Press.

Mukhopadhyay, Trailokyanath (1967). *Damarucharit.* In *Trailokya rachanavali* (seventh story), edited by Pramathanath Bisi. Calcutta : Mitra and Ghosh.

Murshid, Gholam (1983). *The Reluctant debutante. Response of Bengali women to modernization : 1849-1905.* Rajshahi : Sahitya Samsad, Rajshahi University.

Ray, Bharati (1991). Meyelitta o shishukanya shiksha (Womanliness and the education of the girl child). In *Eksathe*, edited by Kanak Mukherjee. Calcutta (Autumn 1990) : 51-57.

Ray, Paramesh Prasanna (1908). *Meyeli bratakatha* (Feminine rituals). Calcutta.

Roy, Manisha (1993). *Bengali Women.* Calcutta : Stree.

Roy, Rammohan (1818-19; 1992). *Sahamaran bishay prabartak nibartak samvad* (Catechism on widow immolation). In *Pratirodh*, edited by Debiprasad Chattopadhyay. Calcutta : Utsa Manush.

Sangavi, Kumkum and Sudeh Vaid (1989). *Recasting women : Essays in colonial history.* Delhi : Kali for women.

Sarkar, Tanika (1987). Nationalist iconography. Image of women in nineteenth century Bengali literature. *Economic and Political Weekly* (21 Nov) : 2011-15.

Vidyasagar, Ishwarchandra (1855; 1976). *Marriage of Hindu widows*, edited by Arabinda Poddar. Calcutta : K.P. Bagchi.

2
THE ENDANGERED SEX
A SELECTED SURVEY OF LITERATURE

The intensive search into the plight of women that was undertaken when the Commitee on the Status of Women's Report was being prepared in 1974 alerted the planners, concerned citizens and social scientists to the danger facing the girl child. While the Status Report did not have a separate slot for the girl child, there was clear evidence of the naturalization of the devaluation of the female child and its consequent social devastation. A brief survey of analyses of the girl child made in the context of West Bengal since 1974 follows. Though not exhaustive, the survey will highlight some of the major trends.

I THE DEMOGRAPHIC WARNING

In 1974 and 1975 there were two articles in *The Economic and Political Weekly* on what Pranab Bardhan called 'a matter of life and death' (Bardhan 1974; Dandekar 1975). Both pointed to the secular decline in the male-female sex ratio as recorded in the Census from 1901 to 1971, a problem which had worried demographers for some time. Bardhan pointed a telling finger at the neglect of the female child. From his table of female-to-male mortality ratios in rural India, 1969, Bardhan observed that in the areas of relatively high female death rates, such as Uttar Pradesh, Punjab, Rajasthan and Gujarat, the female-male ratio of death rates was higher for the age group 0-4 years than for all age groups taken together. This could indicate that the general neglect of little girls might be more important than maternal deaths in governing the sex-differential in mortality (Bardhan 1974:1303). Bardhan found such neglect of the girl child less prevalent in eastern or southern India, and tentatively offered the hypothesis that in the paddy growing areas female labour was valued and hence the neglect of the female child was less acute.

> Could it be that, in areas with paddy agriculture, the economic value of a woman is more than in other areas—so that the female child is regarded less of a liability than in, say, North and North-West India (Bardhan 1974:1304).

In the following year in *The Economic and Political Weekly* Kumudini Dandekar sounded another note of caution: Why has the proportion of women in India's population been declining? Her findings prompted her to state:

> Most of the younger age-groups—except the first year of age—shows the worsening of the female position . . . the younger females are much more handicapped vis-à-vis males: one is even tempted to conclude that the female in the 1960s had a relatively more inferior position vis-à-vis the male, as compared to half a century ago (Dandekar 1975 : 1667).

Strewn in the pages of the Status Report there are hints about the adverse cultural setting into which the girl child is born in India. It is given a place of prominence among the possible causes of the declining sex ratio (*Towards Equality* : 11). In 1981 Barbara D. Miller wrote *The Endangered Sex*. Though the book specifically deals with the neglect of the girl child in rural North India, she makes a special mention of West Bengal:

> There is some indication that the proportion of females in India is on the decline (Dandekar 1975) particularly in West Bengal (Miller 1981: 168).

In 1983 Amartya Sen and Sunil Sengupta published their article 'Malnutrition and Rural Children and the Sex Bias' in the annual number of *The Economic and Political Weekly*. Two villages in the Birbhum district in West Bengal—Sahajpur and Kuchi—were surveyed to study the nature of malnutrition among children of 0-5 years and the way sex bias works against women. The survey studied altogether 236 children below five years, in relation to the socioeconomic background of the families the children belonged to, taking into consideration economic factors like greater availability of land due to land reforms, greater education of mothers, the caste division and proximity to urban centres. One of the major findings that is of interest to our survey is that girls are more undernourished if they are fed only within the family. Sen and Sengupta concluded:

> It is worth emphasizing that direct nutritional intervention through supplementary feeding has the additional advantage of combatting the sex bias in nutrition within the family . . . Increasing the income of the rural family

may be an inadequate instrument in combatting the
unequal deprivation of the girl child (Sen and Sengupta
1983: 863).

Amartya Sen's work in this field has given many fresh insights
into the nutritional disadvantages of girl children within families.
The neglect of the girl child is not yet seen as the sole cause for
the demographic imbalance as the declining sex ratio indicates.
In the last decade and a half it has been orchestrated from
different quarters.

II THREE REPRESENTATIONS

In the post-independence era the problem of the girl child is
increasingly seen as that of deprivation due to poverty. Three
representations of the Bengali girl child in three different kinds of
media are presented here to bring out the multiple facets of this
form of gender exploitation.

(i) PATHER PANCHALI

The tragedy of the girl child in rural Bengal is captured, without
anyone realizing its significance, in the still photograph from
Satyajit Ray's *Pather Panchali,* which was included in the exhibi-
tion called (ironically enough) *The Family of Man.* The photograph
shows Durga, the girl child, helping her mother to dress up her
younger brother, Apu, to go to school. While Apu, the protagonist
of the film, is considered the legitimate claimant of the scant
resources of this very poor family, Durga wastes her time,
scrounging for things to fulfil the cravings of her growing years.
She is her mother's embarrassment as she is caught stealing
green mangoes from the rich man's gardens. She even steals
beads from the neighbour's daughter as her family is too poor to
buy her any. She finally dies of fever; the doctor who practises
traditional medicine is called in too late. Durga is a victim, not of
parental cruelty, for there is sufficient indication of their affection
and concern, but of the social system that considers her needs to
be second in importance to her brother's. Since it is the son who
is the social security of the parents with scarce resources, he has
to be coaxed to go to school or to eat properly. *Pather Panchali* is
a classic of the Indian cinema, but is only lately seen as a film
about the neglect of a girl child (Chattopadhyay 1982: 30-35; Bose
1992: 140-141; Sen 1992: 106-107).

(ii) MEYE DILE SAJIYE

The second presentation of a girl child is taken from an experimental play written by Malini Bhattacharya, for Sachetana, a women's activist group, as part of an anti-dowry campaign. The play is a brilliant subversion of Bankimchandra Chattopadhyay's *Devi Choudhurani* in which a beautiful but poor girl bride is turned out by her father-in-law, the rich zaminder, because the neighbours had spread false rumours about the sexual immorality of her poor widowed mother. The young girl then becomes one of the legendary dacoit queens, punishing the rich and helping the poor. By introducing this as a fantasy motif in her play, and adapting it to the present situation, Malini Bhattacharya lashes out against the socialization process that permits the dowry system to devalue the girl child. Using the original story, the girl child is made to sit on judgement, not only on the rich father-in-law, who demands dowry, but on the poor father who feels obliged to give away the bride fully decked out. The play ends with a vow, sung as a song based on the model of a folk song tradition in North Bengal known as 'Tushu', which is usually sung by women :

> I will not arrange Tushu's marriage.
> Tushu will go to school,
> Wagging her little pigtails.
> Will learn to read and write,
> And not burst into tears.
> Whatever you may say,
> Giving money and jewels,
> I will not arrange Tushu's marriage.

(iii) KONI

This is a novel about a poor girl child of north Calcutta, who becomes a champion swimmer. Written by the Bengali best-selling novelist Moti Nandy, who writes novels about sports, Koni was made into a successful film by the West Bengal Government in its bid to promote cinema. Koni, a natural swimmer, is a poor girl who lives in the slums of Calcutta. She is picked up by a determined leader in her neighbourhood who fights against all the odds of a class-ridden society to help her to qualify for the highest competition in the country, where she comes out on top. What is moving in the depiction is the way physical talents, specially in girls from the lower strata, are often starved out of existence. Lack of facilities like swimming costumes, nutritious food and absence of the right outlook for promoting such non-traditional roles for girls gradually render girls like Koni invisible.

III   SURVEY OF RECENT ANALYSES

Statistical Pocketbook contains the most useful sources of information. Published by the NIPCCD in collaboration with the Department of Women and Child Development, the second revised edition, *The Pocketbook on Statistics on Children in India*, 1991, is the most comprehensive 'ready source of data', extremely useful for policy planners, voluntary organizations and scholars alike.

Situational Analysis of Women and Children in West Bengal, sponsored by UNICEF in 1989 is the comparable sourcebook for West Bengal. The report, consisting of ten chapters, though primarily slanted towards health planners, contains valuable information about illiteracy and female work participation in West Bengal. There is a useful appendix on child labour in Calcutta.

CHAPTER 1: Demographic Profile, includes a useful section on children, pointing out lower child survival rates in the rural than in urban areas. What is noticeable is that there is no attempt to locate the girl child nor to trace the sex ratio.

CHAPTER 2: Vital statistics, deals with infant mortality; no gender break-up is available.

CHAPTER 3: Disability. There are sexwise break-ups in Table 16 dealing with locomotor disability (1981) and Table 17 on totally disabled persons (1981).

CHAPTER 4: Socioeconomic setting with emphasis on literacy and female work participation. The section on literacy gives tables based on 1971 and 1981 Censuses with break-up. Work participation by women is larger among the tribals in Darjeeling, Jalpaiguri and Purulia districts. Female work participation rates are lower in more prosperous districts like Barddhaman, Hooghly, the 24-Parganas and Birbhum (Table 23 gives districtwise, sexwise and the rural-urban break-up). There is a useful section on 'child worker' (Table 26 shows the total employment of child workers up to 14 years in various occupational categories with sex break-up).

CHAPTERS 5-9: Health-related issues such as 'Medical Infrastructure', 'Expanded Programme on Immunisation' (EPI), 'Nutrition', 'Mother and Child Care in the Poverty Pockets of the Calcutta Metropolitan Area' (CMA), and ICDS projects.

CHAPTER 10: Field studies done in Silguri and Purulia. Sample surveys conducted in some villages of Barddhaman Block, Purulia District, Falakata Block of Jalpaiguri District available.

The first nine chapters reproduce eighty tables from various well-known sources. Apart from the appendix on child labour in Calcutta, already mentioned, there is a second appendix on CMDA's Health Programme for the Poor in Calcutta Metropolitan Area. The report, unfortunately, is not adequately *sensitized* to the needs of the girl child.

During the last four years there have been several reports published from seminars and surveys conducted by government sources and voluntary organizations. Some are summarized:

State Level Workshop on Girl Child, 20-22 June 1988, sponsored by CINI, Calcutta. UNICEF, 1988, 34pp.

Papers included in the volume discussed various topics including legal status, child labour, nutritional and social aspects, the origins of discrimination, gender bias, and the inactive role of girls in children's literature, causes of sexual exploitation, child marriage and prostitution and the plight of young unwed mothers.

Suggestions included a call for a holistic approach by government and other organizations, social mobilization for advocacy, relevant profile-creation based on disaggregated data, restriction on sexist advertising and a positive bias in favour of the girl child in the existing programmes in the media.

Health for the Millions, CINI, 1989. A study on girl children in 8 villages of Bishnupur Blocks I and II, South 24-Parganas was done. There were 1377 children from 438 families, below the poverty line, who were interviewed.

SAARC Kanya Sishu Dasak/Sishu Samaj, Paschim Banga, 1991. This book was released at a workshop conducted by the Social Welfare Department, Government of West Bengal.

Survey in the Districts of Howrah and Hooghly on Girl Children by PIRA (Peoples Institute for Rural Action) in 1988 (PIRA, 1990).

In 1988, PIRA undertook an extensive survey in some villages under seven remote blocks of Howrah and Hooghly districts and found that at least 33.33 percent of girl children were murdered at ages 14-17 and the victims included both married and unmarried girls. In 92.86 percent of the cases, the killers and their associates have received political protection, while the rest have gone undergound (p.17).Of the unmarried girl children who gave birth, 57.14 percent had to accept their babies in spite of their unwillingness; most of them belonged to the scheduled castes.

Among the girls below sixteen, 16.32 percent committed suicide; they were unmarried; while among those between 11 and 17 years, 88.85 percent were forced to accept early marriage, though such a marriage is a punishable offence. Early marriage led to desertion by husbands. The PIRA survey shows that 76.92 percent girls were deserted by their husbands (p.19).

The survey found the respondents in the selected level blocks engaged in 20 different indoor and outdoor work. These were: looking after siblings, collection of fuel and fodder from the jungles and fields, scooping of animal dung, making and drying of dung cakes, netting fish with small nets, collection of herbs from marshy lands (risking possibility of snake bite, especially from black cobra) cooking food, carrying lunch to planting or harvesting sites for the males, collection of fortnightly ration, collection of kerosene, shopping, shepherding, bathing and feeding the cattle, floor sweeping, cleaning utensils, washing, cleaning lanterns, boiling and drying rice, collecting drinking water, washing, gardening, entertaining guests and selling labour to others as maid-servants (pp.25-28). The PIRA booklet also presents an all-India picture of the status of a girl child compared to that of a boy child: 'In India, the average longevity of the boys is 52.6 years, while that of the girls, is 51.6' (p.6).

Another survey shows that 64 percent of the boys have access to medical treatment, while only 48 percent of girls do. The figures for malnutrition show that 28.6 percent of boys suffer from malutrition; for the girls, it is 71.4 percent. A 1971 survey shows that 56 percent of guardians are unwilling to provide education to their girl children beyond the school level (p.7).

A 1971 survey shows that 13.6 percent of the married girls were of the 10-14 age range. In a district (province not mentioned) there were 400,000 widows below 15, indicating the prevalence of widespread early marriage (p.7).

Girl Street Children in Calcutta (Mukhopadhyay 1992). Where do they come from and why?

The study showed that almost all the families of the respondents numbering about one thousand, living in the city-streets, had migrated from various villages for reasons mostly linked to extreme poverty and unemployment or underemployment. Families of 82 percent of the children in general, boy and girl inclusive, pointed to poverty as the main push factor for migration. Most of the parents of the respondents were land-poor or wage labourers, and had migrated to Calcutta when their means of living in the villages failed to support them any longer. Fathers of 85 percent of the children, boys and girls inclusive, had been found to be doing some kind of work, but most of them were not earning more than Rs.300 per month. Only 5.5 percent of the fathers earned more than Rs.500 a month.

The income of the fathers was, however, supplemented by that of the mothers, of whom, 93 percent did some kind of work but their income was very low. A large percentage of children, 60 percent, had mothers who earned about Rs. 100 per month (pp.40-41).

IPER's inventory specifically prepared for the Girl Street Children (GSC) and applied on 1000 girls showed that 93 percent of them lived with their parents and only 7 percent with relatives and others.

Age Group: From 6 to 18 years. Girls above 15 were very few in number either because they got married or/were sent back home to stay with relatives or friends. When marriage or living at home was not possible, the GSC was compelled to live on the streets. Marriages were not properly planned and many did not last long. GSC of broken marriages generally found no other place to go to, but adopted prostitution to support themselves. Many were directly inducted to this trade.

Nature of Shelter: 96.7 percent lived on streets, while only 3.3 percent lived in rooms; 30.5 percent lived in covered shelters; 69.5 percent lived on open streets without any cover over their heads.

Most of the GSC spent their nights in unprotected conditions. Though parents and brothers and other relatives slept by them, the girls were liable for assault by antisocials because of the complete lack of protection.

In fact, when the survey was being done, on many occasions touts, pimps, musclemen, street vendors and middlemen who used these children for their own vested interests, protested and even prevented the surveyors from talking to the GSC. In the case of teenaged girls, many women who acted as touts and exploited them in exchange of means and protection, resisted the surveyors, apprehending loss of their source of earning.

Working GSC: Half of the GSC responding to the survey, were found engaged in some kind of work. Though 66.6 percent worked for not more than 6 hours a day, 22.4 percent worked for 7 to 9 hours and the remaining 11 percent worked for more than 10 hours. But the pay was poor. Over 22 per cent of the respondents got Rs 50 per month, 19.3 percent got between 50 and Rs 75, and 57 percent got above Rs 75 a month.

The day-to-day life of the GSC was fraught with myriads of problems. Though 56.9 percent girls reported that their needs for meals, clothings and others were met by parents, 43.3 percent said that they themselves managed the bare necessities to the best of their abilities.

Health: Far from satisfactory; only 8.6 percent of the GSC were found to have good health, 32.9 percent had moderately good health, while 58.5 percent suffered from very bad health. In spite of illness, malnutrition and retarded growth, 47.9 percent of the GSC did not have access to any medical facility. Another 49.7 percent had access to medical care provided by the government, but the unpleasant manner of the doctors, non-medical staff of the hospitals and the general public, detered them from seeking any medical help even when the situation warranted it. Only 2.9 percent of the GSCs were treated by private medical practitioners, when they fell sick.

Clothing: 98.8 percent of the respondents did not have proper clothing and wore used clothes of the well-off classes as under-garments like tape-frocks, shorts and the like.

Bath and Toilet: Among the GSC, 97 percent did not have any regular toilet facility. Only 2.9 percent enjoyed such privileges because of their association with the rich employers and a handful of benevolent beings. As many as 92.7 percent of the GSC used municipal taps or tubewells on open streets, which made them more vulnerable to the pimps, local touts and other anti-social elements. Older GSC, therefore, took their baths very early in the morning. Only 1.4 percent of the respondents enjoyed a good bath in the neighbours' or employers' houses.

Attitude of the Neighbours: 26.1 percent of the girls described their neighbours as hostile, bad, debauched, and so on; 64.7 percent as indifferent; only 9.2 percent thought that neighbours were sympathetic.

Attitude towards Parents: 16.5 percent stated that they were ill-treated by their parents; 26.5 percent stated they were ex-ploited. Their complaints were usually on two counts. They were overworked and they are neglected.

Harassment by the Police and the Municipal Corporation: 86.9 percent resented the behaviour of the police who regularly raided their sites, kicked away their belongings and used abusive lan-guage and even beat them. This apart, there was 'teasing' by the local boys: 85.9 percent complained that teasing by the local boys had become a common feature and only a few of the passers-by or residents cared to come to their rescue. As many as 86.7 percent of the GSC felt that living on the street was very humili-ating for any growing girl and they should have better shelters from the point of view of comfort and security. And 90.2 percent of the GSC said it was the duty of society to take care of them and rehabilitate them instead of being totally indifferent to them. Though lacking a clear sense of social justice, the GSCs were conscious that they were deprived of rights and privileges that were their due. Most of the working GSCs rarely got rest hours during work; 17 percent did not get any rest at all, while 49 percent got rest only for an hour.

Facility for Training, Education: GSCs were almost totally deprived of opportunities for training and education. All of them complained that they did not get any chance to study in schools. Without an exception they were tired and disgusted with the life they led and all asserted they were very eager to change their lives. When asked what needs they wanted to be fulfilled, they responded (pp.59-70):

Needs	Percent
Education	35
Vocational Training	18.5
Job/Employment	28.7
Financial Assistance	17.8

Love and Affection: A very vital psychological need, essential for proper mental growth of any child—rich or poor. In spite of their extreme physical deprivation, they seem to possess an urge to survive and a little love and affection could motivate them to make a better future for themselves.

Recommendations: Environmental support for proper expression of creativity is seriously lacking. Though some of the GSCs are found possessing creative talents, they have failed to cultivate them because of the absence of an environmental support.

It is clear that the older GSCs, compelled to live on streets, are the worst sufferers of the whole lot of the destitute children. They not only undergo severe hardships, at the physical level, but are also victims of deep psychological sufferings and frustrations. They openly blame their parents and the society at large for their wretched condition. Spending the whole day before the eyes of the passers by, without proper food and clothing, they develop a strong sense of anger and disgust. It is obvious that a planned programme must be undertaken for the GSCs, not only to give them a decent mode of life but also to protect them from the pimps and other anti-socials waiting to pounce on any unprotected older girl.

One effective measure may be a short-term training course in productive crafts like tailoring, doll-making and other jobs suitable for girls, and this should be accompanied by a monthly stipend to encourage the trainees to complete their course. Since the GSCs do not get any nutritious food, the centres may supply tiffin-packs and also one or two sets of clothing. Such incentives will definitely attract the GSC to the training course and will prevent them dropping out (pp.103-105).

GIRL CHILD IN PERIODICALS PUBLISHED BY WOMEN'S ORGANIZATIONS IN CALCUTTA

During the Year of the Girl Child, several special numbers were published. We are highlighting two of these: *Eksathe*, the journal of the Ganatantrik Mahila Samity, and *Sachetana*, the eponymous journal of the activists' group, mentioned earlier, that has functioned since 1982.

EKSATHE

Jasodhara Bagchi. 1992. '*Vidyasagar O kanyashishu*' (Vidyasagar and the Girl Child)

This article re-examines the crucial role played by Ishwarchandra Vidyasagar for the improvement of the social status of the girl child in our society. The girl child remains at the centre of most of his social reform: the spread of women's education by opening schools; protest against the polygamy of brahmin *kulins* resulting in numerous child widows, and finally his most militant battle against brahminical orthodoxy resulting in the legislation for widow remarriage in 1856. His campaign that extended from the domestic sphere to the state machinery is worth remembering even today. It tried to liberate many caste Hindu girl children from the unbearable shackles of forced ignorance and confinement.

Banani Biswas. 1991. '*Shishu kanyake raksha karo*' (Protect the Girl Child)

This article was read out at a seminar on the Girl Child Decade held on 3 August 1991, at Sramik Bhavan, Calcutta.

In 1990, the SAARC countries gave a call to 'Save the Girl Child' and had extended the time limit of the Girl Child Decade up to the end of the year 2000. India is the second largest populated country in the world where one hundred babies per thousand die within a year of their birth. Of them, the majority are girl children. From the point of view of food and nutrition, girls in India are being discriminated against, receiving 15 to 20 percent less calorie and protein than boys. During adolescence, when girls need maximum care and affection, they meet with indifference, negligence and exploitation. Thus, physically or mentally underdeveloped, they cannot be healthy mothers. As a result they suffer miscarriages, give birth to rickety children, and there is a high mortality rate among the newly born. The prevailing socioeconomic conditions which stand responsible for this gross injustice are also reflected in the sphere of education and job opportunities.

A 1981 survey shows that whereas 46 percent men are literate in the country, in the case of the women it is only 24 percent. A 1991 survey suggests the national literacy rate to be 52 percent, where the men's share is 63 percent against the women's 39 percent. According to a 1980-82 estimate, there were 4.45 crore boys in primary education, whereas the girls' share was 3 crores. The drop-out rate for girls at the primary level was 55.5 percent. According to a 1981 finding, excluding the drop-outs, 75 percent of the girl children were illiterate.

There has been no universal right to education in our national planning. Moreover, the prevalence of the feudalistic agricultural practices which control the rural economy opposes the expansion of education, particularly among the girl children. Poverty and starvation in particular cause girls to drop-out. From a tender age, they start their lives as beasts of burden, attending to numerous duties. They are excluded from any sort of amusement.

Whenever a girl is born, she is considered an unwanted being in the context of the need to marry her off, provide her with a dowry, and so on. Often a father incurs debt to get his daughter married, yet the situation seldom improves. The girl falls a prey to the greed of her husband and his in-laws, which often culminates in her murder.

There are 54 percent of Indians who are below the poverty line, which cripples opportunities in every sphere, particularly for girls. Though legally declared equal, women are not given the same status by society. The perpetuation of this inequitable situation has resulted in stagnation; and preparing for change itself requires continuous social and political movements, through which the slogan: 'Save the Girl Child' can be made a reality.

Mrinalini Dasgupta. 1991.'*Sadyasakshar narir samajik bhumika*' (The social role of the neoliterate woman).

Right from the age of six or seven, girl children in rural areas are forced to attend to various household chores and outdoor work, ranging from looking after younger siblings to cattle grazing. There are innumerable instances, where the parents themselves exploit their daughters, depriving them from schooling and amusements or force them to work in other families for earning money. The injustice continues because the womenfolk themselves are not organized. Had there been an act making primary education compulsory, the situation would have been different. In that case, every girl would have had to be given time for schooling and study. The existing social structure that has been created and protected by capitalism has to go. Otherwise, women's emancipation will remain a distant dream.

There are many illiterate mothers, each with three or four illiterate daughters. These women have to be inspired to participate in the literacy campaign. And once that is done, they themselves will inspire their daughters to come out of their cocoon of ignorance. A literate mother can protect her children from superstitions, epidemics, ultimely death and lifelong slavery to rich people. Once made literate, the women themselves will be able to recognize the system of exploitation around them. They will then unite and pull it down and work towards a better human society.

Manjari Gupta. 1990. 'Shisukanya bachao. Samajke bachao' (Save the girl child. Save society).

Gender identification and female foeticide not only amount to a great offence against women throughout the world, but also at the same time amount to a gross misuse of expensive scientific innovations in the medical sciences. Though the amniocentesis test is still confined to the upper and middle classes of Indian society, the majority of the parents; seem to have the same mentality, that is, a girl child is a liability and a boy, an asset. One girl and one boy form an 'ideal family', two boys 'not too bad', but two girls, oh, no. If it happens, it is the end of all hopes and aspirations of the parents. This attitude towards the girl child reflects the prevalent socioeconomic and cultural forces that provide no room for the healthy growth of girls.

Besides planned prevention of the birth of the girl child, the disparity in health care and nutrition, mentioned in other studies earlier, continues. This is how an utter imbalance is created, which in turn weakens society as a whole and retards the growth of a healthy demographic pattern.

Girl children are also discriminated against in spheres of education, culture and employment. Table 2.1 stands as a proof.

Instead of being reared with care and affection until the age of fourteen so that the girl child is equipped to inherit the rich cultural heritage of the country, the actual picture is totally different. Even at the age of five or six, the poor girl child is being forced to hard labour inside and outside her house. She is allowed very little scope for the healthy growth of her body and mind. At the work site, there is no job security. She is constantly haunted by the fear of retrenchment, suspension and other punishments. At home, she is berated by her parents or guardians for being a liability.'Gender justice' and 'gender exploitation' are vague terms. In reality, boys and girls in an exploited community are equally [sic] deprived of their rights and privileges. Exploitation emanates from the existing socioeconomic situation, and there is a need for immediate action.

Renuka Ray. 1991. 'Shishukanya barsher bhabona' (Thoughts in the Year of the Girl Child).
Man and woman produce a baby, create and develop a society. But when a girl is born, the social situation does not give her an equal status with the boy child. Thus a very responsible section of human society finds itself deprived from the very beginning, and gradually sinks into depression and inactivity.

The greedy, selfish society, which has no lofty principle to be guided by, stands responsible for the wrongs being done to a girl child. Through the ages, many sages, statesmen and reformers have advised mankind about the cruelties being perpetrated on women and girl children. We observe their birth and death anniversaries, read out their statements, their experiences, we swear in their names and we forget. Society continues to exploit women. Because society itself is based on exploitation.

Table 2.1. Discrimination of Girl Child

Year	Boys	Girls
Primary Education		
1982-83	4.75 crore	3 crore
1984-85	little over 5 crore	3.25 crore
Secondary Education		
1982-83	1.50 crore	1 crore
1984-85	2 crore	1.10 crore
High School		
1982-83	75 lakh	50 lakh
1984-85	80 lakh	60 lakh
Higher Secondary		
1982-83	5 lakh	3 lakh
1984-85	10 lakh	2.5 lakh

Extreme socioeconomic deprivation in countries like India constantly pumps fundamentalism, communalism, superstitions and sheer opportunism into society. The condition of a girl child is going to worsen under the prevailing circumstances. As soon as a girl is born, her parents or guardians label her as a liability and estimate how much she will require for her marriage in terms of dowry and other expenses. They never think that the girl is actually an asset of society and hence she deserves equal treatment with a boy in every respect, be it education, sports, physical and mental growth and recreation. This mentality has to be changed and the sooner it is done, the better.

It is the absence of security that makes parents afraid and this fear makes girl children feel unwanted. But this is a mere transitory phase. If the rights of women are recognized, if they are extended equal status with men in every sphere, parents and girl children will not feel insecure. Legal protection exists, but their implementation requires a strong and disciplined administration.

Bharati Ray. 1991. '*Meyelitta o shishukanya siksha*' (Womanliness and the education of the girl child).

The author severely lashes out at the traditions which have made women subservient to men inside and outside the family. Girls, through the ages, have been taught allegiance to the opposite sex and even unconditional surrender of their personal opinions, likes or dislikes and aspirations. True, the women's emancipation movements in the nineteenth century were spearheaded by men, but the real motive had nothing to do with the welfare of women, but the making of good mothers, good housewives or good daughters. At that time the native gentry of Bengal, which was created and patronized by the British rulers for the smooth running of the colonial administration, had themselves treated their womenfolk in the same way, remoulding them to suit their own desire. Women were given Western education but were seldom allowed to drop their femininity.

After fifty years after independence, when the nation needs equal labour from both men and women for developing the economy, should we continue casting the latter in the same mould? The government must change the curriculum from primary to postgraduate levels so that a relationship of mutual respect develops between men and women. Students have got to go through this realization that gender differentiation does not help growing up in a human society. Men and women should have equal status everywhere and in every respect.

SACHETANA

Sachetana (October-December, 1990). The girl child number of this journal contains several valuable analyses of the problem. The editorial calls attention, in no uncertain terms, to the right of the girl child. The increase in the number of girl children in the labour market has several adverse implications for the girl child, specially in poor families. With boys being enrolled in school, girl children are being harnessed to do the work that boys used to do. Referring to newspaper sources it points out that girls under fourteen account for 8 percent of the total labour force, boys 4 percent; adolescent girls under twenty account for 20 percent, boys 14 percent. There is an increase in the demand of the girl child in domestic service, as cheap and compliant labour. There has also been a rise in the recruitment of girls in the flesh trade.

The special number contains several poems on the girl child, both original and in translation. A reprint of a short story by a woman writer of the turn of the century (Saratkumari Chaudhurani) about a doll's marriage reflects the trials in the life of a girl child (pp.4-8). There is a historical analysis of the dowry system as it evolved under colonial rule (Sanyal 1990:16-19). In a substantial contribution (Banerjee and Bandyopadhyay 1990: 12-15) the ideological notion of '*kanyadai*' (the daughter-burden) is deconstructed and its implicit economic assumptions unearthed. Focusing on the new forms of female infanticide being practised in our society, the authors mention the hideous forms of son-preference that is commonly seen in our society. Citing an all India statistical table on the sex and age break-up of the infant mortality rate, they show how discrimination against girl children contributes to a reversal of the medical expectations of child survival rates in India. After an examination of the regional variation in infant mortality rates and the way casteism still practised in some parts of the country contribute to higher mortality among girls, the authors claim that the neglect of girl children and mothers of girl children is resulting in countrywide decimation of the girl child population. Amniocentesis is also discussed to indicate the way science provides a new and modern version of female infanticide.

'*Janmasutre aparadhi?*' (Guilty by birth? pp.39-40) is a translation based on a report entitled 'Juvenile Injustice', prepared for the Lawyers's Collective of Bombay by Sanwar Keshwar. It gives a historical account of the framing of laws on juvenile delinquents, pointing out the bias within laws themselves that result in greater criminalization of children.

'*Amar baro icchhe chhilo parar!*' (How I wished to study!) is based on an interview with an eleven-year-old girl child, Phullara—Phuli, in short. She has had to give up school in order to feed the family and look after the schooling of two brothers. Her father is the caretaker in a school and is too sick to earn a full month's wage. She earns Rs 320 per month working in four different households.

In the section on health Krishna Banerjee does a health profile of twelve-year-old Subala who has had to give up school and stay at home to look after her siblings and do the housework. She is constantly told off by her family for being born a girl. This is a relative privilege, because in a place like Rajasthan she would probably have been killed off by now. Subala suffers from anaemia and cannot see properly. She will lose her eyesight if she does not get food with vitamins. But who cares and who will provide, even if they do ? (Banerjee 1990: 46)

'*Kanyashishubarsha : kayekti prashna*' (Year of the Girl Child: A few questions). The problem of discrimination against the girl child is most visible in lower middle class families. The girl child has come to accept the discrimination in good grace.' After all, he is the brother', is all she says when she is deprived.

BOOKS/ARTICLES IN BOOKS

While the earlier history of the girl child in Bengal has received attention in books or articles in books, a great deal of the plight of the girl child today is relatively untouched in book-length studies or articles. A book belonging to the earlier part of the period covered has given us a number of case histories of girls who are pavement dwellers (Mukhopadhyay 1974: 90-97; 116-118). Comparatively speaking, girl child labour in Calcutta has received some attention. Bela Bandyopadhyay gives valuable case studies of girl children engaged in different industries and services of the unorganized sector, such as bulb factories, rubber cutting, cutting nylon pieces. They are all piece-rate workers working at home. She comments on the extremely unhygienic condition of work, the exploitative wage rates, and the lack of any labour legislation. Most of the girls engaged in these works have had to give up school to help out their respective families (Bandyopadhyay 1989). A more generalized study on child labour in Calcutta contains some information on the girl child (Sinha 1991).

A refreshing addition to this section is an analysis on the writings of some girl children in children's magazines (Chanda 1992). This article is based mainly on these sources : (*a*) the monthly magazine *Children's World*, (*b*) the children's page in the

Sunday Miscellany in *The Statesman*, and (c) the Bengali monthly *Suktara*. Those who write in English, though they focus more readily on the girl child, write under a double bind : the linguistic registers are both masculine and foreign. The pressure of the school curricula, with its emphasis on Romantic and Victorian poetry also percolates in these writings. Mothers are a strong presence in these wrtings. Once they move out of the orbit of the family, the writings rely very heavily on the stereotypes available in the media. There is silence over urgent areas in the lives of the girls such as the physical changes and the way in which girls cope These are their own voices which remind the author of her journey as she wrote herself into being a woman.

NEWSPAPER ARTICLES

[There has been a quantum leap in the newspaper coverage on the girl child. We conclude this chapter by highlighting a few of these.]

Char jelar kishorider janya prashikshan prakalpa, Ananda Bazar Patrika, 30.3.92

The central government finds adolescent girls in four West Bengal districts : Murshidabad, Malda, Purulia and Jalpaiguri— much more neglected than those in other parts of the state. The Government of India has introduced two special projects for these girls in 41 blocks of the concerned districts.

One of the projects is for the girls of 11-15 age range. *Char jelar kishorider janya* (for adolescent girls between 15 and 18).

Both the projects aim at providing nutrition and other health care for the girls concerned and enable them to be educated and vocationally trained.

Maitreyee Chatterjee. 1989. *Kono surjar alo ekhono pouchayni. Ananda Bazar Patrika,* Calcutta, 11.6.89.

The article speaks of child marriage abuse in Howrah District and refers to the activities of PIRA.

Premananda Ghosh. 1987. *Sundarbaner gram theke meye pachar hochhe uttarpradeshe. Bartaman.* 27.11.87.

The article speaks of the trafficking in women to Uttar Pradesh from remote villages in the Sundarbans. The victims are mostly girl children.

Jayanta Das. *Kanyabarshe shishu kanya sramikra. Jugantar,* Calcutta, 3.12.90.

According to the 1981 Census, West Bengal had 5,23,000 child workers below the age of 14 of whom 60 percent were girls. They were engaged in varieties of work.

Female foeticide is on the increase in the state: West Bengal stands fourth in the list with Maharashtra as the first.

Arunava Sinha. 1990. The scared children of Sealdah. *The Telegraph*, Calcutta, 9.12.90.

Teenage girls, aged between 8-15, found to be victims of regular sexual abuses on railway station platforms. Runaways from home or deserted by parents, these pre-puberty girls are paid Rs 7-15 by the clients. Some of them save part of the money and send it home.

REFERENCES

Most of this material has been meticulously researched and compiled by Dr. Ashim Mukhopadhyay on behalf of the project on the Girl Child and the Family, conducted by the School of Women's Studies, Jadavpur University. Sucharita Sahu, Baby Das and Sarbani Goswami have also helped with the collection of this material. Jashodhara Bagchi, however, accepts responsibility for any omission or commission of errors.

Bagchi, Jasodhara. 1992. *Vidyasagar o kanya shishu* (Vidyasagar and the girl child). *Eksathe*, ed. Kanak Mukherji, May.

Bandyopadhyay, Bela. 1989. *Abahelita kajer meyera* (Women in marginal work). In Ratnabali Chattopadhyay and Goutam Niyogi, eds., *Bharat itihase nari* (Women in Indian history) Calcutta: K.P.Bagchi.

Banerjee, Krishna.1990. *Subalear kahini* (Subala's story). *Sachetana*, Sept-Dec.

Banerji, Nirmala, and Bela Bandyopadyay. 1990. *Kanyadai baro dai* (The daughter-obligation is the worst). *Sachetana*, Sept-Dec:12-15.

Bardhan, Pranab. 1974. *On life and death problems. Economic and Political Weekly*, 32-34 (August):1293-1308.

Bhattacharya, Malini. (n.d.) *Meye dile sajiye*, edited by Sukumari Bhattacharji. Calcutta: Sachetana.

Bose, Debika. 1992. The girl child in early Bengali literature. In Vinay Kirpal, ed., *The girl child in twentieth century literature*, pp. 63-77. New Delhi: Sterling.

Chanda, Ipsita. 1992. Hearing voices once our own : Writing of girl children considered. In Vinay Kirpal, ed., *The girl child in twentieth century literature*. New Delhi: Sterling.

Char jelar kishorider janya prashikshan prakalpa. 1992 (Training programme for adolescent girls in four districts). *Ananda Bazar Patrika* 30 March.

Chatterjee, Maitreyee.1989. *Kono surjer alo pouchayni* (No sunshine reached here). *Ananda Bazar Patrika* 11 June.

Chattopadhyay, Amitabha.1982. *Chalachchitra, samaj o Satyajit Ray.* Asansol: Film Study Centre. Committee on the Status of Wmen, 1974.

Committee on the Status of Women, 1974. *Towards Equality* (Government of India).

Dandekar, Kumudini.1975. Why has the proportion of women in India's population been declining? *Economic and Political Weekly,* 9, 42 (Oct. 18): 1663-87.

Das, Jayanta. 1990. *Kanyabarshe shishukanya sramikra* (Girl child as labour in the year of the girl child). *Jugantar,* 3 December.

Dasgupta, Mrinalini.1991. *Sadyasakshar narir samajik bhumika* (The social role of the neoliterate women). *Eksathe,* ed. Kanak Mukherji, Oct:.120-23.

Ghosh, Premananda.1987. *Sundarbaner gram theke meye pachar hochhe uttarpradeshe* (Girl children are being abducted from Sunderbans and taken to Uttar Pradesh). *Bartaman,* 27 November.

Girl Child. 1988. State Level Workshop sponsored by CINI and UNICEF, 20-22 June, pp.34.

Gupta, Manjari. 1990. *Shisukanya bachao, samajke bachao* (Save the girl child, save the society), *Eksathe,* April:34-37; 40.

*Health for Millions.*1989. Generating awareness on the girl child : An overview. New Delhi, 15 June. pp.11-14.

Miller, Barbara, D. 1981. *The endangered sex: Neglect of female children in rural North India.* Ithaca: Cornell University Press.

Mukhopadhyay, Ashim.1974. *Footpather basinda* (The pavement dwellers).

____.1992. Compilation of material on girl street children of Calcutta.

Nandy, Moti. *Koni* (Calcutta: Ananda).

NIPCCD (National Institute of Public Co-operation and Child Development). 1990; 1991.*The pocketbook of statistics on child in India.*

PIRA (People's Institute of Rural Action). 1990. *Prasanga shishukanya* (Subject : Girl child). Report based on a survey in the districts of Howrah and Hoogly on girl children in 1988.

Ray, Bharati.1991. *Meyelitta o shisukanya shiksha* (Womanliness and the education of the girl child). *Eksathe,* ed. Kanak Mukherji, Oct:51-54.

Ray, Renuka. 1991. *Shisukanya barshe bhabona* (Thoughts on the year of the girl child).*Eksathe,* ed. Kanak Mukherji, Oct.

*Sachetana.*1990. *Shishukanya: janmasutre apradhi?* (Girl child : Guilty by birth?). *Sachetana* special no, Sept-Dec.

Sanyal, Manaswita. 1990. *Unabingsha shatabdir prekshapate panpratha* (The dowry system on the backdrop of the nineteenth century). *Sachetana,* Sept-Dec:16-19.

Shirali, Nina. 1990. *Kanyashishubarsha: kayekti prashna* (The year of the girl child : a few questions) *Sachetana*, Sept-Dec: 47.

Sen, Rushati.1992. *Ekti abadharita mrityu* (An inevitable death). *Baromash*, Autumn.

Sinha, Arunava. 1990. The scared children of Sealdah. *The Telegraph*, 9 December.

Sinha, Swapan. 1991. *Child labour in Calcutta.* Calcutta: Naya Prokash.

Situational analysis of women and children in West Bengal. 1989. Sponsored by UNICEF. Conducted by T. K. Banerjee, Jt. Director, Institute of Local Government and Urban Studies (ILGUS) and A.M.Chakraborty, Special Secretary, Calcutta Metropolitan Development Authority (CMDA).

Situational analysis of girl children in the city of Calcutta. 1989-90. Survey conducted by IPER (Institute of Psycholigical and Education Reserach), Calcutta.

Sen, Amartya. *Family and food : Sex bias in poverty*, mimeographed, Oxford University.

3
THE SAMPLE

METHODOLOGY AND CHOICE OF THE SAMPLE

The sample consisted of 600 households, drawn from four villages and two urban areas in West Bengal. A four-stage stratified random sampling process was used. The sampling units at the different stages were :

(i) district
(ii) village for rural areas/ward for urban areas
(iii) household
(iv) girl child

Stratification was used at two stages: first, at the district level and second, at the village or ward level. At the first stage, the districts were chosen. Two districts, one developed and the other underdeveloped, were chosen on the basis of their levels of economic development, as indicated in the Centre for Monitoring Indian Economy report (CMIE 1985). Other general development indicators were also considered during the selection.

In West Bengal, there are 17 districts varying widely in their levels of development. Of these, Barddhaman, which ranked second according to the CMIE index of economic development, both in 1980 and 1985, was chosen as the developed district.

The South 24-Parganas was chosen as the underdeveloped district from West Bengal. The erstwhile district of 24-Parganas has recently been divided into two districts, North 24-Parganas and South 24-Parganas, a division that reflects their different natures and levels of development. The North 24-Parganas is highly industrialized and well developed, whereas the South 24-Parganas is underdeveloped in several respects. Since these, however, have been recently declared as separate new districts, there is a scarcity of data for these districts individually. All available sources of reference say that South 24-Parganas belongs to the relatively underdeveloped group of districts in West Bengal. It has relatively low levels of per capita income and industrialization; no well-developed transport and communication systems over extensive areas and single cropping in agriculture. A substantial part of this district, which lies in the coastal areas of the state, has a very low level of development. Salinity poses special problems in agriculture as well as in the availability of potable water, which is of special concern for the women in the region. Employment opportunities are minimal. Though the old district of 24-Parganas does not rank very low down according to the CMIE index, South 24-Parganas would rank among the bottom 25 percent and was hence chosen as the underdeveloped district for the study.

Calcutta was chosen as the urban area to be surveyed for the sake of convenience, as our centre is located in Calcutta.

The second stage of stratification was in the selection of villages in the rural areas and in the selection of wards from the urban centre. Four villages, two each from Barddhaman and the South 24-Parganas, and two wards from Calcutta were chosen for the survey, keeping in mind a selected women's status indicator: female literacy. From each district two villages were chosen, one with a relatively high female literacy rate, and the other with a relatively low female literacy rate. The two urban wards were also chosen on the basis of their rank according to the female literacy rate: one with a relatively high female literacy rate, and the other with a relatively low female literacy rate.

Data on female literacy rates were obtained from the *District Census Handbooks* (1981), which listed the police stations in each distirct and provided information about each with respect to various socioeconomic indicators, female literacy rate included. In each district, the police stations were ranked in descending order of their female literacy rates, and two police stations were chosen, from the top 25 percent of the lists: Raina in Barddhaman district and Sonarpur in South 24-Parganas district. Similarly, two police stations were chosen from the bottom 25 percent of the lists: Ausgram, from Barddhaman district and Basanti from the South 24-Parganas.

Next, a list of all the villages in these four police stations was formed, once again ranking the villages in descending order of their female literacy rates. From Raina (Barddhaman) and Sonarpur (South 24-Parganas), the police stations with high female literacy rates, two villages, one from each police station, were chosen; each village belonging to the top 25 percent of their lists. Similarly, from Ausgram (Barddhaman) and Basanti (South 24-Parganas) two low female literacy rate villages were selected.

All the villages were selected, keeping in mind two other considerations as well: (i) the availability of scheduled caste/scheduled tribe (SC/ST) households; and (ii) the availability of at least 200 households in each village. The four villages so chosen were:

(a) Gunar from Raina, Barddhaman
(b) Pichkuri from Ausgram, Barddhaman
(c) Kustia from Sonarpur, South 24-Parganas
(d) Phulmalancha from Basanti, South 24-Parganas

Gunar and Kustia were the two villages with high female literacy rates; and Pichkuri and Phulmalancha were the two villages with low female literacy rates.

The four villages thus represented the following combinations:

(a) Positive development index and high female literacy: Gunar
(b) Positive development index, but low female literacy: Pichkuri
(c) Negative development index, but high female literacy: Kustia
(d) Negative development index and low female literacy: Phul-malancha

For Calcutta, too, two wards were chosen for survey, one with high female literacy and the other with low female literacy. *The District Census Handbook for Calcutta* (1981) provided information about the female literacy rates of all the wards in the city, which were then arranged in the descending order of their female literacy rates. Ward No. 96, in the Jadavpur area, was chosen as the high female literacy ward from the top 25 percent of the list; and Ward No. 79, in the Khidirpur area, was chosen as the low female literacy ward, from the bottom 25 percent of the list.

Within each selected village and ward, 100 households were chosen for survey, around 15 percent of which belonged to the schedule castes (SC) and scheduled tribes (ST) families. Both in the villages and in the urban wards, the households were chosen using the technique of systematic random sampling.

The sample drawn from each village and ward consisted of about 15 SC/ST households and about 85 non-SC/ST households. In drawing the sample of 100 households from each urban ward, two localities were selected: one primarily consisting of lower socioeconomic status households and the other primarily consisting of middle socioeconomic status households. During the selection of the two localities, care was taken to ensure that there were a sufficient number of SC/ST households.

The high female literacy ward, Ward No. 96, had no contiguous area of slum settlements. So the low socioeconomic status households were selected from the refugee colonies in the area, which housed resettled refugees from East Bengal (now Bangladesh). Forty such households were selected. The middle socioeconomic status households were selected from other areas of the ward. These households also largely of families who had their origins in

East Bengal (now Bangladesh), but these families had a considerably higher income level as compared to the families living in the refugee colonies. Sixty were included.

The low female literacy ward, Ward No. 79, had large areas of contiguous slum dwellings. One such slum was selected for the survey, keeping in mind the availability not only of SC/ST households but also of households belonging to different religious groups. The middle socioeconomic status households were chosen from the non-slum areas of the ward. Fifty households were selected for survey from each of the areas.

In order to draw the sample from a village, first, a list of all the households was obtained from the Gram Panchayat office. Two separate lists were then compiled, one consisting of all the SC/ST households and the other comprising the non-SC/ST households. For the two urban wards, first the voters' lists of each of them was obtained from the Corporation office, from which the lists of households, both SC/ST and non-SC/ST, were prepared. The required number of sample households were then selected from the respective lists using a systematic random sampling technique.

The method of drawing the sample is described by taking an example. If, for instance, the number of SC/ST households in a village was 1055, from which a sample of 85 households was to be drawn, the households would be selected systematically according to a fixed interval. This interval would first be calculated thus:

> interval = *total no of households ÷ sample size*
> This means that the interval = $1055 ÷ 85 = 12.4$.
> The figure 12.4 is rounded off to 12, which becomes the
> interval at which the sample is drawn.

Now, out of the first 12 households in the list (since 12 was the interval), one household was taken at random. This could be done by drawing one slip out of twelve slips of paper, each containing one number, ranging from 1 to 12.

If we assumed that the slip contained serial no.7, then we started from the household no.7 in the household list, and went on selecting every twelfth household from the list thereafter. The list of selected households thus became: 7, 19, 31, 43 . . . 1027 . . . and so on.

There always remained the possiblity, however, that a household so selected in the sample might not have a girl child between the ages of 6 to 18 years. To guard against such instances, a few extra households needed to be selected, so that such a household might be easily substituted by other households in the list. Around 10 additional households were thus chosen for inclusion in the sample in each area.

After reaching the end of the household list (i.e., no. 1055, in this instance), the counting was continued by going to the beginning of the list once again. The counting was continued till the requisite number of households had been drawn. In the example just discussed, after serial no.1027, the list would read as, 1039, 1051, 9, 22 . . . and so on. Care would be taken to exclude those households from the counting which had already been included in the sample. That was why, households at serial nos.7 and 19 had been excluded from the counting in this round. A similar procedure was adopted for drawing the sample of the 15 SC/ST households. In the two urban wards too, the same procedure was used to draw the sample of the requisite number of households from each locality. Here, also, the samples of SC/ST and non-SC/ST households were drawn separately, with a few extra households for substitution.

After selecting the 600 households, the next step was to select one girl child in the age group of 6-18 years from each household. In a household with more than one girl child, a simple random sample of one girl child from that household was selected out of the available girl children by the method of drawing slips, as described earlier. This was done to ensure the inclusion of girl children of various age groups as well as of different orders of birth (i.e., eldest, middle child, youngest, and so on).

In each household, a total of three questionnaries were filled up. One was addressed to the girl child herself, seeking her ideas, opinions and perceptions about her health, education, socialization and work status. One questionnaire related to the household as a whole and sought to obtain information in general about the background of the girl child, her living conditions and the other members of the family. The third questionnaire was addressed to the mother (or mother substitute, in case the biological mother was not available) of the girl child, which sought information about the mother herself, the respondent girl child, and the other children in the family. Particular care was taken to observe the gender dimensions of the responses.

In addition to these questionnaries there were also separate schedules to be filled up giving the characteristics of each area surveyed. That is, six primary schedules were filled up, containing detailed information about the four villages and two urban wards that were chosen for survey.

AREA PROFILES

GUNAR

As mentioned earlier, the village of Gunar, which belongs to the district of Barddhaman, was chosen for our survey as the high female literacy village from the developed district. Its area is roughly 425 acres, of which close to 400 acres are cultivated. The residential area consists of about 15 acres with the houses arranged in three or four clusters of varying sizes.

The environment

The village is built on a slightly elevated land mass, which slopes downwards toward the principal approach to the village and the paved main road, which is also the bus route. The main road lies actually about half a kilometre away from the village, passing at this point through Gunar Boropukur. Though a wide *kutcha* road leads up from the main road to the village, all pathways within the village itself are extremely narrow, permitting travel by foot or bicycle only—and sometimes not even the latter. This is a flood prone area; indeed, a heavy shower is enough to make the roads so muddy and slushy as to render them almost unusable.

The houses are clustered largely according to caste, with the SC, ST and other castes forming separate settlements. Most of the houses are kutcha and the few *pucca* houses that exist either belong to very large farmers or to rich businessmen. The nearest city, Barddhaman, which is also the district headquarters, is at a distance of 37 km. from the village.

Water and electricity

The village is electrified, though the voltage at all times is extremely low, and the area suffers from daily power-cuts which last for several hours at a stretch.Of the 400 acres of cultivated land, only 13 acres are irrigated: the main sources of water for irrigation are some ponds, six water tanks and ten shallow tubewells. However, not all the shallow tubewells are operative. Five tubewells are diesel-operated and five operated by electricity. Of the latter five, three have been disconnected by the government. All other sources, that is, the government canal and the electrified deep tubewell are non-functional. Even the river Ajoy, which flows by the village, is dry most of the year. Drinking water comes mainly from the seventy-six handpumps, six of which have been installed by the government and the rest are privately owned. Water for all other purposes comes from the fifteen ponds in the village, only four of which are used for purposes of irrigation.

Health and education

The closest public health centre (PHC) is situated at the village of Maheshbati, 5 km. away from Gunar, and the nearest government hospital is at Raina II, which is about the same distance away. There is, however, a PHC sub-centre at the neighbouring village of Sanktia, about half a kilometre away. For all other medical facilities, the villagers have to travel to Bardhhaman.

There is an anganwadi/ICDS centre within the village, as well as a primary school. The nearest high school is at Sanktia. The closest college is to be found at Shyamsundar, a small town, about 7 km. away.

Population

The total population of the village is around 1229 (Census 1981), of which 656 are males and 573 females, residing in 212 households. An exclusively Hindu settlement, there are 33 SC and 30 ST households, the rest belonging to the other castes. The major occupation of the residents is cultivation (including share cropping and agricultural labour), though there are a few businessmen and service-holders. Almost all the children are enrolled in school, and attend either the village primary school or the high school at Sanktia. There are a few drop-outs, but practically all of them have been enrolled in school at one time or another.

Panchayat

The village has a panchayat which is extremely active and has implemented the following programmes: *(a)* Integrated Rural Development Programme (IRDP) and Rural Labour Employment Generation Programme (RLEGP); *(b)* afforestation; *(c)* advancement of irrigation; *(d)* production of HYV; and *(e)* relief operations. Moreover, adult literacy classes were being held under the National Literacy Programme, and had received widespread support from all quarters.

Conclusion

Gunar is a reasonably affluent village. It is well connected by road and rail to many towns in Barddhaman and even to Calcutta, lying as it does, right off the Barddhaman Road. Boys and girls have easy access to schools and colleges since economic conditions are not a constraint in most cases. All these are likely to be positive influences on the condition of the girl child. A serious problem is that the area is prone to flooding. The muddy condition of the roads increases the drop-out rate among the girls substantially.

PICHKURI

The village of Pichkuri, belonging to the district of Barddhaman, was chosen, as mentioned earlier, as the village with low female literacy in a developed district.

The environment

The total area of the village is around 945 acres, of which 900 acres are cultivated, and about 23 acres comprise the residential area. The village is large and sprawling with wide kutcha roads criss-crossing its area. The main road is, however, quite a distance away, and the nearest bus stop is at least 3 km. away. The railway station is closer, about 1 km. away, but the road from the railway station to the village is so narrow that the only means of travel are walking or riding a bicycle. The nearest town is Guskara, at a distance of 7 km. away. Bolpur town, which is also the station for Santiniketan, is about 12 km. away.

Water and electricity

There are two rivers flowing past the village, Ajoy and Kunur. Because the Ajoy is mostly dry during the year, water from the Kunur is used for irrigation. All the 900 acres of cultivated land are irrigated, the chief source of water being the 120 diesel-operated shallow tubewells. There are also 21 water tanks, one government canal and 8 deep tubewells (of which 4 have been installed by the government), all of which are used for irrigation. The chief sources of drinking water are the 31 hand-pumps of which 20 are privately owned. Only 2 of the 60 ponds are used for irrigation, the rest being put to use for other purposes. There are no electrical connections in the area and hence no electrified deep tubewells, either.

Health and education

The closest PHC is at Baunabagram, a village 15 km. away. However, there is a DMC-subcentre within the village itself. The nearest government hospital is located at Guskara. All other medical facilities are available either at Bolpur or at Barddhaman, the district headquarters, which is at a distance of 40 km. away. There is however a sub-health centre at Ukta, the village next to Pichkuri, about 0.5 km. away, and there are six community health workers in the village itself.

There is an Anganwadi/ICDS Centre in the village as well as a primary school. Ukta-Pichkuri High School lies practically within the village and serves both Pichkuri and Ukta. Guskara has a high school as well as a college to which students from Pichkuri travel. There is also a madrassa for Muslim students.

Population

The total population of the village is 2286 (Census 1981), of which 1210 are male and 1076 female, residing in 312 households. The settlement is predominantly Muslim, with 235 Muslim households, 41 SC households, 31 ST households and with only 5 households belonging to the other castes. Almost all the residents are cultivators, sharecroppers or agricultural labourers. Only a few are small businessmen (e.g. shopowners) and service holders. At the time of the survey there were 200 children enrolled in the primary school (110 male and 90 female) and 300 in the high school (230 male and 70 female). In addition there currently 55 children at the ICDS centre, 40 boys and girls studying at the madrassa and 32 children enrolled in the literacy classes.

Panchayat

The village has a panchayat government which has implemented a few schemes under the IRDP, some health and children-oriented programmes, and has initiated two adult education centres under the National Literacy Programme.

Conclusion

Pichkuri is situated at one end of Barddhaman, almost on the Birbhum border. Transport facilities are poor, and usually the only means of reaching this area is by walking from the railway station or bus stop. The general economic condition is rather poor.

KUSTIA

The village of Kustia, South 24-Parganas, was chosen for survey as the high female literacy village in an underdeveloped district.

The environment

The total area of the village is about 183 acres of which 142.25 are cultivated.The main road passes through Chakberia, which is about 0.5 km. away from Kustia. All the roads within the village are either kutcha or brick-paved. This is an extremely picturesque village with trees, flourishing fields and numerous ponds. At first glance the area appears to be rather well developed, with well-kept cottages, most of which are electrified, with handpumps here and there and even a few television antennae. However, one later realizes that all the development has occurred in the area surrounding the panchayat office, which is predominantly an upper class Hindu settlement. The SC and the Muslims have separate settlements at the two extremities of the village, which are largely in poor condition. The nearest city is Calcutta and the nearest town Rajpur.

Water and Electricity

The chief sources of drinking water are the 25 or 26 privately owned handpumps. The shallow tubewells are also occasionally used for this purpose.Most of the cultivated area is unirrigated; about 42.2 hectares are supplied by irrigational sources. There are three canals, of which one does not function througout the year. A major disadvantage is that water from the canals overflow during the monsoon. The river Vidyadhari is also used for purposes of irrigation. The other major sources of irrigational water are the shallow tubewells, about 8-10 in number. The village is electrified.

Health and education

The closest PHC is at Subhasgram, 12 km. from the village, and there is a sub-health centre at Kasinathpur, which is about 4 km. from Kustia. For all other medical facilities, including government hospitals, one has to travel to Calcutta. The village has one primary school as well as a private English-medium primary institution. There are high schools at Champahati and Kalikapur, both being about 4 km. away.

Population

The total population of the village is about 1128 (Census 1981), of which 577 are male and 551 female, residing in about 272 households. The main occupation is cultivation, most of the cultivators belonging to the class of upper caste Hindus, who own most of the cultivable land. The agricultural labourers come mostly from the SC and Muslim families. There are quite a few service-holders among the caste Hindus, who work in Calcutta. There are some businessmen as well. The Muslims who are not agricultural labourers are either small poultry farmers or work as masons. Among the SC families the chief occupational groups are wage labourers, artisans, and so on. Apart from this, several of them have availed of government loans to buy van-rickshaws, which serve as a means of livelihood.

Panchayat

The village has a panchayat, which has implemented several schemes under the District Rural Development Authority (DRDA) programme. There are also adult education and family welfare programmes in the village, though the former has not been very effective.

Conclusion

Kustia is located quite close to Calcutta and is well connected to the city by both road and rail. Urban influences are quite visible in the people, both in their demeanour and in the nature of their possessions, specially among upper caste Hindu households. Exposure to radio and television is quite high. The poverty-stricken, unhygienic conditions in the Muslim and SC settlements present a sharp contrast to the rest of the village.

PHULMALANCHA

The village of Phulmalancha, South 24-Parganas, was chosen for our survey as the village with low female literacy from an under-developed district.

The environment

It is a fairly large village with a total area of about 1992 acres. The total cultivated area amounts to 1672 acres of which only 172 acres are irrigated. The village lies in the Sundarban area and is close to the mouth of the Ganga and the Bay of Bengal. The river Matla flows nearby.The main road is quite far away, the closest bus stop is Canning, at a distance of 22 km. The nearest railway station, Basanti, is also 22 km. away. The only mode of transport from the bus stop or the railway station are the van-rickshaws which travel to and fro. All the roads within the village are kutcha roads, mostly of mud, while some of them are brick-paved.

Water and Electricity

The major sources of irrigation are the two canals and the numerous ponds which are found all over the village. There is an acute shortage of drinking water in the area; the chief source being the handpumps, of which there are only nine in the entire village.

Health and education

The closest PHC is at Basanti, 22 km. from the village, but there is a PHC sub-centre at Kathalberia which is about 7 km. away. There are government hospitals both at Canning and Basanti. For all other medical facilities, one has to travel to the district headquaters, located in the state capital, Calcutta, which is 90 km. away. There are a Balwadi centre and an Anganwadi/ICDS centre. There are two primary schools within the village, one of them run by Christian missionaries, and Phulmalancha Junior High School. There is a madrassa at Nirdeshkhali, at a distance of 3.50 km. from the village.

Population

The total population of the village is 8148, of which 4066 (from Panchayat Records) are male and 4082 female, residing in 1444 households. There are 539 Muslim households, 155 Christain households, 598 Hindu households (of which 544 belong to the scheduled caste) and 162 scheduled tribe households—the settlements being separate for each religious group and caste. Most of the residents are cultivators or agricultural labourers. Some non-agricultural labourers and fishermen are also to be found.

Panchayat

The panchayat has implemented several schemes under the IRDP: cultivation of vegetables, processing of paddy, granting loans for the purchase of van-rickshaws and setting up of tea stalls, promoting fishing and fishing-net weaving, and so on. There are health programmes for mother and child and adult education classes. The National Afforestation Programme is also underway.

Conclusion

Phulmalancha is a large, sprawling village. General economic conditions are very poor. Transport and communication system to and from this area is not at all well developed.There is a drinking water problem in this village and women and girl children have to travel long distances to fetch water.

CALCUTTA : WARD NO. 79

Ward No. 79 in Calcutta was chosen for the survey as the urban area with low female literacy. It lies in the Khidirpur area of the city, and the 100 households in the sample were divided into two groups of 50 each, one group being chosen from the slum area of Hossain Shah Road and the other group being chosen from some non-slum, middle class areas of the ward.

The environment

The total area of the ward is 3.2 sq. km. and it has about 10 km. of paved roads. The exceptions are the slums and the settlements (quarters) of the low-income group port and dock workers.There are about three or four large slum settlements, one of them entirely Hindu and the others have a mix of many religions, groups and communities. The slum chosen for our survey has a mixed population of Hindus, Muslims, Christains, Sikhs and even some Buddhists. This slum has houses built extremely close to one another—some are kutcha and some are pucca houses, but the greatest number are of the combination type. Most of them have just one room, which is used for all purposes, even for cooking and the bathing of girls and women. There is an acute shortage of drinking water in the slum area with only 120 public taps, and each serves about 30 households. Houses in the non-slum areas, however, have individual tap-points provided by the government. Public toilets are also very few in number, one privy being provided for about 50-60 slum households.

The non-slum area has wide, paved roads and the residents live in large pucca houses or apartment houses.

Health and Education

There are three primary schools in the ward, six middle schools, of which one is Oriya-medium and two are Urdu-medium, and eight high schools. Enrolment in school also varies sharply according to whether the children belong to the slum or non-slum areas.

There are no PHC or health centres within the ward, nor any government hospital. Private practitioners abound, however, and clinics in the neighbouring wards are easily accessible. There is, however, a private nursing home within the ward and a hospital run by the port authorities, which serves only the port employees. In addition, a mobile medical service is operated by the CMDA.

Population

The ward has a total population of 46,144 (Census 1981) of which 29,936 are males and 16,308 are females, residing in 12,209 households. Most of the residents in the non-slum area are service-holders, though a large number of businessmen can also be found. The chief occupation of the people in the slum area is petty business and trading, though people of almost all occupational groups—labourers who work for daily wages, carpenters, artisans, drivers and even sweepers—are settled here.

Local government

The ward comes under the jurisdiction of the Calcutta Municipal Corporation and has one elected councillor to represent the people. Some employment-generating schemes have been begun by government authorities, but the system does not function very efficiently due to a lack of proper communication between the people and the authorities. Though some sanitary privys and water taps have been provided, the numbers are yet quite insufficient.

Class Contrasts

A sharp contrast is noticeable between the slum and non-slum areas of this ward. In the non-slum, middle class areas, the development of the girl child is not being hindered in any obvious material sense. She generally comes from a well-to-do family, is healthy, well looked after, enrolled in a good school, and has the opportunity to participate in various extracurricular activities. More subtle forms of discrimination, however, are observed in some cases. The girl children from the slum areas are undernourished, over-worked at home, taking on the burden of both housework and care of younger siblings, and live in the most unhygienic of surroundings. About 60 percent of the girl children are enrolled in school, and most of them drop out after the primary or middle level.

CALCUTTA: WARD NO. 96

Ward No. 96 in Calcutta was chosen as the urban area with high female literacy. The ward lies in the Jadavpur area of the city, its total area being about 1.6 sq.km.

The environment

The ward has 12 km. of paved and 1 km. of unpaved roadways. Most of the houses are pucca houses, with a few kutcha houses or *jhopris* scattered here and there. There are no slum settlements in this ward, only a few clusters of hutments of 4/5 households each, distributed over the ward. The main source of drinking water are the handpumps, 42 of which are now operative. In addition, there are 8 deep tubewells and 23 or 24 ponds, though water from the ponds are not used for purposes of drinking. Each house, moreover, has a corporation tap-point, which provides it with running water within the house. This water too, is generally not used for drinking.

Health and education

The ward has a total of 3 schools, one primary and two high schools. It also has one college at Bijoygarh. There is one government hospital within the ward located at Bijoygarh, one CGHS centre at Regent Estate and a municipal dispensary at Layalka.

However, there are a large number of private practitioners and small clinics and diagnostic centres. Moreover, all medical facilities in the neighbouring wards are easily accessible.

Population

The ward has a total population of 27,851 (Census 1981), predominantly Hindus, of which 14,171 are males and 13,680 are females, residing in a total of 5116 households. Most of the residents are service-holders and a few are businessmen. Almost all the children go to school in various parts of the city and most continue to study in colleges and polytechnic institutions after high school.

Local government

The ward comes under the jurisdiction of the Calcutta Municipal Corporation, with one elected councillor to represent the people. There are no government schemes being implemented, in general, in the ward.

Migrants form more than half the population of the ward, having settled here after independence, originally being residents of Bangladesh. Hence, they have had to establish themselves in a new city, starting from scratch which, along with the other migrant qualities of being more mobile and outgoing, also makes them generally more receptive to new ideas and more progressive in thought amd action. Most of the residents are quite well educated, their occupational structure showing a bias towards the service sector, and they are interested in the educational attainment of their children, both boys and girls. The girl child almost never suffers from overt material discrimination and is encouraged to pursue higher education and an independent career right from childhood. Less obvious forms of discrimination, however, may be noticed in some cases.

4
THE FAMILY ENVIRONMENT

The physical environment that the girl child lives in, her socio-cultural setting, the economic condition of her family, the attitudes and the educational level of her parents, all have an important bearing on the quality of her life. We present an overview of this background in which the girl child of our survey is located, divided into two sections: *(i)* the household; and *(ii)* the mother.

It is well known that the primary influence in the life of a child is her/his mother. This is particularly true in the case of the girl child because she spends the largest part of her day in the company of her mother. As such, the mother's educational background, her economic status and her perceptions and attitudes about life play a major role in the development process of her daughter. Details about the health, education and work status of the mother respondents have been given in the next section (p.72) along with some information about her ideas, opinions and attitudes with regard to her children.

In some cases the biological mothers of the girl children concerned were not available. This was because some of the girls were married and had moved to their husbands' homes, or because the girl child worked and lived away from home. A few had lost their mothers. In all these cases the questions addressed to the mother were put to the mother substitutes (other female relatives such as aunt, mother-in-law, sister). There were some questions, however, like the immunization history of the girl child, or the duration of her breastfeeding, which the mother substitutes were not competent to answer and, on these questions, their responses were not included in the analysis but were grouped along with those cases where answers were not available.

THE HOUSEHOLD

This section gives information about the nature of households that the respondent girl children live in.

RELIGION, LANGUAGE AND MIGRATORY STATUS

The first part of this section gives an idea about the general socio-cultural characteristics of the households included in our sample. Table 4.1 shows the distribution of households according to religion. As expected, Hindus form the majority, with a sizeable number of Muslim households and smaller numbers of Christians, Sikhs and Buddhists. In the two households that have been identified in this table as households with mixed religions, the different family members belong to different religious groups.

It is interesting to note that no special effort was made to include all these religious groups in our sample; it occurred naturally during the selection procedure.

Table 4.1 Households: Distribution According
to Religious Groups

	Households No/(%)
Hindu	402 (67.0)
Muslim	135 (22.5)
Christian	15 (2.5)
Other Religious Groups	45 (7.5)
Mixed Religions	2 (0.3)
N.A.	1 (0.2)
Total	600 (100)

The castewise breakdown of the households is shown in Table 4.2. The number of families belonging to the backward classes is minimal, which is as expected in West Bengal.

Table 4.2   Households: Distribution According to Caste

	Households No/(%)
Scheduled Caste	
Higher	107 (17.8)
Lower	52 (8.7)
Other Hindu Castes	
Brahmin	52 (8.7)
Non-Brahmin Upper Castes	189 (31.5)
Other Backward Classes	2 (0.3)
Scheduled Tribe	45 (7.5)
Other Religious Groups	152 (25.3)
N.A.	1 (0.2)
Total	600 (100)

Table 4.3   Households: Distribution According
to Mother Tongue

	Households No/(%)
Bengali	512 (85.3)
Hindi	22 (3.7)
Santhali	33 (5.5)
Kurmali	8 (1.3)
Marwari	7 (1.2)
Others	18 (3.0)
Total	600 (100)

Table 4.3 reveals that the majority of the sample of 600 households were Bengali-speaking. However, we obtained a variety of other mother tongues across the remaining 88 households. Of these, 33 had Santhali as their mother tongue. Almost all the Santhali-speaking households belong to the rural areas, and form the bulk of the scheduled tribe households in our sample. A total of 16 different mother tongues was observed across the 600 families interviewed, including Bengali, Santhali, Hindi, Assamese, English, Garhwali, Bhojpuri, Kurmali, Marwari, Nepali, Malayalam, Oriya, Punjabi, Tamil, Telugu, and Urdu. With the exception of Kurmali, which, like Santhali, is a language spoken predominantly by the ST population in the rural areas, all the other languages related to households in the two urban areas. These areas were much more multilingual in nature, with a liberal mixture of people from all parts of the country. The spectrum of mother tongues, apart from Bengali, occurred naturally in our sample. No special endeavour was made to obtain households with non-Bengali mother tongues.

Table 4.4 Households : Migration Status

	Households No/(%)
Migrant	162 (27.0)
Non-Migrant	432 (72.0)
Once migrant now returned	3 (0.5)
N.A.	3 (0.5)
Total	600 (100)

The migration pattern of the households is shown in Table 4.4. The majority of the migrant population was found in the two urban areas surveyed, especially in Ward 96, in Jadavpur. The largest

number of migrants from the rural areas are from the scheduled
tribes. The scheduled caste households and the households of
other Hindu castes or other religious groups have usually been
settled in the village for several generations.

SOCIOECONOMIC BACKGROUND

Table 4.5 Households : Main Occupation

	Households No/(%)
Piece-rate workers	9 (1.5)
Business	35 (5.8)
Petty business	20 (3.3)
Agriculture/Share cropping	209 (34.8)
Artisan/Craftsman	7 (1.2)
Agricultural Labour	127 (21.2)
Manual wage workers (non-agricultural)	27 (4.5)
Others	8 (1.2)
No specific household occupation	157 (26.2)
N.A.	1 (0.2)
Total	600 (100)

The bulk of the rural households were engaged in agriculture.
(See Table 4.5). The significance of the 157 households that did
not have a definite occupation meant that they did not have a
definite, traditional household occupation which was taken up by
the family members, generation after generation. These households consist of families which are largely service-holders, and the
majority of these families belonged to the urban sector.

In the course of the survey it was observed that about 73
percent households had no subsidiary occupation. In most of the
other households which had a subsidiary occupation, the members worked as manual wage workers, agricultural labourers, or
piece-rate workers. A very small number of households had
fishing and animal husbandry as subsidiary occupations. These
two occupations were however entirely absent from the list of main
occupations of the 600 households in this region.

Table 4.6 Households : Distribution According
to Father's Occupation

	Households No./(%)
Senior professionals	44 (7.3)
Junior professionals and middle level officials	32 (5.3)
Other white collar jobs	26 (4.3)
Service-unspecified	34 (5.7)
Skilled workers	20 (3.3)
Unskilled workers	37 (6.2)
Big farmers: (more than 10 acres of land holding)	14 (2.3)
Medium-size farmers:(5-10 acres of land holding)	9 (1.5)
Marginal farmers:(1-5 acres of land holding)	90 (15.0)
Farmers: (land size unspecified/share cropper)	13 (2.2)
Fishermen	1 (0.2)
Agricultural labourers	106 (17.7)
Large-and medium-size businessmen	40 (6.7)
Petty businessmen	35 (5.8)
Washermen, barbers, cobblers, sweepers and other similar occupations	4 (0.7)
Piece-rate workers (home-based and otherwise)	2 (0.3)
Any other occupation not mentioned above	3 (0.5)
Unemployed	20 (3.3)
Inapplicable : no father or father not alive	36 (6.0)
N.A.	34 (5.6)
Total	600 (100)

The household's occupation and the father's occupation (Table 4.6) have a clear impact on the economic and the socio-cultural environment of the girl child. Of the 126 who were farmers, the majority, 90, were marginal farmers, holding about 1-5 acres of land. Eighteen percent of the girls had fathers who were agricultural labourers. We have seen in Table 4.5, that 209 households, that is, about 35 percent, had agriculture as their main occupation. It was also observed that 127 households had agricultural labour as their main occupation. Comparing Tables 4.5 and 4.6, it is seen that the number of households where the fathers were farmers (21%) is considerably less than the number of households with farming as their household occupation (35%). This shows that quite a lot of agricultural families were, in this generation, diversifying into other occupations, and had either given up farming altogether or practised it only as a subsidiary occupation. It was also seen that the number of families where the fathers were agricultural labourers were fewer than the number of families whose main household occupation was agricultural labour. However, the difference is not as much as the difference obtained in the case of the farming families. For agricultural labourers the difference was only about 3 percent, whereas for farmers, the difference was as much as 14 percent. This shows that though the families of agricultural labourers may have been trying to branch out into other occupational modes, they had not found it as easy as the farming families, possibly because their resources and opportunities were quite severely limited and did not offer too much scope for change.

The fathers of about 22 percent of the girl children were either professionals, or service holders. All of them held white collar jobs and came mostly from urban areas. In over 12 percent of the families the fathers were businessmen. In about 3 percent households, the fathers were unemployed.

ECONOMIC CONDITION OF THE FAMILIES SURVEYED

Information about the economic condition of the families surveyed: the asset position, the household incomes, the extent of indebtedness, and so on are presented.Table 4.7 (condensed from other detailed tables) shows the status of the households with respect to ownership of various assets. Only 46 households, that is, about 8 percent of the total, did not own any house or house plot. All the other families owned some kind of a house or piece of land which could be used for building a house. The largest number (45%) owned only a *kutcha* house. Around 20 percent had *pucca* houses or flats. Evidently these were urban households. Close to 22 percent owned a house as well as another house plot. Out of the 600 households, 252 owned agricultural land and 200 were in the urban sector, the majority of which owned no agricultural land whatsoever. Therefore of the 400 rural households, more than 50 percent owned some agricultural land. However, only 18 households owned more than 5 acres. Sixty-three families owned less than 1 acre of land and not even one household owned more than 20 acres. We observe that 306 households owned either cattle or poultry or other farm animals. This means that 294

households had no cattle or animals at all. Most of these households were from urban areas. With regard to ownership of audio-
visual gadgets we found that 205 households had no audio-visual
gadgets. At least 209 families owned a radio or a transistor; 170
families owned televisions. Most of the households that owned a
TV set owned transistors or radios as well. There is no reason to
assume, however, that those families which own no audio-visual
gadgets were totally cut off from the audio-visual media. These
families belonged either to the poorer sections of the rural population or to the slum areas of Ward No. 79, in the Khidirpur
neighbourhood of Calcutta. It was not uncommon to find a TV
owner's house crowded with neighbours, all gathered to watch TV
together. It may be said that families without a TV or a radio often
had free and easy access to their neighbours' sets and used these
facilities almost as regularly as their owners did.

Table 4.7 Households: Asset Ownership

	Households No/(%)
House/house plot non-agricultural	554 (92.7)
Agricultural land	252 (42.0)
Cattle/farm animal/poultry/fish	306 (51.0)
Audio-visual gadgets	395 (65.8)

Table 4.8 Households: Distribution According to Fathers' Monthly Income

Income	Households No/(%)
No Income	29 (4.8)
Rs. 101-200	2 (0.3)
Rs. 201-300	19 (3.2)
Rs. 301-500	96 (16.0)
Rs. 501-750	67 (11.2)
Rs. 751-1000	84 (14.0)
Rs. 1002-1500	43 (7.2)
Rs. 1501-2000	43 (7.2)
Rs. 2001-3000	30 (5.0)
Rs. 3001-4000	13 (2.2)
Rs. 4001-5000	14 (2.3)
Rs. 5000+	42 (7.0)
Inapplicable : father not alive or not with the family	36 (6.0)
N.A.	82 (13.6)
Total	600 (100)

It becomes clear from Table 4.8 that the majority of respondent girl children in the sample had fathers who earned less than Rs 1000 per month. As much as 24 percent had a monthly income of less than Rs 500. Only in 16.5 percent families did fathers earn more than Rs 2000 per month. This is quite in keeping with the kind of sample that was chosen, with almost all the families coming either from the low or middle socioeconomic sections.

It is evident from Table 4.9 that more than half the households earned less than Rs 1500 per month, which is once again in keeping with the character of the sample.

Table 4.9
Households: Distribution According to Total Monthly Income

Income	Households No/(%)
Less than Rs. 100	1 (0.2)
Rs. 101-200	3 (0.5)
Rs. 201-300	3 (0.5)
Rs. 301-500	34 (5.7)
Rs. 501-750	79 (13.2)
Rs. 751-1000	115 (19.2)
Rs. 1001-1500	91 (15.2)
Rs. 1501-2000	45 (7.5)
Rs. 2001-3000	57 (9.5)
Rs. 3001-4000	25 (4.2)
Rs. 5000+	63 (10.5)
N.A.	67 (11.2)
Total	600 (100)

Enquiries on the issue of the indebtedness position of the households revealed that 283 or 47.2 percent of the sample had no outstanding debts to be paid. Around 12 percent had taken loans of up to Rs 500 and about 7 percent of the households had taken loans of above Rs 5000. In this connection it may be mentioned that the small debts were usually incurred every month because the debtors said their incomes were not sufficient to make both ends meet. Those who had relatively large debts were usually paying off one-time loans borrowed on the occasion of a daughter's marriage or to buy a piece of land and did not incur small debts every month.

LIVING CONDITIONS

This section gives information about the living conditions of the girl child respondents, supplying details about the kind of houses they live in and the nature of amenities available to them.

Living Quarters

The majority of the families (around 81%) lived in houses that they owned. Only about 9 percent lived in rented houses, mainly in the urban areas. It was observed that almost 38 percent of the families lived in one-room houses. In 62 percent of the households, women had a separate room or a space to cook; others cooked in the rooms they lived in.

In the rural areas, families which lived in one-room houses were not confined to that room only throughout the day. They spent a sizeable portion of the day outdoors, and could often do a lot of their work outside the house. They were also accustomed to bathing in nearby ponds. In the slum areas, however, having one room meant staying within the four walls of that room for the entire day. All daily activities, including cooking, would have to be carried out within it. Women and grown-up girls in some cases took their baths also within the room itself. In spite of this, however, the slumdwellers, we have observed, kept their rooms meticulously clean.

SOURCE AND COLLECTION OF WATER

Answering queries about sources of drinking water, 464 households or 77 percent said that they had no source of drinking water within the house. Family members had to bring water from outside. Whether inside or outside the house, taps and handpumps were found to be the chief sources of drinking water. At least 99 percent of the families reported that they did not draw water from ponds or wells for drinking purposes. Some said that these sources would be used only if taps and handpumps were not functioning.

These responses indicate that there is widespread awareness about the importance of using safe water. However, during the survey we observed that the incidence of gastrointestinal diseases was still high. This had two implications. First, the water obtained from the taps and handpumps might not be free of contamination. Second, though the people seemed to be aware that drinking water should be collected only from safe sources, it was possible that they could still be using contaminated water for cooking and for washing utensils. Greater awareness about these matters, as well as improved infrastructural facilities are necessary if the situation is to be changed substantially.

Who Brings the Water?

As expected, in around 60 percent of the households either girls or women were solely responsible for collecting drinking water.

Only 4.3 percent households had male members helping the women to collect water. In about 2 percent of the households it was seen as a man's job exclusively because social and religious taboos confined women to the house. Around 10 percent of the households had hired help to collect drinking water. These were mainly urban households where either the maidservants or paid *bhistiwallahs* brought water for the family.

How Far Do Women and Girls Have to Go to Go to Bring Water for Drinking?

About 17 percent of the households reported that their source of water was just outside the house and around 35 percent collected water from the neighbourhood. Another 25 percent had their source of water within the village itself, but at quite a distance. A little over 22 percent had their sources of water within their own houses. Only about 0.3 percent of households had to travel up to 2 km. to collect water from outside their own villages.

In interpreting these results, however, it must be remembered, that two of the villages surveyed, Pichkuri and Phulmalancha, were extremely large and spread-out. Often, those collecting water had to travel more than 2-3 km. to fetch water from within the village itself. Girl children in these two areas often had to spend a large part of the day fetching water—sometimes even missing school to do so. The figures by themselves may not reflect the real situation.

The problem in the slum and low socioeconomic status areas of the two urban wards is of a different nature. Though one does not have to travel large distances to collect water, the taps and handpumps are so few in number, that there are long queues to collect water, and it takes a person an enormous amount of time every day to collect his or her share. Often, the taps run dry before everyone has been able to collect water, and skirmishes are quite common.

Toilet Facilities

As many as 351 households had no facilities of any kind. These people were forced to use the fields and wash up in the nearby ponds, which made the environment extremely unhygienic. These households belonged almost entirely to the rural sector. About 26 percent households had flush toilets. These were mainly urban households or affluent rural ones. About 7 percent used public latrines or Sulabh Shauchalayas. They belonged to Ward 79 of Calcutta, which is in the slum area of Khidirpur, where about 50/60 households together shared one public toilet. The remaining 8.5 percent households had other toilet arrangements, such as dry toilets, pit latrines, and so on.

ELECTRIFICATION

Out of the six localities surveyed, two were not electrified. These were the villages of Pichkuri in Barddhaman and Phulmalancha in the South 24-Parganas. Both were in a poor economic condition with low female literacy rates. Out of the 400 households in the four electrified localities (i.e. two villages and two urban areas), 165 households did not have any electrical connections in their homes: only 231 families out of 600 had electricity, a majority of these were in the urban areas.

COOKING FUEL

The type and source of fuel used in a family is of particular concern for women and girl children. In our sample, the majority of households, about 84 percent, used conventional types of fuel, which category included, wood, cowdung cakes, coal and kerosene, for purposes of cooking. Poor families, it must be remembered, could not afford to buy fuel. Coal and kerosene were usually beyond their means. These families, therefore, depended mostly on fuel material that could be gathered from their surroundings: wood, leaves, twigs and agricultural and animal wastes. The girl child spent much of her time in collecting these materials. Even the cowdung cakes that were used were made by the women and girls of the household. Cooking time was, therefore, greatly increased because the fuel needed constant tending while food was being cooked.

A different kind of situation was observed in Pichkuri, in Barddhaman district. Here, there was widespread use of small and broken pieces of coal as cooking fuel. This coal, we were told, spilled over from the wagons of the trains that passed through the area. Small children, especially girls, spent a large portion of their day in travelling to the railway tracks every morning and afternoon, collecting these pieces of coal.

Twelve precent of the households used gas or electricity to cook with. These belonged exclusively to the urban areas. Almost none of the households used non-conventional energy sources.

THE FAMILY

This sub-section describes some characteristics of the kind of families that the girl children come from.

Information is provided about the nature of the family (whether joint or nuclear, for example), the family size, the educational background of the father, and so on. Four broad family types have been identified in the areas surveyed:

(a) nuclear families;
(b) supplemented nuclear families (i.e. nuclear families with dependent relative);
(c) joint families (i.e. husband, wife, unmarried sons or daughters, married sons, their wives and children); and
(d) extended families (i.e. all other family types not included so far).

In our sample, as much as 66.3 percent of the households had nuclear families. This shows the changing social character of the family as an institution, even among the low and middle socioeconomic sections of our society. It is evident that joint families are now on the decline, with only about 16 percent of the sample households still living within the joint family system. Most families are nuclear in character, with, at the most, one or two dependent parents or relatives to support in some cases. It is significant that this trend is noticeable even in the rural areas now, where more and more families opt for the nuclear family mode.

We also found that 74 percent of the households had a separate kitchen for each family unit. Only 26 percent of the households shared a joint or common kitchen with the rest of the family. Among the 202 joint/extended/supplemented nuclear families surveyed, which lived under the same roof and shared the same premises, not all households had a common kitchen. Only 156 households shared a common kitchen; the others had separate cooking arrangements for each unit living in the same house.

This finding forcefully brings to light a particular social trend. Not only are joint families giving way to nuclear families, both in the rural and in the urban areas, but even among those families who share the same premises, many prefer to have their own, separate cooking arrangements.

Who Were the Heads of the Households We Surveyed?

The majority of households, about 81 percent, had the father as the head of the family. There were only 32 female-headed households, which is a little over 5 percent of the total sample. Of these, mothers headed 27 households. In most cases, women become heads of households only when there are no other male family members who might take up that role.

Table 4.10 Total Number of Household Members

	Households Number/(%)
Two	4 (0.7)
Three	29 (4.8)
Four	133 (22.2)
Five	121 (20.2)
Six	103 (17.2)
Seven	72 (12.0)
Eight	47 (7.8)
Nine	28 (4.7)
Ten or more	63 [10.5]
Total	600 (100)

The majority of houeholds, 76 percent, had up to 7 members (Table 4.10). About 22 percent had only four household members, 20 percent had five household members, and around 17 percent had no more than six family members. Thus, it is seen that very large families are no longer the norm. Most of the families were small, with husband, wife and between two and four children. Sometimes, there might have been dependent parents to support.

Table 4.11 Households:Distribution According to Fathers' Education

	Households No/(%)
Illiterate	131 (21.8)
Up to Primary	99 (16.5)
Up to Middle	92 (15.3)
Up to High School/H.S.level	93 (15.5)
College. No degree	11 (1.8)
Graduate	57 (9.5)
Post-graduate	6 (1.0)
Technical/professional diploma or degree	42 (7.0)
Inapplicable: father not alive/not with family	36 (6.0)
N.A.	33 (5.5)
Total	600 (100)

The level of parental education is an important influencing factor in the matter of educational and overall development accessible to the girl child. Table 4.11 shows that in 6 percent of the households there were no fathers, meaning that they were either not alive during the time of the survey or that they had deserted their families. In almost 22 percent of the households the fathers were illiterate. About 16 percent of the fathers were educated up to the primary level, 15 percent up to the middle, and 15.5 percent up to high school. Only 9.5 percent were graduates, but another 7 percent had some sort of technical or professional degree or diploma.

Outings

How often women and girls go on an outing is an indication of the extent of the freedom they possess, not only within the family, but also within the social system they live in. It may reflect their economic and social status and also throw light on the degree of conservatism they are subject to. The women and girls in our sample were questioned about this aspect of their lives. It is significant that 29.5 percent of the women and the girls did not go on any outings at all. Around 40 percent went on outings occasionally, which in this case meant less than once a year; and around 14 percent went about once or twice a year. When interpreting the results, however, it must be kept in mind that the households in this sample came from the low and middle socio-economic strata of society. The fact that there were many households in which women did not go on outings frequently might simply mean that the family could not afford the time or expense involved. Women in these households were extremely busy in income-earning activities and with domestic chores.

It is likely that the majority of mothers of the girl children in our sample may have had many restrictions imposed on their movements. What did she herself feel about her daughters going outside the home for study, work, and so on? In 42 percent of the households, mothers were of the opinion that going out was good for a girl's mental growth and cultural development. About 21 percent of the mothers felt that girls should go out only if it were absolutely necessary. In 6 percent of the households, however, mothers said that it was necessary for girls to go out if they were to earn and become self-sufficient. On the other extreme were the 20 percent of mothers who believed that girls should not go out of the house at all, whatever the circumstances. Around 6 percent felt that it was not safe for girls to go out. We see, therefore, that opinion about girls leaving home to work or to study was almost sharply divided down the middle: 50 percent of the mothers were categorical in their approval for it, whereas the other 50 percent were equally vehement in their opposition to the idea.

THE MOTHER

HEALTH

The state of the mother's health, especially when she is pregnant, has an important bearing on the child's health status. It is well known that children of mothers who receive ante-natal care are far healthier than those of mothers who do not. One of our objectives during this survey was, therefore, to obtain information about this aspect of the life of the mother.

It appears that in many households mothers had no check-ups at all during pregnancy. This is true for more than 44 percent of the households. In about 38 percent of the households, however, mothers had regular check-ups during all their pregnancies. Mothers in the other households said that they went to the doctor only when they had a problem or were feeling unwell. A few consulted physicians only during the first pregnancy but not during subsequent ones. Mothers who did not take any dose of ATS for any of the pregnancies amounted to 43 percent, while 42 percent took all doses. It thus appears that in almost 45 percent of the households, rudimentary medical attention during pregnancy is lacking even today. This has serious implications for the health of both mothers and children and highlights the need for generating awareness in this sphere and for providing necessary facilities in a form which is physically and financially accessible to the underpriviledged sections of our society.

The majority of mothers said that they did not suffer from any serious problems either before, during or after pregnancy, and most of them also said that they delivered healthy babies.This should not, however, be accepted at face value. Most women from rural areas or from the urban slums are used to discomfort during pregnancy. Nausea, weakness, backaches or even oedema are considered normal and they do not connect these symptoms with ill health. As for delivering healthy babies—most of our respondents had hardly any perception that babies with low birth weight or babies born with illnesses such as jaundice were less than normal. Unless the new born child was visibly deformed or acutely ill they considered it as normal and healthy.

In over 52 percent of the households, the couple did not use any birth-control measures. Around 6 percent did not do so because they lacked information about the available methods of contraception and about 2 percent did not believe in practising birth control while 44 percent of the couples refused to elaborate on their answers.

About 44 percent of the couples currently practised birth-control. In 35 percent of the families it was the women's responsibility to take care of the matter. In only about 7 percent of the households did men take protective measures. In 2 percent of the families, both husband and wife used birth-control measures.

Contraception is thus observed to be chiefly the woman's reponsibility. This was so because it was the woman who was actually involved in caring for and rearing the child, and it was she who constantly saw the effect of scarcity on the health and development of the child, not to speak of the effect of frequent child-bearing on her own health. Even though contraception was far easier for the male, most men had reservations about it, and the onus of birth control fell almost exclusively on the women. A few women did not answer any question regarding contraception.

It must be mentioned in this connection that many women were ambivalent in their responses to inquiries about contraceptive practices. This was because most harboured ambivalent feelings about the issue. In many families contraception was not permitted on religious grounds. Almost all the women believed that children were gifts from God and any process which interfered with this was bad. Therefore, even if they used some form of contraception, they concealed the fact from their family and friends and would not admit to it when asked. Many, on the other hand, were aware that contraception was a 'desirable' thing; it was recommended on TV, the health centres gave incentives to those who had their fallopian tubes tied; perhaps the educated investigators would consider the affirmative answer to be the 'right' one. So very often they said they used contraceptives even when they did not. In sum, there was overstatement and understatement in both the figures. It was difficult to assess on balance what the real situation was.

It also emerged that the mothers had mostly heard about birth control measures either from friends, neighbours and relatives, or from advertisements on TV, radio or magazines. Some had been informed by their doctors, or by the nurses in nearby health centres and hospitals. Only about 10 percent were informed by their husbands.

The majority of mothers, about 76 percent, felt that the 'small family' norm was a good one. According to most mothers, the ideal family size varied between 4-6 members, with 2-4 children in each family unit. About 44 percent were of the opinion that it was best to have two children only; 17 percent preferred three; and about 19 percent wanted four children.

EDUCATION

It is widely acknowledged that the education of the mother may have a significant impact on the nurturing and life chances of her children in general, and of the girl child in particular. How are the girl children in our sample placed in this regard? Table 4.12 gives an overview of this aspect. In almost 47 percent of the households the mothers were illiterate. Many of those who claimed to be literate and had indeed attended school up to Classes 4 or 5 had actually lapsed back into illiteracy by the time of the survey. Mothers educated above the graduate level belonged to the two urban centres.

Table 4.12 Households : Distribution According to Mothers' Education

	Households No/(%)
Illiterate	281 (46.8)
Literate/read and write	21 (3.5)
Up to Primary	69 (11.5)
Up to Middle	110 (18.3)
Up to High School /H.S. level	52 (8.7)
College, no degree	1 (0.2)
Graduate	46 (7.7)
Postgraduate	12 (2.0)
Technical/Professional diploma/degree	4 (0.7)
N.A./D.K.	4 (0.7)
Total	600 (100)

It emerged that most mothers felt that they could not, or were not allowed to, study up to the level that they had aspired to. Many of them, almost 27 percent, said that their families, and the community they lived in did not approve of or value girls' education. About 26 percent were married off too early and could not complete their education. Another 19 percent could not go to school or had to drop out early because their families were too poor to support their education. About 3 percent could not attend school due to the pressure of household chores. It is evident, therefore, that besides poverty, perceptions about a girl's role in life and her education were also a major constraint to school-going in these cases.

With regard to the ambitions the mothers may have had in their childhood, we found that most of them, around 36 percent, had never thought about it; 17 percent wanted to be good housewives and about 13 percent wanted only to be well educated. Most of the mothers, in this last group, viewed education either as a prerequisite to making a good marriage or as a non-essential supplement to marriage. Only about 9 percent of the mothers spoke about ambitions in the direction of a profession, job or career. About 4 percent had wanted to join some service, but were undecided about the choice. The remaining wanted to be doctors, school teachers or artists. About 14 percent did not answer the question. Most of them could not even conceive of the idea of a woman with ambitions.

What Levels of Education Do Mothers Want for Their Children?

What are their perceptions in the matter of the desired levels of education for boys and girls? Some interesting contrasts emerge (Table 4.13). It seems that 4.5 per cent mothers felt there was no point in educating girls, but only 0.5 percent felt the same way about boys. Around 19 percent said that it was enough to educate girls up to the primary level or just to teach them to read and write. Less than 4 percent mothers felt similarly about boys. Only around 2 percent wished to educate girls up to the postgraduation level or encouraged them to obtain a professional degree, but 6.5 percent wanted their sons to acquire education up to these levels.

Table 4.13 Desired Levels of Education for Children
in Mothers' Perceptions

	For Girls	For Boys
	Mothers No. (%)	Mothers No. (%)
No use educating/education not necessary	27 (4.5)	3 (0.5)
Up to primary/read and write	116 (19.3)	22 (3.7)
Up to Mddle School	47 (7.8)	41 (6.8)
Up to Matric/High School/Higher Secondary	108 (18.0)	92 (15.3)
Intermediate up to Graduation	49 (8.2)	56 (9.3)
Up-to Postgraduation/professional degree	14 (2.3)	39 (6.5)
Diploma-technical/Vocational	1 (0.2)	5 (0.8)
As far as they can/want	201 (33.5)	296 (49.3)
D.K.	7 (1.2)	8 (1.3)
N.A.	30 (5.0)	38 (6.3)
Total	600 (100)	600 (100)

Whereas about 33 percent mothers wanted their daughters to study as much as they aspired to, around 49 percent wanted this for their sons. This confirms that even today girls' education is not valued as much as boys' education, and this is one of the major reasons why girls are still lagging so far behind boys in this field.

Some children in our sample had never been to school.Others dropped out before the completion of their school education. We asked their mothers the reasons for this. The primary reason for both non-enrolment and drop-out was stated to be poverty at home. The pressure of household work on girl children was also cited as one of the most important constraints. Many felt that it was not important to educate girls. A sizeable number, however, said that though the family had been encouraging and supportive, the girl children themselves chose not to go to school because they were not interested in studies.

WORK

The occupation of the mother often plays an important role in determining the kind of life her children have. In our sample about 72 percent of the mothers were purely housewives. Among the 167 mothers who worked, the majority, that is, 85 of them, were agricultural labourers; 29 were piece-rate workers; and 14 were domestic servants (Table 4.14). Most of the mothers who worked belonged to the poorer sections of society both in the rural and in the urban areas. Very few held white collar jobs. In the middle income families of our sample — rural and urban — it appears that it is still not the norm for women to go out to work. In such families women work only when it is absolutely necessary to supplement the family income.

Table 4.14 Occupation of Mothers	
	Households No/(%)
Housewife	433 (75.2)
Junior professionals and middle level officials, inspectors, social workers, priests, artists, musicians	10 (1.7)
Agricultural labourers	85 (14.2)
Piece-rate workers (home based; otherwise)	29 (4.8)
Domestic workers	14 (2.3)
Other occupations	10 (1.7)
Total	600 (100)

How much do the working mothers earn? Among those who are engaged in income-earning occupations, the majority earn less than Rs 500 per month (see Table 4.15). Only 13 out of the 167 working mothers are able to earn more than Rs 1000 every month. This is as expected, given the nature of work most of them are engaged in.

Table 4.15 Monthly Income of Mothers	Mothers No (%)
Inapplicable—housework only/other work for which no separate income received	433 (72.3)
Less than Rs. 50	6 (1.0)
Rs. 51-100	3 (0.5)
Rs. 101-200	12 (2.0)
Rs. 201-300	47 (7.8)
Rs. 301-500	37 (6.2)
Rs. 501-1000	13 (2.2)
N.A.	36 (6.1)
Total	600 (100)

Our survey reveals that about 83 percent of the mothers had some practical skill or the other. The majority, about 30 percent, were skilled in food processing, cooking, and so on. Knitting, stitching and embroidery accounted for another 28 percent. About 17 percent had no skills at all. However, though 83 percent of mothers had one or more skills, more than 55 percent did not use any of their skills for economic gain.

This means that though most women possess some kind of skill, they usually do not utilize it for any income-earning activity. Their skills are used at home, of course, but for this they get neither payment nor recognition. It is taken, as a matter of course, as part of the woman's household work, which is so grossly under-rated as being an unproductive activity.

As far as mother's housework was concerned, it was primarily the majority of household chores that were her sole responsibility, and she performed most of these activities either alone or with the help of other female members of the family, including the girl child

(Table 4.16). The few household activities in which the male members of the household helped and participated in were going to the market, running errands and taking the cattle out for grazing. Cleaning, cooking, looking after children, fetching fuel and water are all women's jobs and no help from the male members is usually forthcoming. Gender-specific role stereotyping comes through quite clearly from our survey results.

Apart from income-earning occupations outside the home, there is also the question as to the extent to which the women in the sample households have been able to extend their activities beyond their domestic spheres socially or through involvement in politics. The majority, around 92 percent, were not members of any organization at all. No one was a member of more than one organization. Nine mothers belonged to mahila mandals; 8 worked in voluntary organizations; 4 were members of the panchayats; and 2 belonged to women's cooperatives. Seventeen mothers were members of various other types of organizations; no one, however, held any official post.

SOCIALIZATION

Social conditioning and familial pressures determine, to a large extent, the mother's preference with regard to the number and gender of her children. Over 50 percent of the mothers said that it was best to have either one son and daughter or two sons and two daughters. In about 15 percent of the households the mothers said that they wanted two sons and one daughter. It was taking a risk, they said, to have only one son—what if something happened to him? There would be no one left to carry on the family name. And who would look after the parents in their old age? Such possibilities were not considered to be a risk in the case of daughters, however. Two percent mothers wanted sons exclusively.

It may appear that daughters are not as unwanted today as they were earlier. One might even infer that mothers generally want an equal number of boys and girls. However, these results must be interpreted with caution. In answer to questions of this nature respondents often give answers which they think are expected of them. Mothers may give one kind of answer in response to a hypothetical question of this nature, but when the time for child-birth comes, we may find that in many cases they actually desire to give birth to sons. Around 48 percent of the mothers have clearly said that they hoped for a son during their first pregnancy. Forty-one percent said that they did not have any particular expectations about the gender of the child. It was evident, however, from our conversation with them that most of these women really wanted a son. They did not want to say so because they were afraid that this might tempt fate to do otherwise. The strongly entrenched son preference came out clearly in the course of conversation.

Enquiries were also made about the expectations of other family members with regard to the sex of the first child. The son preference was even more clearly reflected in this context—in more than 50 percent households a son was desired from the first pregnancy of the mother.

In the areas that we surveyed in West Bengal, the practice of sex-determination was practically non-existent. In 92 percent of the households, no sex-determination methods were ever tried. In only about 2 percent of the households was any form of sex-determination attempted. These families were rural, tribal families and they had their own 'traditional' methods of doing so. Most of the families that we spoke to had not even heard of sex-selection or amniocentesis. In about 6 percent of the households the mothers were not the respondents and so the question was not placed before them.

Mothers' perceptions were sought with regard to the qualities that they valued in a good boy, a good girl and a good daughter-in-law. A substantial number of mothers said that the qualities expected in a good girl are that she should be well educated and have an interest in studies; be good-natured, well mannered and well behaved. Obedience and respect towards elders were also highly valued. The other qualities that were considered to be important were humility and politeness, a willingness to share and assist in household work, and a tolerant and adjustable nature. It was also felt that girls should not be allowed to socialize too freely with members of the opposite sex. It is interesting to note that qualities such as honesty, the ability to get a good job or to be economically independent have not been given any significance. Also, in very few households have the mothers said that they expect their daughters to share in family responsibilities or to help the family financially. It is another matter that girls, in most cases, do both, and the family accepts the help as a matter of course.

As expected, in the case of a boy, being well-educated was considered to be very important. Qualities such as a good nature, good manners, obedience and a respectful attitude towards elders were thought to be desirable. Only about 10 percent of the mothers felt that a good earning capacity was a necessary 'good' quality for a good boy. No one expected boys to help with housework. Qualities such as honesty and good/respectful behaviour with women have been considered important by very few.

When mothers gave their opinions about the kind of brides they would want for their sons, most felt that they should be good looking, smart and appealing (about 20%). Another 12 percent felt that it was very important for them to help with household work. Close to 8 percent stressed on qualities such as good manners and an adjustable nature. Only about 3 percent thought that it was important that the bride come from a family of similar social background and status. It is important to note that issues such as caste, religion and the necessity of matching horoscopes have not figured at all in the criteria set by mothers for the selection of a bride; nor have qualities such as an affectionate nature. About 14 percent of the mothers have stressed on educational accomplishment.

The mothers' opinions were sought on the age at which boys and girls should be married. Almost 35 percent mothers responded that they would want their daughters married between the ages of 18 and 22 years; 24.5 percent mothers wanted their daughters married between the ages of 15 and 18 years, while in almost 17 percent households mothers would have liked their daughters to be married between 12 and 15 years of age. In about 18 percent of the households the mothers had no objections to marrying their daughters after the age of 22 years.

For boys, the situation was quite different. Almost 50 percent of the mothers did not want their sons married before the age of 25 years; 17 percent preferred to have them married between the ages 22 and 25 years; and a little over 23 percent of the mothers wanted them married between the ages of 18 and 22 years. In only about 3 percent of the households have mothers stated that they wanted their sons married before they attained 18 years of age.

The sons' and daughters' own opinions about the age when they would wish to get married were not considered to be very important by their mothers. They would leave the decision to their sons in only 2.5 percent of the cases, and to their daughters in only 0.3 percent of the cases.

Mothers were also asked about the reasons which prompted them to decide on a certain age as the 'right' age for the marriage of their sons and daughters. As far as daughters' marriages were concerned the greatest number of mothers, about 22 percent, answered that they felt that a particular age was 'right' or 'proper' for marriage because by then their daughters would have attained maturity and would be able to understand the responsibilities of marriage. Close to 10 percent decided upon a particular age because of social, religious or familial pressures, or simply to conform to the norm in their community. Some mothers (about 9%) believed that it was unsafe for girls to remain unmarried for too long. Around 4 percent wanted their daughters married young to avoid paying a higher rate of dowry. In only 10.5 percent of the households were mothers willing to wait till their daughters had completed their education, and in only 2.5 percent households did mothers want their daughters married after they had become economically independent.

For boys, as expected, the situation was quite different. Over 53 percent of mothers wanted their sons married only after they had started to earn and were economically independent. Around 6 percent felt that boys should be married after a certain age because that was the 'proper' age for boys to be married, and otherwise they might be lured into undesirable company if they were single for too long.

In the region surveyed, over 80 percent households never had any tradition of bride-price. In 8.5 percent households this tradition had been prevalent a long time ago, but has now become obsolete. Of the 8 percent families who still had the practice of paying bride-price, the majority belonged to the scheduled tribe households of the rural areas.

As far as the issue of dowry was concerned, more than 75 percent mothers answered in the affirmative when asked whether they paid or accepted dowry in their families and communities. Only about 22 percent families did not have the custom of paying dowry in their communities.

Opinion about whether it was right or proper to pay dowry varied widely. Almost 30 percent of the mothers had no objection to paying dowry. Some felt that their tradition and customs necessitated it. Others said that it was necessary to pay a dowry to obtain a good match for their girls. About 9 percent mothers were of the opinion that the payment of dowry was a necessary evil. Though they were against the idea of paying a dowry in principle, they were quite prepared to do so in order to get a 'good' match for their daughter.

Almost 42 percent of the mothers, however, were vehemently opposed to the practice of paying dowry. They felt that getting a girl married with the help of a dowry was tantamount to buying her happiness by bribing the groom and his family. Seven percent of the mothers agreed that paying a dowry was a social evil. However, social norms dictated that they do so even though it was difficult for poor families such as theirs to arrange for this money.

Table 4.16 Mothers and Housework

	Fetching			Sweeping	Errands	Marketing	Care of Cattle
	Fuel	Fodder	Water				
	Households No. (%)						
No such housework/done only by servants	3.3	52.0	5.7	2.8	2.2	2.2	50.3
Self, alone	7.7	5.3	10.2	22.3	10.5	9.0	6.7
Self, assisted by servants	0.2	0.5	0.5	0.5	0.5	0.2	0.3
Self, assisted by male family members	3.5	3.5	0.7	1.3	8.3	8.7	5.5
Self, assisted by female family members	22.7	4.5	36.5	54.8	6.2	2.2	7.7
Self, assisted by male and female members	4.7	5.3	4.2	1.8	12.2	5.2	12.2
Work done by male family members	10.2	14.2	1.3	0.3	32.3	46.7	4.2
Work done by other female family members	5.7	1.5	11.0	10.5	6.0	4.3	2.7
Work done by male and other female family members	1.7	4.0	1.5	0.3	5.8	4.2	2.3
N.A.	40.5	9.2	26.5	5.2	16.0	17.5	8.2
Total	100%	100%	100%	100%	100%	100%	100%

Table 4.16 (contd.) Mothers and Housework

	Cooking	Care of Children	Plastering Walls, Floors	Cottage Industry	Agriculture	Washing Clothes
			Households No. (%)			
No such housework/done only by servants	0.2	24.2	34.2	76.0	50.7	1.3
Self, alone	42.3	19.0	16.2	3.3	1.8	4.2
Self, assisted by servants	—	—	0.2	—	—	0.2
Self, assisted by male family members	0.5	0.5	0.7	0.5	4.0	—
Self, assisted by female family members	49.2	34.5	35.7	3.2	0.8	49.2
Self, assisted by male and female members	1.0	1.5	0.7	1.5	4.8	0.2
Work done by male family members	0.5	0.2	0.2	0.7	10.5	—
Work done by other female family members	3.8	4.8	5.2	1.0	0.3	1.5
Work done by male and other female family members	—	0.7	0.3	—	0.7	—
N.A.	2.5	14.7	6.8	13.8	26.3	43.4
Total	100%	100%	100%	100%	100%	100%

Table 4.17 Decision-Makers on the Following Issues

	Spending	Children's Education	Recreation	Puberty Rituals	Marriage
			Households No. (%)		
Inapplicable: no spending/not working/ no payment/no such occasion	435 (72.5)	29 (4.8)	42 (7.0)	386 (64.3)	125 (20.8)
Self	61 (10.2)	122 (20.3)	121 (20.2)	100 (16.7)	67 (11.2)
Parent/Parent-in-law	2 (0.3)	192 (32.0)	153 (25.5)	13 (2.2)	106 (17.7)
Husband	15 (2.5)	179 (29.8)	156 (26.0)	19 (3.2)	182 (30.3)
Son/Son-in-law	1 (0.2)	30 (5.0)	27 (4.5)	3 (0.5)	52 (8.7)
Daughter/Daughter-in-law	- (-)	5 (0.8)	11 (1.8)	- (-)	3 (0.5)
Self and others	55 (9.2)	-(-)	2 (0.3)	9 (1.5)	2 (0.3)
Husband and others	2 (0.3)	11 (1.8)	16 (2.7)	9 (1.5)	14 (2.3)
Others/no one in particular	4 (0.7)	19 (3.2)	39 (6.5)	10 (1.7)	31 (5.2)
N.A.	25 (4.2)	13 (2.2)	33 (5.5)	51 (8.5)	18 (3.0)
Total	600 (100)	600 (100)	600 (100)	600 (100)	600 (100)

Table 4.17 (contd.) Decision-Makers on the Following Issues

	Religious Ceremonies	Using Resources	Property Matters	Legal Matters
	Households No. (%)			
Inapplicable: no spending /not working /no payment /no such occasion	41 (6.8)	1 (0.2)	169 (28.2)	264 (44.0)
Self	207 (34.5)	113 (18.8)	52 (8.7)	46 (7.7)
Parent/Parent-in-law	72 (12.0)	228 (38.0)	173 (28.8)	132 (22.0)
Husband	158 (26.3)	155 (25.8)	100 (16.7)	57 (9.5)
Son/Son-in-law	10 (1.7)	60 (10.0)	55 (9.2)	33 (5.5)
Daughter/Daughter-in-law	4 (0.7)	10 (1.7)	6 (1.0)	4 (0.7)
Self and others	3 (0.5)	2 (0.3)	2 (0.3)	2 (0.3)
Husband and others	21 (3.5)	13 (2.2)	12 (2.0)	11 (1.8)
Others/no one in particular	57 (9.5)	9 (1.5)	11 (1.8)	10 (1.7)
N.A.	27 (4.5)	9 (1.5)	20 (3.3)	41 (6.8)
Total	600 (100)	600 (100)	600 (100)	600 (100)

It is interesting to note that the tribal people who pay bride-price complained bitterly about the rate at which the bride-price was increasing every day, just as the others complained about the increasing rate of dowry that they had to pay.

One of the significant indicators of the status of an individual in the household is the role he/she has in the decision-making process within the family. How does the woman in the family, the mother, that is, fare in this regard? Table 4.17 reveals that about 20 percent of the women were permitted some say in such matters as children's education, recreation, puberty rituals, and so on. Around 10 percent of the mothers participated in decisions about legal or property matters, household expenditure or children's marriage. Women had a participatory role in the decision-making process only with regard to religious ceremonies—in about 34 percent of households women took decisions on these issues.

5
THE GIRL CHILD
SOME STATISTICS

HEALTH

It is well known that the quality of health services available to the people in the rural areas and in the less affluent urban areas is very poor. Children in these regions are, in fact, handicapped right from birth. Firstly, pregnant women usually do not receive adequate food and nutritional supplements, which results in the birth of low-weight infants who are physically underdeveloped and easily susceptible to disease. Simple preventive measures like the administration of anti-tetanus vaccines are lacking in many cases. This alone would help in drastically reducing the number of deaths caused by neonatal tetanus. It is common knowledge that children born to mothers who have not received any antenatal care have a significantly higher risk of infant mortality.

Secondly, these children suffer from malnutrition—a direct consequence of not having enough to eat. Though all children in poor families are deprived in this regard, it is well known that girls are particularly discriminated against in the distribution of food within the family.

Moreover, the insanitary environment in which they live increases their susceptibility to infections and diseases. Parents who are largely illiterate are unaware of the need for and the means to secure safe sanitation and a clean environment. They also lack awareness about preventive and curative health care for their children. In the first place, few children are immunized. Then again once they fall ill, proper medical attention is often not sought unless the matter is very serious. Both in the case of immunization and in the case of treatment of disease, girl children receive less care than boys because sons have always been valued more. The lack of adequate health-care facilities is also a serious constraint. We shall look into some of these aspects relating to the health condition of the girl child as reflected in our sample.

IMMUNIZATION

Above 40 percent of the girl children in our sample had received no immunization. It is indeed a cause for concern that parents in so many families are still unaware that the lack of these essential vaccines can leave their children open to many infections which, though not always fatal, can seriously undermine their health. It is not just a matter of awareness, however. In many areas the absence of necessary facilities could also be a serious problem.

Around 40 percent of the respondent girl children had been given at least one vaccine: BCG, DPT, polio or MMR. Another 20 percent had received some form of immunization, but no specific details were available as to the type of vaccine. It is possible, however, that some of these girls had only been given the smallpox vaccine and that was considered complete 'immunization' by their mothers. We gained the impression that in some cases the affirmative answers to the question of whether the girl child had been immunized did not correctly reflect the true state of affairs. It seemed that these parents were aware that in the current environment immunization was in general considered to be a desirable thing, so that the expected answer to such questions from urban investigators would be the positive one. But they actually lacked the conviction and awareness about the critical need for such preventive measures. Therefore, they had not really bothered much about actually immunizing the girl, but when asked they gave the 'appropriate' affirmative answer. Hence, there may be some overstatement in the 20-percent category.

Mothers of even those girl children who had been immunized, were found, in essence, to be ignorant about the different modes of immunization and about the need for administering different kinds of vaccines to prevent different kinds of illnesses. For many mothers, the process of inoculation seemed to mean a single point intervention. If a child had been given the BCG vaccine (against tuberculosis), for instance, the mother was often unaware that she also needed to be given the MMR vaccine for protection against other diseases like measles, mumps and rubella. Most mothers had never even heard of booster doses. Several were under the impression that inoculation against smallpox was all that there was to vaccination or immunization. Some also believed that since social workers no longer went visiting from house to house with smallpox vaccines, the process of immunization was obsolete and children no longer needed to be vaccinated. A few were of the opinion that vaccination was bad for a child's health since it caused a high fever. Among the immunizations for BCG, DPT and/or polio and measles the polio vaccine was the one most commonly administered. This was perhaps because it is taken orally and therefore considered to be a simpler procedure than an injection. Mothers were far less apprehensive about giving their children oral medicine than having them inoculated. Mothers whose girl children were not immunized usually could give no reason for this oversight. Most said it had not seemed important at that time. Evidently the health centres and the health service staff in these areas were not very active. Many families were not even aware of the crucial need for immunization.

BREASTFEEDING

It has long been recognized that breastfeeding establishes the nutritional foundation of a child's future development. The duration of breastfeeding would therefore be one of the important indicators of the future health status of a child. In our sample, nearly 32 percent of the girls were breastfed for more than two years and 33 percent for a period ranging between one year and two years. Very few were breastfed for less than six months.

When asked about the reasons for breastfeeding for such long periods, most mothers responded that it had never occurred to them to do otherwise. What else would they have fed the child? Baby food, milk powder or formulas were expensive and also difficult to obtain in the rural areas. They could not afford such luxuries. Mothers in these families acted according to traditional wisdom and practices and recognized that breast milk was good for the child's health in the initial stages of her/his life.

The problems arising out of inadequate breastfeeding were not observed in these families. This problem occurred mainly in the affluent section of society and its effects had not significantly percolated down to the households in this sample. Those mothers who had nursed their daughters for six months or less said that they did so only because they had insufficient breastmilk. It was inconceivable to them that a mother would even consider giving her baby other kinds of food when breastmilk was available. Breastfeeding is so entwined with the concept of motherhood that most women suffer from feelings of inadequacy if they cannot for some reason nurse their children. Social conditioning apart, it is generally accepted that breastmilk is good for a baby and also available free of cost; children should be allowed access to it for as long as it is available.

The cost to the mother's health was disregarded in most cases. In the poorer households, for instance, the majority of lactating mothers did not receive adequate food or nutritional supplements. Breastfeeding for such long periods, therefore, had a severely detrimental effect on their health and aggravated their malnourishment. The problem was often compounded by the fact that other toddlers also breastfed together with the newborn baby. Because the gap between two consequent births was small, the older child easily fell back into the breastfeeding habit as soon as the new birth occurred. Indeed, the concept of weaning a child was absent in these families.

Since the mothers were undernourished, the breast milk generated was sometimes of insufficient quantity for the needs of the children. It could have also lacked all the nutrients necessary for the healthy development of the child. The fact that the child might be receiving insufficient nutrition usually went undetected because the infant's health was hardly ever monitored. The majority of children also did not receive any supplementary nutrition in the first few months after birth. These mothers simply did not know that a child needed additional food such as fruits, vegetables and cereals after a few months. The children went on to solid food directly and usually did not drink milk once they had started eating regular food—their families could not afford to buy any. Consequently, they suffered from malnutrition from early childhood and soon started showing signs of growth retardation.

Surveys in many parts of the country have shown that girl children suffer more than boys because unlike the latter they are breastfed less frequently, for shorter durations and over shorter periods. They are also weaned earlier. From the responses to questions in this connection it appears that boy and girl children were breastfed for approximately similar periods of time. Our general impression, however, obtained from casual conversation with the mothers was that girl children were discriminated against in this matter to a greater or lesser extent in most families.

FOOD

It was found that children, both boys and girls, in the majority of households belonging to the low socioeconomic strata lived largely on cereals, that is, rice, which was generally eaten with pulses or with vegetables that were cheaply available, like potatoes or home-grown *sag* or spinach. Fish was not a part of the everyday diet in most households and was eaten only on special occasions. No explicit mention was made of gender-based discrimination made in respect of the number of meals taken or the type of food generally eaten by children in the overwhelming majority of households. However, girls were usually denied delicacies. Traditionally boys have always been given the best of what was available. We noted that girls were discriminated against in the distribution of food within the family in quality more than in quantity.

It must be borne in mind, however, that parents and the majority of girl-children were extremely conscious of what the 'proper' answer should be. They usually conformed to these expected answers and the truth in many cases might well have been the reverse of the answers given. On occasions a girl child away from her own home would confide that she was often denied food and delicacies. She could eat only after her father and brothers had finished, and sometimes had to go hungry because there was little left over. But the same child when questioned again in the presence of her parents would deny that any differentiation was made between her and her brothers. Therefore, though the results show no significant discrimination in food consumption by boy and girl children, it must be remembered that there is evidence of serious under-reporting in this regard.

About 57 percent of the girls said that they had never felt that they did not have enough to eat and 20 percent said that they went hungry only sometimes. Only about 12 percent said that they often had to go without food. We note, however, that we are dealing here, in most cases, with the peceptions of many girls who have grown accustomed to eating less than a full meal. They are so used to doing without food that they have been able to suppress feelings of deprivation or even hunger effectively. We cannot accept at face value their statement that they always had enough to eat or that they rarely had to go hungry.

DISEASE AND TREATMENT

As shown in Table 5.1, most girls did not report any illness during, or even two or three years before the survey. Of the 237 girls who said that they had been ill during this period, the majority suffered from common ailments. However, it must be noted that our sample was drawn chiefly from the rural areas and the middle and low socioeconomic status urban households.

In these families, girls, or even their parents, usually did not have any awareness of ill health as we understand it. Their circumstances did not permit missing work due to illnesses such as a recurrent fever, chronic cough, weakness or stomach problems. Even severe diseases such as asthma or bronchitis were ignored until the person affected actually took to her bed. Since no one reported being ill, ailments often went undetected and untreated. For instance, diarrhoea and related infections are not considered serious unless they become fatal and claim a child's life. Girls in general are taught not to take their illnesses seriously. Unless a girl is so sick that she is physically unable to carry on with her daily activities, she does not perceive that there is anything wrong with her. Feeling a little under the weather is regarded as normal in many cases. Thus, it would not be proper to conclude from the evidence in this table that the sample of 600 girls was a generally healthy sample. The possibility of underestimation of morbidity must be borne in mind when interpreting the results.

Table: 5.1 Diseases Suffered by the Girl Child	
	Girls No. (%)
Ordinary ailment [1]	76(12.7)
Serious ailment [2]	73[12.2)
Infectious diseases [3]	49 (8.2)
Chronic diseases [4]	10 (1.7)
Gynaecological diseases	1 (0.2)
Cancer/Heart disease	2 (0.3)
Mental illness [5]	2 (0.3)
Inapplicable—no disease	358[59.7)
Any other	24 (4.0)
N.A.	5 (0.8)
Total	600 (100)

Notes

[1] Cough, cold, fever, stomach disorder, allergy and so on; [2] Cholera, typhoid, blood infection, skin diseases, jaundice, liver disorder, diptheria, urinary infection, dengu fever, bronchitis, whooping cough and so on; [3] Smallpox, chicken pox, tuberculosis and so on; [4] Asthma, arthritis, ulcer, chronic anaemia and so on; [5] Nervous breakdown, hysteria and so on.

The girl children were also asked where they and their brothers were taken for treatment when they fell ill. The same question was put to their mothers. The answers were similar. The mothers said that they preferred hospitals and private practitioners to health centres because, firstly, access to health centres was difficult; in most cases they were quite far away. Secondly, even if one took a sick child to a health centre, there was no guarantee that he or she would receive proper treatment there; the health centres were, in most cases, hopelessly understaffed and suffered from a severe lack of medical supplies. Even basic necessities such as disinfectants and bandage rolls were usually found to be in short supply. Under such circumstances, parents preferred to take their children to the nearest hospital even if that meant travelling long distances. If they could afford to incur the expenditure involved, they called in a private practitioner.

When asked what form of treatment was preferred, the majority of parents said that they used more than one method of treatment for their children. Allopathy was the most common, but homeopathic medicines were used as well. Many believed that allopathy was effective in cases of severe illness where it gave quick relief to the sick child. Homeopathic treatment was preferred in cases of chronic diseases as it was believed to eradicate the illness completely. Allopathy, it was felt, merely suppressed the symptoms. Ayurvedic and Unani treatment were not in much demand. In some cases healing herbs, home remedies and therapeutic stones were used and *ojhas* were also called in. Exclusive reliance, however, was not placed on the efficacy of such remedies and they were mostly used together with allopathic and homeopathic treatments.

There did not appear to be any discrimination made between boys and girls either with respect to the place of treatment or with respect to the form of treatment given. Discrimination was present, however, in a much more subtle fashion. It became quite evident during the survey that there was serious under-reporting of ailments in the case of girls. Mothers were anxious to seek our help and advice about a sick son, but a visibly undernourished and sick daughter caused little concern. Casual conversation with the mothers also revealed that a boy child's illness received more immediate attention than that of a girl child. A doctor's help was sought quickly for a boy, whereas a girl often received home remedies for a prolonged period before institutional care was arranged for her. Many were hesitant about taking girls above the age of ten years to a male physician. The general feeling in most families was that the sick boy child needed immediate attention. The girl child, it was felt, would as a matter of course be sickly and prone to illness because she belonged to the weaker sex. Moreover, it was her lot to bear pain in silence. The fact that such illness often prevented her from doing useful work at home was the only inconvenience in this regard.

MENSTRUATION

Matters connected with menstruation influence the life of a girl child in various ways. About 290 girls out of our sample of 600 had started menstruating. Most of them started their menses between the ages of 12 and 16 years. Of these 290 girls, only about 60 had any prior knowledge about menses, the majority having been informed by their friends and neighbours. Others obtained information from either their sisters/sisters-in-law or, in urban areas, from their teachers in biology classes. Very few were informed about these matters by their mothers or other older female relatives. In fact, of the 290 girls who had started menstruating, 263 informed other members of their families at the onset of menses and sought help from them. Seventeen girls did not respond to our question. The remaining learnt to manage somehow alone.

Seventy-four girls reported having problems during menses. Most did nothing about it. A few admitted taking self-prescribed painkillers and other medicines. However, it must be noted that most girls accept a certain amount of pain and discomfort as normal at such times. That is what they have been taught by their mothers, and their perceptions have developed accordingly. This is the reason why most often they do not report any feelings of illness during this period, even though they may actually feel quite unwell. Besides, most girls from rural areas or poorer urban areas have no idea that menstrual irregularities, such as early or late menses, heavy bleeding, intermittent spotting or heavy leucorrheal discharge are abnormalities that need medical attention. Hence these too are not usually reported, unless the discomfort actually hampers their daily work. Though the majority of girls said that they had no problems after they started menstruating, many felt frightened at the onset of menses. A great number, however, had no special feelings and had no difficulty in coming to terms with this change.

EDUCATION

What are the factors that promote or inhibit school enrolment of girl children? What are the reaons for non-enrolment and dropout? What are the girl child's perceptions about education or schooling? What are her hopes and ambitions? These are some of the issues discussed in this section.

LITERACY

Almost 32 percent of the girl children in our sample were illiterate. About 29 percent could read and write in their mother tongue only; in this case, the language was usually Bengali. Close to 32 percent knew how to read and write in one or more languages in addition to their mother tongue; in most cases these girls had referred to English learnt in their schools as a second language. Some girls also knew either Hindi or Sanskrit, once again learnt as a part of course work in school. About 7 percent of the girls said that they could only read and write in languages other than their mother tongues. Such answers were obtained from girls who could speak their mother tongues but had not been taught how to read or write it. They knew only those languages that they had been taught compulsorily. Most of these girls belonged to non-

Bengali families in the urban areas and came from households that were reasonably better off. They usually went to English-medium schools and learnt either Bengali or Hindi as their second languages. They used their mother tongue only during conversation at home.

ENROLMENT

Table 5.2 gives the enrolment situation of the girl children within the sample. It appears that 65.1 percent of the respondent girl children were enrolled in school; a little over 18 percent were never enrolled at all; and around 16 percent had dropped out before the completion of their school education. Thus close to 35 percent of children were out of the school system either because they were never enrolled or because they were drop-outs.

Table 5.2 Girl Children and Their Schooling

	Girls No. (%)
Currently attending school	391 (65.1)
Never attended school	110 (18.4)
Drop-out	99 (16.5)
Total	600 (100)

NON-ENROLMENT

There are many possible reasons for non-enrolment. The primary one is the acute poverty of a large section of the people in our country. They often cannot afford the direct and indirect costs of education for their children. Although in West Bengal, education is formally free up to the Higher Secondary level, that is, Class 12, in effect it means simply that no tuition fees have to be paid by students in government schools. Parents have to bear substantial costs by way of books, notebooks, pencils, and other learning aids. More often than not, teaching is inadequate and private coaching has to be arranged or the children are likely to fail in school. For daughters, there is also the additional expense of providing proper clothes for school. A boy could conceivably go to school clad only in a pair of shorts, but under no circumstances would a girl be allowed to do so.

In addition, there are the indirect costs in the form of earnings forgone by the child who might have worked if he or she were not attending school. When household income is low compared to the size of the family, children have to work to supplement family income. Though this factor affects all children, the girl child suffers additional disadvantages. Parents who cannot afford to send all their children to school, usually prefer to educate the sons and not the daughters. Educating a son is perceived to be of greater value to the family as a whole since the son is expected to look after his parents in their old age.

At home, too, the girl child is weighed down by the burden of housework and spends a large portion of her time helping her mother and caring for younger siblings. This means that she does not usually have time to attend school, especially at the preset, specific hours in which the schools function. Since boys are not expected to help at home, they do not suffer this additional handicap. The social bias against girls' education may also be one of the major causes of non-enrolment of girl children.

Factors internal to the school system also influence the decision on children's school enrolment. Lack of schools within walking distance, dearth of female teachers, lack of facilities such as separate toilets for girls and so on, are often major deterrents to school going. We examine the situation in West Bengal as obtained by our survey.

Table 5.3 shows the various reasons for which some of the respondent girl children in our sample could never attend school. The possible reasons have been divided into five main categories: economic; socio-cultural; personal; familial; and infrastructural or situational. Of the 110 girl children who never enrolled in school, about 36 cited economic reasons; 24 of them said their parents were too poor to provide money for school. Five others reported that the family had other more pressing demands, and seven had to work to supplement the family income and were therefore kept out of the school system.

Table 5.3 Why Girls Were Never Enrolled in School

Reasons Given	Girls No (%)
Economic	36 (32.7)
Socio-cultural	11 (9.9)
Personal	11 (9.9)
Familial	55 (49.9)
Infrastructural	3 (2.7)

Note: There is some overlapping in the answers given with respect to the categories listed: e.g. the reasons for enrolment may be both economic and familial. Since both reasons have been tabulated for the same girl, the total number of girls in the table is 116, i.e. more than 110 who were never enrolled (see Table 5.2). The percentages, however, have been calculated on 110.

Eleven girls said that they could not go to school largely because of socio-cultural contraints. In most cases the respondents felt that girls' education was not valued or considered important. Parents were often of the opinion that it was pointless to educate a girl child since she would have to be given away in marriage and so the investment made on her schooling would be wasted. Besides, it would be of no use to her in her role as wife and daughter-in-law in which cooking, cleaning and looking after the household would take up all her time. That a girl might conceivably have a role in life other than being a wife and a mother did not register in their consciousness at all.

Another eleven girls did not go to school due to their own personal problems. These girls suffered from a low self-image and lacked the motivation to go to school. Though these have been tabulated as personal problems, the nature of the problems observed indicate that it is the social system which is actually responsible. There is no reason why a young girl under the age of ten should have a low self-image unless such perceptions were inculcated in her early in life. Also, an improvement in the school system itself, especially in the quality and the relevance of the education offered would help to motivate the girls to go to school.

The majority (49.9%) of girls who have never attended school could not do so due to familial problems. In seven cases the family did not approve of girls' education. Twenty-four girls had to stay at home because there was either too much housework to do, or because they had to look after their siblings. Eighteen said that their parents did not enrol them in school because one or both parents were addicted to gambling, liquor, and so on, which used up scarce economic resources. Almost none of the girls cited situational reasons as the cause for their non-enrolment. Only two have said that they refused to go to school because they had heard that the teachers were extremely harsh in their behaviour.

The major reasons for non-enrolment that have been obtained for the girl children in this sample are: poverty (29 girls); parents' addiction to liquor and gambling (18 girls); burden of housework (16 girls); lack of interest in girls' education and traditional beliefs regarding their role in life (11 girls); responsibility for siblings (8 girls); necessity to work in income-earning capacity (7 girls); and low self-image and lack of motivation (7 girls).

DROP-OUT

The persistently high drop-out among girls is a major cause for concern. The associated factors are similar to those for non-enrolment (see Table 5.4). Poverty is again one of the major reasons for drop-out. Other factors, such as bias against girls' education, the burden of domestic chores and the poor quality of education available are also important contributory factors. Girl children are often enrolled in school when they are very young (about 6-7 years), and of not much use at home. As they grow older and become capable of either working outside the house or of taking responsibility of household chores and younger siblings, they are increasingly kept back from school and put to work in these capacities. For older girls, it is not socially acceptable to study in coeducational schools under male teachers and in schools which are far away. The school system too leaves a lot to be desired.

Table 5.4 Class from Which Girls Dropped Out of School

	Girls No. (%)
STD 1	29 (29.4)
STD 2	11 (11.1)
STD 3	8 (8.1)
STD 4	12 (12.1)
STD 5	10 (10.1)
STD 6	13 (13.2)
STD 7	5 (5.0)
STD 8	1 (1.0)
STD 9	3 (3.0)
STD 10	3 (3.0)
N.A	4 (4.0)
Total	99 (100)

Our survey revealed that the majority of the girls dropped out in Class 1 itself. There was a significant and steady rate of drop-out in Classes 2-6, after which a sharp fall was observed in the drop-out rate. This implied that the reasons which compel a girl to drop out of school are present right from the beginning and the problems manifest themselves in the initial stages of schooling. Though the rate of drop-out decreased somewhat after Class 1, the number of girls who left school at all levels of primary school was still considerable. Interestingly though, once this watershed was crossed, that is, Class 6, there was a major reduction in the drop-out figures, which suggests that those who can resist dropping out in the first few levels of schooling will perhaps stay on for the remaining years till they have completed school.

Table 5.5 Reasons Why Girls Dropped Out of School	
Reasons given	Girls No (%)
Economic	30 (30.3)
Socio-cultural	11 (11.0)
Personal	26 (26.3)
Familial	42 (42.4)
Infrastructral	18 (18.2)

Note: There is some overlapping in the answers given with respect to the categories listed: e.g., a girl may have dropped out due to both socio-cultural and economic reasons. Since both reasons have been tabulated for the same girl, the total number of girls in the table adds up to 127, i.e., more than 99, the number of drop-outs (see Table 5.2). The percentages, however, have been calculated on 99.

The general reasons why girl children in this sample dropped out of school are once again classified into five main categories (see Table 5.5). Of the 99 girls who dropped out of school, 30 said they had done so because of economic reasons. Of these, in 24 cases, the parents were too poor to keep the girls in school; three girls said that the family's resources were needed for other purposes; and three had to drop out because they had to go to work. Eleven girls had to drop out because of socio-cultural reasons. Of these, five got married early and were not allowed to go to school after marriage. In other cases a girl's family and her community did not approve of her being educated and were instrumental in her being withdrawn. Twenty-six girls dropped out because of personal problems. The majority suffered either from a low self-image and lack of motivation or from a fear of examinations. The majority (42 girls) who had dropped out due to familial reasons did so because there was too much work to be done at home. The others said that their family members disapproved of girls' education. As far as situational reasons are concerned, the most significant one for which girl children dropped out of school appears to be the harsh behaviour of teachers. Several girls reported that their teachers were frequently absent, indifferent in class and were often physically abusive towards the children. In brief, the three most important reasons for drop-out were poverty of parents (27 girls); the pressure of domestic chores (22 girls); and bias against girls'education (9 girls). For five girls the problem was early marriage. The girl children's fear of failure in school and the treatment received from harsh teachers were also major deterrents (see Tables 5.4 and 5.5).

The girl children who were currently not attending school were asked whether they would like to return to school if they were given a chance. The majority, almost 57 percent of the 209 girls out of school (both non-enrolled and drop-outs) answered in the affirmative. Over 40 percent of the girls, however, said that they did not want to go back to school. Some were already married or engaged to be married and said that it was absurd even to think of such a possibility. A few said that they would not like to re-enrol because they had grown far too old. It was shameful to think of going to school with boys and girls so much younger than them.They would much rather stay at home than face such an embarrassing situation. Some girls also said that they simply would not be allowed to go back to school because their families did not consider it proper for grown up girls to travel to school, even if the school was in the locality itself.

Some girl children said that their families were not in a position to spare them for school, either because they took care of a large part of the household chores or because their parents could not afford to forgo the income they brought in. Their families were far too poor to consider educating them at all. We tried to explain to them that we were talking about a hypothetical situation: would they like to go to school if the present obstacles were removed? The idea was met by incomprehension on the part of these girls. The difficulty of their circumstances was so ingrained in their minds that they could not even imagine that these might conceivably change. They continued to insist that their poverty would not permit their going to school.

CURRENTLY ATTENDING OR EVER ATTENDED SCHOOL

We have tried to get an idea about the nature of education and related facilities available to those girls who were enrolled or had enrolled at some time but had later dropped out. Out of the 490 girls who had attended school at some time, 333 girls or 67.9 percent had studied in coeducational schools; and 152 or 31.1 percent had studied exclusively at all-girls' schools. The latter belonged mainly to the families settled in the urban areas. In the rural areas, usually only one school is available for both boys and girls, and those who are sent to school have no choice in this matter. At the high school level this sometimes becomes a reason for girls dropping out of school. Most of the girls, that is, 269 out of the 490, who had ever been enrolled, attended schools within their village or locality. This answer was obtained usually from the younger girls who were enrolled in the village primary schools or from Muslim girls in the slum areas who attended Urdu-medium schools within their locality. Many, 151, attended schools in nearby villages or localities; the schools were situated within a radius of about 2 km. In the rural areas, these girls were generally the older ones, attending upper primary or high schools. In the urban areas the girls came from both slum and non-slum areas.

Sixty-seven girls answered that they had to travel more than 2.5 km to reach school. These were girls from the two non-slum urban areas who travelled to school either by school bus or by some other means of transport. It would appear from these findings that the non-existence of schools or distance of school from home were not the major deterrent to school enrolment in the areas surveyed. The majority of girl children said that they had no problems in travelling to school. Bad roads during the monsoons affected school attendance of about 8 to 10 percent of the girls, especially in Gunar and Phulmalancha villages. About 2 percent of the girl children reported problems due to lack of a companion or an escort when travelling to school. These girls belonged to conservative families who did not approve of girl children going out of the house alone.

It was observed that of the majority of the girls attending school, about 78.5 percent received education in their mother tongue. Very few, about 4 percent, were educated in a regional language which was not their mother tongue. About 15 percent of the girls went to English-medium schools. These girls belonged chiefly to the middle class families in the urban areas who could afford to send their daughters to privately run schools.

Inquiries about the availability of infrastructural facilities of schools revealed that about 7 percent of the girls attended schools that had no playgrounds. More than 58 percent went to schools that did not have a library. Almost all the children, however, said that they participated in games and sports. Those who had no playgrounds in their schools played indoor games or were taken to open spaces nearby for outdoor activities. However, only about 31 percent of girl children reported using libraries. Some girls said that they were not allowed into the school libraries because they were still too young.

This underlines the serious inadequacy in the provision of library facilities and the urgent need for improvement in this direction. Books outside the school syllabus would encourage the children to develop a reading habit and would increase their interests in subjects outside their textbooks. This might stand them in good stead in later life after they have completed their school education. It would also prevent the tendency, especially in girls, of dropping back into illiteracy once they left school. A girl who had developed a reading habit would presumably still be interested in books even if she were no longer in school. However, in the absence of a library, she would have no other source which would provide her with books because most girls come from poor families who would not be able to buy their children any. A school is the natural place to have a library. That there is such a major lack of this basic facility is indeed a serious cause for concern.

With regard to extracurricular activities, about 14 percent participated in school plays, 42 percent took music lessons, close to 31 percent attended sewing classes and about 6 percent were enrolled as girl guides. Other activities were dancing, recitation, debates, quizzes, and so on. Most of the girls who took part in such activities came from the urban areas. Schools in the villages surveyed had no such facilities.

When our respondents were asked whether they had time at home to study or to finish their homework, the majority, about 85 percent, answered in the affirmative. Only about 13 percent categorically said that they had too much work at home to be able to spare any time for books or homework after school. It must be noted here that when they were asked about their brothers, only around 1.5 percent of the girls said that their brothers too had no time at home to study. This clearly brings out the distinction in treatment between the girl child and the boy child. A greater number of girl children are overburdened with work at home and so can spare less time than boys to complete their school work. As a result, their performance in class suffers, and at the end of the academic year they often fail to make the grade. Eventually these girls drop out of school altogether. This is one explanation for the greater tendency among girl children to drop out of school.

To questions about who provided them with books and other learning material, about 70 percent of the girls answered that their parents—either father or mother or both—bought them their books. Twenty-four percent of the girls said that their schools and the village panchayats provided them with some books and their parents and other relatives had to buy the remainder. The others were given books by relatives and friends. Schools, panchayats and similar agencies, without the aid of parents, gave books to only around 3 percent of the girls. This implies that it is chiefly the girl child's family which has to provide her with books, notebooks, pencils, and so on, for the purposes of schooling. Schools do not provide books to the majority of children. This means a substantial additional cost which most parents find difficult to bear. This could well be one of the reasons for non-enrolment and early drop-out.

Table 5.6 Persons Helping Girl Child with Homework

	Girls No (%)
Self	98 (20.0)
Parents and/or other relatives	145 (29.6)
Tutor/Coaching class	233 (47.6)
Other	8 (1.6)
N.A.	6 (1.2)
Total	490 (100)

In West Bengal, government schools offer education free of tuition fees up to Class 12 level. Officially, they also provide textbooks free of cost to the children in these schools. Our survey shows that these books do not actually reach the children they are meant for, which means that much of the effort made in this direction and the resources earmarked for this purpose are being wasted. This is an important matter which needs attention.

Table 5.6 shows that close to 48 percent of the girls needed to be tutored privately (43.7%) or in coaching classes (3.9%). It thus becomes evident that the nature and quality of teaching in class was such that the girls needed additional help. Parents who wish to keep their daughters in school and expect them to pass examinations have to make provisions for this requirement.Tuition fees amount to a considerable burden on the already scarce resources and negate to a considerable extent the benefits of 'free' education. Poor parents often do not enrol their children, especially daughters, in school simply because they cannot afford private tuition fees. As they are largely illiterate, they cannot coach their children themselves. As observed from the table, less than 30 percent of the parents help their daughters with school work; they are from the socioeconomically better off sections of the urban areas. Girls coming from two categories, amounting to 20 percent, said that they received no help at home whatsoever. Some belonged to the middle class families of the urban areas and went to the better schools, and could manage their homework on their own. The others came from the poorer rural areas and the urban slums. When they said that they did their school work by themselves it usually meant that there was no one to supervise them and they had to manage as best they could. In many cases these girls attended school irregularly and dropped out early. They often failed to pass the end of term examinations, and no one much cared if they did not.

PERCEPTIONS OF THE GIRL CHILD

Do the girl children like school? Forty-one of the girls said that they did not like going to school at all. Among those who professed to like school, the majority, about 54 percent, said that they did so because school gave them an opportunity to learn and to improve their skills and knowledge. They felt that going to school raised their ability to cope with life substantially and also helped them to become self-reliant. Around 26 percent of the girls said that they liked going to school because it meant meeting friends and a chance of socializing with new people. About 6 percent liked school because their schools had large playgrounds where they could play and because school offered them a chance to join in extracurricular activities. Around 3 percent of the girls said that they preferred going to school to staying at home because it meant relief from excessive domestic work. These girls belonged chiefly to rural scheduled tribe families, who, in addition to school and housework had also to earn money usually as agricultural labourers.

Of the 41 girls who did not like school, 8, that is, almost 20 percent, said that the reason was the harsh behaviour, incompetence or indifference of the teachers. About 12 percent suffered from ill-health or from problems of low self-image and were afraid that they would fail in school. Some said that they did not like going to school because no one else in the locality did so; going to school meant missing out on the games that they could have otherwise played. Older girls who had dropped out said that they had failed to realize the importance of schooling when they were young and so had tried to stay away from school.

Motivation or the lack of it is sometimes an important determining factor in the matter of the level or quality of education the girl child receives. In order to assess the girl child's situation in this regard, we tried to find out about her perceptions.

It is encouraging to note that most girl children who were currently attending school (391, see Table 5.2) had high aspirations for themselves (see Table 5.7). A large number wished to study at least up to the Higher Secondary level. Most of the girls from the urban non-slum areas said that they would study at least up to the graduation level. Those who said that they would study as much as they were allowed to were mostly girls who belonged to conservative families and apprehended that their education might be discontinued when they reached puberty.

Table 5.7 Girl Child and Desired Education Levels of Girls

	Girls No (%)
Up to primary/read and write	11 (2.8)
Up to middle	25 (6.8)
High School/Higher Secondary/Intermediate	77 (19.6)
Graduation	100 (25.6)
Postgraduation/Doctorate/Professional degree	66 (16.8)
Diploma—Technical/Vocational	9 (2.3)
As far as I can/am allowed to	74 (18.8)
D.K.	19 (4.8)
N.A.	10 (2.5)
Total	391 (100)

Around 24 percent of the girl children were of the opinion that boys should be more educated than girls. When we asked them why they felt so, the answers we received all pointed to the fact that from childhood most girls had been conditioned to believe that men were superior to women and boys to girls, they worked and looked after the family and so their education was more important. Educating a son today meant enhanced earnings tomorrow and so it was worthwhile to send a son to school, many of them said. Daughters would after all be married off, and would not be of any use to their parents' families.

In response to the question about the advantages of being able to read and write, almost 50 percent said that literacy helped in their personal development. Being literate gave them a greater sense of self-confidence and enabled them to communicate with others in a more intelligible manner. Another 17.5 percent of the girls felt that employment prospects were considerably improved for those who were literate. It also helped their career advancement. Over 6 percent of the respondents felt that literacy improved their social status and almost 5 percent felt that it helped them to educate and help other children. It must be noted, however, that 9 percent of the girls could not answer the question, either because they had not thought about the problem at all, or because they could not perceive any advantage in being literate. Four percent of the girls clearly stated that literacy yielded no special benefit at all.

What about the disadvantages of being illiterate? About 80 percent recognized that illiteracy was a major handicap; 54 percent felt that illiteracy led to a low self-image and left them unable to deal with day to day activities. They were not able to maintain their daily accounts, for instance. They could not understand what change they should get back when they went out to shop. They could not read their own letters or teach their younger brothers and sisters the alphabet. When they went out they could not even read the street names or the numbers on the buses and so were always afraid of getting lost. As a result, they never dared to go out anywhere without an escort. People considered them stupid because they could not read. About 8 percent felt that being illiterate made it difficult for them to get good jobs. About 15 percent said that they suffered from feelings of inferiority because they were illiterate. It restricted their knowledge and development of what went on around them. Close to 9 percent of the girls could not answer the question and over 6 percent perceived no disadvantage in being illiterate.

We attempted to find out what the girl children's future ambitions and aspirations were. Their answers were revealing. Most of the girls restricted their answers to professions that were predominantly feminine. For instance, 108 girls, or around 18 percent of the sample wanted to become school teachers, a profession that is considered feminine by the majority of people. Close to 8 percent said that they wanted to become 'well educated'. They had no idea what they would do afterwards, whether they would be able to make use of it. Their attitude suggested that they felt that for a woman it was enough to be granted permission to be educated. What more could a woman aspire to? Around 13 percent clearly and unambiguously wanted to become housewives. More than 10 percent of the girls said that they had not formed any definite idea about a profession and around 4 percent said that they did not aspire to any particular profession. These girls too belonged to the category of those who wanted to become housewives; their attitudes reflected the view that there was no need for them to consider any vocation or career for themselves, their roles were clearly marked out: their parents would get them married when the time came. What else could a woman be but a housewife?

Among the 10 percent of the girls who wanted to become doctors, some were daughters of doctors themselves and wanted to follow in their parents' footsteps. Others thought of it as a 'noble' profession. Very few girls wanted to become nurses, however.

Engineering, which is clearly considered to be a very 'masculine' profession, was, as expected, the choice of very few girls. Besides, in poorer families, even boys could hardly aspire to such professions. Almost 9 percent said that they would like to get some sort of a job after they finished studying, but had not yet decided

definitely on the kind of job they wanted. Finally, about 12 percent
of the girls were not able to answer this question. They were either
too young or could not understand the concept that women might
have a choice about their futures.

Did the girls have any particular reasons for their career choices?
Around 21 percent replied that they aspired to a particular kind
of life because it satisfied them and that was what they wanted to
be. Another 3.5 percent said that they had no specific reason for
their choice. Only about 8 percent said that their purpose was to
attain economic independence. About 2 percent of the girls said
that they would have to work to support their families, while 5
percent had made their choices according to their parents' wishes.
More than 8 percent felt that they would serve society and the
nation, and over 6 percent only wanted to live up to social
expectations about women's roles. About 4 percent of the girls
said that they wanted to become educated enough to be able to
teach their own children or hoped to become school teachers
because they liked teaching.

What, if any, were the girl children's ideas about their parents'
aspirations for them? It was observed that the greatest number of
girls, about 21 percent, felt that their parents wanted them to
become good housewives. Almost 20 percent of the girls said that
their parents did not want them to take up any job and had no
career aspirations for them, or at least, had not mentioned
anything in particular to them. Close to 14 percent said that their
parents told them to study well either because it was the first step
towards achieving any ambition or because they themselves had
not had the opportunity of completing their education and they
wanted their daughters to have this chance. Around 6-7 percent
of the parents wanted their daughters to be doctors. Almost the
same number wanted their daughters to be school teachers. Close
to 7 percent wanted their daughters to be engaged in some kind
of service, but no further details were supplied. In all, 19.5 percent
of the girls felt that their parents wanted them to work in an
income-earning capacity.

When comparing the figures on the girls' own ambitions with
those of their parents on their behalf, it is observed that over 40
percent of the girl children in the sample would choose an
income-earning career if the choice were left to them. However,
only 19.5 percent girls were encouraged by their parents to do so.
This is certainly heartening and shows that more girls today are
breaking out of the traditional framework that confines women
within the four walls of the home. This is also reflected in the fact
that though more than 21 percent of the parents wanted their

daughters to become only good housewives, less than 13 percent of the girls actually said that this was all they aspired to.

The majority of the girl children could not say why their parents wanted them to choose a particular way of life. Some felt that their parents wanted them to behave according to accepted social norms. Only about 5 percent said that their parents encouraged them to be economically independent. Two percent said that their parents had got them engaged in income-earning work to help support the family. Less than 5 percent said that their parents wanted them to pursue any career that they chose simply because it would make their daughters happy.

WORK

In the underpriviledged sections of our society, child labour is a common feature. Children are often put to work so that they can earn and supplement the family income. They usually start working when very young, often before they are legally old enough to work. Many work for very long hours, under conditions that are extremely hazardous for their physical and mental health. Coming from families where any addition to the household income is welcome, and working mostly in the unorganized sector, these children have no choice but to accept very low payment for their work. There is usually no opportunity to learn any skill which might improve their future job prospects.

As soon as the decision is taken to engage a child in some income-earning activity, a decision, in effect, is also made about her/his educational opportunities. The child is denied her/his basic right to education. Working girl children are additionally burdened with housework. They work strenuously for long hours, but get no extra credit or consideration for this dual burden, as it is considered to be 'natural'. A girl child's chances of getting any kind of education is clearly even less than that of the boy child in similar circumstances.

ECONOMIC ACTIVITY

What is the condition of the working girl children in our sample? It is seen that 528 girls report no economic activity, that is, 88 percent of the households did not have any respondent girl children working in any income-earning capacity. Of those who did work (72), the majority were agricultural labourers (see Table 5.8). There were others engaged in home-based work activities and they were all paid at piece-rates. Some girls made floor mats and cane mattresses. Others prepared puffed rice (*muri*) from paddy. In the urban slums, some girls helped to make papads, some made

envelopes or helped in the packaging trade which their parents
were engaged in. Other activities included weaving and stitching,
petty business and working as domestic help in more affluent
houses. Three girls who belonged to the non-slum, low socioeconomic status area of Calcutta coached younger children at home.

Table 5.8 Types of Economic Activity

	Girls No (%)
Weaving/basket-making	6 (8.4)
Tailoring/embroidery/knitting	4 (5.6)
Other crafts	2 (2.8)
Agricultural labourer	28 (38.7)
Petty business/hawker/vendor	4 (5.6)
Piece-rate worker (home-based)	17 (23.6)
Domestic worker	5 (6.9)
Tuitions/teaching	3 (4.2)
N.A.	3 (4.2)
Total	72 (100)

Economic activity has been defined as any work which yields
some economic benefit. Payment for the work done might have
been made directly to the girl child who was engaged in doing that
work or if she had been simply assisting other family members in
their work, she may have got part payment, or sometimes no
payment at all. She might be paid in cash or kind, or both.

Table 5.9 shows the nature of employment of the working girl
children. It is seen that the majority of the girls were salaried
employees. In the rural areas they were often engaged in work such
as making paper bags, muri, and so on. In the urban areas they
usually worked as domestic servants. Since they were paid on a
monthly basis, they chose to call themselves salaried employees.

Table 5.9 Girl Child: Nature of Employment

	Girls No (%)
Self-employed (for economic benefit)	11 (15.3)
Salaried employee	36 (50.0)
Working with family (piece wages)	7 (9.7)
Productive activity at home/assisting family-members (no separate payments)	12 (16.7)
Casual worker	2 (2.8)
D.K.	1 (1.3)
N.A.	3 (4.2)
Total	72 (100)

Table 5.10 Working Girl Child: Monthly Income*	
	Girls No (%)
Less than Rs. 50	4 (6.7)
Rs. 51-100	11 (18.3)
Rs. 101-200	10 (16.7)
Rs. 201-300	12 (20.0)
Rs. 301-500	12 (20.0)
N.A	11 (18.3)
Total	60 (100)

* Out of the 72 working girl children, 12 did not receive any payment in cash or in kind and therefore their answers have not been included.

From Table 5.10 we get an idea about the monthly income of the working girl child. A significant fact emerges from this table. It is seen that over 41 percent earned less than Rs 200 per month while no one was able to earn more than Rs 500 per month.

It is generally expected that employees received some benefits and amenities at their place of work, but we noticed that these girls did not have any clear understanding of this concept. Since most of the girls worked at home, rudimentary facilities, such as drinking water, light and ventilation, were available to the majority of them. Most of them were also given a period of rest during work. It must be remembered, however, that the girls gave their answers according to their perceptions of these amenities. Most of them lived in one-roomed or two-roomed houses which had no light or ventilation and, which were, additionally, cramped with a large number of family members. In the urban slums, especially, the living conditions were highly unsanitary. Even, the 'period of rest' that these girl professed to have, was usually spent doing house-hold chores, such as cooking, cleaning and looking after younger siblings.

The facilities that were largely not available to the working girl children were benefits such as free medical expenses, bonus or festival bonus. Paid holidays, maternity leave, skill training or education at place of work were also not available to the majority. Some respondents were not able to answer these questions. This could be due to two reasons : (a) because they were not able to perceive, at all, that these facilities could be available to anyone at their place of work, or, (b) because they themselves had so far had no occasion to avail of these benefits, they simply did not know whether these existed (maternity benefits, for example).

During the survey it was found that most of the working girl children spent between 6 to 10 hours at work, every day. About 27 girls spent between 6 to 8 hours and 9 girls between 8 to 10 hours at work every day. Nineteen girls had no fixed hours of work.

Most girls worked during the daytime. A few worked during the day, as well as in the late evenings. These were the girls who worked as domestic servants. Quite a number had no fixed timings of work. Almost all of them worked all seven days of the week and had no holidays.

Most of the girl children did their income-earning work at home. Some worked outside the home, but within their own locality. The remaining, 27 girls in all, had to travel between 2 and 6 km to reach their work-place, most of them walking all the way. These girls needed between 30 minutes to 2 hours to reach their place of work, depending upon the distance they had to travel.

It has been found that most of the girls received their payment in cash. Some were paid partly in cash and partly in kind. They were mainly from the group of agricultural labourers. A substantial number of girls received daily wages. Some were paid weekly; the remainder were paid either at the end of the month, or on completion of the job given to them. Almost all the working girls received their payment themselves. Parents or guardians collected the earnings of very few. The money earned however was, in almost all cases, spent on family expenses; the decision about spending being taken usually by parents or older relatives in the household. Only 10 girls were able to participate in the decision-making process regarding the spending of their own money. In most cases, they too, actually spent the entire amount on the family. It is clear, therefore, that the girl children were sent out to work by their parents in the interest of the family. The children themselves rarely had any choice or control over the decision to work or over their own earnings.

In addition to their jobs outside the home, the working girls also had to shoulder a lot of responsibilities in their own homes. This not only placed the dual burden of work on them, but also effectively robbed them of any time or opportunity for schooling or education. In fact, the girls did not even have time for leisure. Also, working in no way improved their bargaining power within the home. They were not treated better in any way because they contributed to the family income.

Most of the working girls did, however, receive pocket-money, which they spent either on themselves or on gifts for other members of the family. This was not a special favour bestowed on working girls, though. When resources permitted, all children in the family, boys, more than girls, were given small sums of money when they asked for it, and which they were allowed to spend in any way they wished.

It becomes evident from the survey that about 45 percent of the working girls liked whatever work they were engaged in and about 41 percent either disliked their work or were indifferent to it.

Among the girls who professed to like their work the greatest number (15%) did so because of the economic independence that working permitted. Some liked working because it gave them an opportunity to go out and mix with others. A few (close to 7%) responded that they liked working because it gave them a chance to learn a skill that could be of gainful use one day. A few (5%) worked outside the home to escape the drudgery of domestic work.

We also found that the compulsion to work in order to supplement family income was one of the more important reasons that made girls dislike the work they were forced to do. Others disliked working because of the long and difficult journey to the workplace, the risk to health due to the nature of the work and the drudgery that the work involved. A few, usually domestic servants, also felt that the work they did was socially demeaning. There was scope for providing more than one reason for liking or disliking work, but the majority had no second or third response.

It is interesting to note, however, that none of the girls said that they disliked working because they were ill-paid or paid less than the boys who did the same work. None even stated that they felt overburdened with work both at home and outside the house. Not even one girl brought up the issue of sexual harassment. However, when these questions were put to them specifically, several expressed dissatisfaction about payment, gender discrimination (regarding wages and conditions) and sexual harassment. This was probably because the girls did not perceive these as major problems worth mentioning, or, because they accepted the presence of such problems as 'natural' in all workplaces. It must be remembered, however, that sexual harassment, here, refers to moderate to severe eve-teasing. In our perception, actual molestation or the possibility of rape have not emerged as serious threats to the girl children in our sample. Most girls, it appears, would be happier simply if the atmosphere in the workplace became a little more friendly and congenial.

SKILL

Even the girl children who were then not in an earning job might have needed to find some work in the future. Because skilled workers get higher payment for their work than unskilled workers, we tried to find out whether our girl child respondents had got the opportunity to acquire any skills which would improve their income-earning potential. Interestingly, only 29 percent of the girl children were found to have aquired no skills whatsoever. Of the others, the majority were skilled in stitching, embroidery, knitting, and so on, while about 13 percent were skilled in music, dance and painting. The latter group came from the urban areas surveyed, where there are opportunities to pursue such activities. Almost 6 percent of the girls were skilled in food processing and allied activities. These girls belonged to the rural sector and food processing meant either making muri from paddy, or husking paddy after it has been cut and dried. Most of the girls, however, did not use any of their skills for economic benefit. Only about 9 percent did so, and almost all of them came from the rural areas.

Parental perceptions with regard to the kind of skills which boys and girls in the family were expected to acquire, determined to a large extent the opportunities that were made available to them to acquire these skills. A rigid compartmentalization in the minds of the parents with regard to their ideas about masculine and feminine skills conditions children to accepting as normal such role models for themselves. This is the beginning of gender-based role stereotyping that is so widely prevalent in our society. Because children become conditioned to believing that there are definite gender-specific expectations from them in the matter of skill formation, they choose only to learn those skills which fulfil these expectations. A boy, for instance, rarely chooses knitting as a hobby; similarly, a girl seldom wants to learn carpentry. Both might be equally good at either skill, but knitting is usually regarded as a feminine skill, just as carpentry is considered a masculine occupation. It is such categorization in skill formation that leads to job-stereotyping later.

What skills were expected from the boys and the girls by their parents? It is evident, that the majority of parents, about 56 percent, expected both sons and daughters to be proficient in reading/writing. Only about 14 percent expected this from boys exclusively. Skills such as music and dance were considered to be exclusively for girls. In fact, the majority of parents did not expect either sons or daughters to acquire expertise in these fields. In poorer households these were luxuries which their meagre resources did not permit. Sewing and cooking were, as expected, the girls' preserve. However, as far as participation in the traditional household occupation was concerned, about 54 percent of the parents did not want either child to take it up and about 31 percent expected only boys to do so.

HOUSEHOLD WORK

Girl children grew up helping their mothers at home. They became proficient at work such as cooking, cleaning, looking after children, and so on, from an early age. As they grew older they were increasingly entrusted with the responsibility of domestic chores, often to the point of being kept back from school to take care of such matters. Boy children, however, were not expected by parents or by society to do household work and had a minimal involvement in these activities.

For most girl children, there was no choice in the matter of housework. Working within the household was a necessity, either because their mothers went out to work, or because the mothers were so over-burdened with work that they were unable to manage on their own. In any case, girl children were expected to earn their keep by at least making themselves useful within the house. They were, in fact, unrecognized child labourers and though they were not able to earn wages for this labour, they did make a significant economic contribution to the maintenance of their families simply by freeing their mothers from the burden of domestic chores and by making it possible for them to go out to work. The variety of work and responsibilities that they shouldered, and the amount of time that they had to spend in work at home effectively put an end to any aspirations of schooling that these girls might have had. In fact, the pressure of housework is one of the major contributory factors to the low female enrolment and early drop-out.

It is observed that fetching fuel and water was done usually to a far greater extent by girls than by boys. Work, such as cooking, cleaning the house, and looking after younger children was almost exclusively girls' work and boys did not spend any time on these activities. Cleaning utensils and washing clothes was also 'women's work'. As far as running errands was concerned, boys and girls were equally active. Boys were sent to the market to a greater extent than girls were. In households where both children spent no time at all on domestic work, either the women of the family performed these tasks or, in the case of fairly affluent families, services of hired help were used. The latter is true, particularly, of the middle class urban families and the economically better off rural families. In general, the traditional gender-based role stereotyping in the matter of household work continues unchanged.

SOCIALIZATION

An attempt has been made to study the different influences which may act upon the socialization process of the girl child.

BIRTH RITUALS

The majority of households, over 55 percent, had the same birth rituals for boys and girls and professed to make no difference between sons and daughters in this respect. Only about 10 percent families said that boys were given greater importance and birth celebrations were either held only for them or were much more elaborate. However, casual conversations with the mothers and other family members revealed that in many cases, though the ritual itself may have been the same for both sexes, there was much greater jubilation and gaiety with the birth of a male child. As many as 30 percent of the girls were not able to answer this question, usually because they were much too young to understand its import.

EATING ORDER

The sequence in which the family members are given their meals is an important indicator of the status of these members within the family. In patriarchal societies there is usually a definite hierarchical pattern observed in the eating order of the various family members. The male members of the family are traditionally served their food first. Women and older girls eat after all the other family members have eaten. One of our objectives during this survey was to find out whether there had been any change in this behavioural pattern.

In over 50 percent of the families, the mother of the girl child respondent (with or without the other female members of the family) was the one who was last to eat. Girl children in the age group of ten and above usually accompanied their mothers. In about 46 percent of the households, the fathers ate first, either on their own, or with the other male members of the family or with the children. In about 16 percent of the families children were served their food first, before either parent. The entire family ate together in around 19 percent of the households. Another 13-14 percent of the families said that the members did not have any fixed eating order, each ate according to his or her convenience.

Thus we see that the general trend is for the women in the families to eat last, serving food first to the male members, and sometimes to the children as well, irrespective of sex. In most cases, it has been our experience that girl children above the age of ten are not considered children any more and they eat only after the male members have eaten.

These girls, therefore become used to eating whatever is left over after their fathers' and brothers' meals. And in most poor families, very little is actually left over. This means that not only do the women eat less nutritious food, but they also make do with less than adequate quantities of food, both of which have serious implications for their health. What is more, this is regarded as normal by both men and women. As a result, the girl children who become accustomed to such practices from childhood, also become conditioned to regarding their status within the family as inferior to that of their male counterparts. When they, in turn, grow up and have families of their own, they too inculcate the same biases in their daughters' psyches, consequently perpetuating this mode of behaviour in future generations.

SOCIALIZING WITHIN THE FAMILY

How does the girl child relate to the other members of her household? Does she get the opportunity to spend any time with her parents? Is she able to play with her brothers? Our findings show that only 10.4 percent of the girls have ever had the opportunity to play with their parents; and among these, about 4-5 percent have played only with their mothers. In barely 4 percent of the families did the girl children spend time with their parents in activities such as listening to music, and so on.

Some of the girl children were helped by their parents with their homework. It appears that parents were minimally involved with their daughters in activities other than compulsory school work.

The role of the father in caring for a young boy or girl is negligible in our society. It is the mother who retains the responsibility of looking after her young child. This is all the more true in the case of the girl child, because even if the father takes an interest in his son, who is expected to be his heir and successor, and to whom he is expected to be a role model, with the intention of initiating him into manly pursuits, he usually has nothing whatsoever to do with his little daughter, and takes no part in her rearing or development. Girl children grow up at home in their mothers' company. In fact, as soon as the girls are six or seven years old, they start helping their mothers with the household work and pick up skills such as stitching or weaving.

In our sample, too, similar phenomena were observed. Though about 50 percent of the girls received skill training from their mothers and over 80 percent spent time helping their mothers with the domestic chores, less than 3 percent of the fathers participated in the skill-training of their daughters, and, as expected, a negligible number of fathers shared in any household work. One notable change, perhaps, was that 42 percent of the girl children ate meals with their fathers.

The survey reveals that this kind of sex-role stereotyping persists by and large in the majority of households in our sample. Daughters are still expected by society, and even by their own parents, to grow up in the image of their mothers: learning womanly skills and feminine virtues. Housework is still entirely a woman's responsibility, and daughters are expected to take on the mantle after their mothers.

Did the girl children play with their brothers? As many as 43 percent did not play at all with their brothers. Many of the girls phrased the answer in the reverse and said that their brothers never played with them either because their brothers were a great deal older or because they refused to play with mere girls. Several girl children, however, did play with their younger brothers. About 18 percent girls said that they played with their brothers sometimes, and about 22 percent said that they played often with their brothers. It is possible that many of these girls have interpreted sibling care as 'playing' with their brothers because in almost all cases whenever the girl child responded in the affirmative, the brother was very young. Given the responsibility of looking after small brothers and sisters at home, they played with them to keep them entertained and out of their mothers' way.

Boys and girls seldom played outdoor games together, both in the urban as well as in the rural areas. They usually preferred the company of children of their own age and sex. When they played together, they usually did so because of the lack of any other activity or the dearth of companionship of the same sex.

Gender stereotyping was observed to a great extent in the kind of games that they played. Girls liked to play feminine games, for example, to play 'house', dressed up as their mothers, with a family of dolls to care for. Some liked to play 'teacher', usually girls who had been recently enrolled in school. Otherwise, they preferred to play with their skipping ropes or at different variations of hide and seek. Boys, on the other hand, had their own typical games, football and cricket being the favourites. Boys and girls usually moved around in separate groups, and were, in fact, urged to do so by their parents and elders.

ENTERTAINMENT

With regard to entertainment we found that in 65 percent households, girls had access to radios and in 58 percent households they were able to watch TV. This, however, does not mean that all these families had their own radios or TV sets. As mentioned earlier, both in the urban and the rural areas, the sets of their more affluent neighbours were easily accessible and were regularly used by those who did not own them. Both girls and boys spent time watching TV or listening to the radio. However, boys did seem to have fewer restrictions than girls on visits to the cinema or to friends' houses.

More girls listened to the radio than they watched TV. The favourite radio programmes in order of popularity, were film songs, plays or serials and other musical programmes. Very few listened to news oriented programmes. Only 1 child out of 600 liked listening to children's programmes and not even one girl child listened to either educational or women's programmes.

In the case of television programmes, too, film songs (*Chitrahar*) topped the list, with plays/serials/films coming a close second. There was almost no viewership of other programmes. Once again, no one watched women's programmes. However, this response should not be judged at face value, because often girls who watched women's programmes, especially in the slums or in the villages, failed to identify such items as 'women's programmes'. These programmes, which are usually telecast in the form of plays or serials with a message in them pertaining to certain issues that concern women, were usually viewed simply as another play or serial and accepted as such. Children's programmes and educational programmes on television had negligible viewership.

The fact that there was no or negligible viewership and listenership for children's programmes and educational programmes on radio and TV indicates that there is a serious mismatch between programme planning and audience/viewer preference. Either these programmes were aired/shown at times when the children were away at school or work, or they were so uninteresting that the children did not like them. The audio-visual medium was an extremely powerful one and can play an important role in imparting knowledge as well as in changing or influencing ideas and perceptions. This is especially true today when almost every household owns a transistor radio and many have fairly easy access to television. With programmes that are framed in an interesting manner, it should be easy to capture the attention of the children so as to bring about desired changes in their outlook, perceptions and way of thinking. Extensive recasting of programme formats and schedules is necessary if the situation is to be improved in any way.

RESTRICTIONS AND PUNISHMENTS

Information was sought about the nature of punishments and rewards given to the boys and girls and whether any gender bias was observed in such matters. No explicit mention was made of any differentiated mode of conduct. Parents only admitted to restricting the movement of girls outside the home and said that they did disapprove of girls socializing too much with boys. Apart from that girls, they said, were treated no differently from boys. However, casual conversation revealed that girls were expected to mould themselves in the traditional feminine role model. The only concession in some cases was that they were allowed to go to school and were also expected to do well in class. Otherwise, tradition decreed that they stay at home, learn womanly trades like sewing and knitting, talk softly, walk lightly and be obedient and subservient to their parents and elders. Boys, however, were expected to be boys. For the same breach of conduct, a boy would get away with having his wrists rapped; a girl would be severely punished. Girls were taught to be tolerant; boys had no such expectations imposed on them.

RESTRICTIONS AFTER PUBERTY

The onset of puberty is considered as synoymous with 'growing up'. Girls are assumed to be on their way to being adults once they have started menstruating. As such, in many cases, traditionally certain rules and restrictions are imposed upon their movements when they reach puberty. In our sample the majority of girls were told that it was not befitting for them to move around or to play freely. They should take small steps, dress properly and behave in a demure fashion. Social contact with boys was to be avoided as far as possible.

Some rules and restrictions were imposed also during the period of menses. A few were restricted from playing strenuous games. For almost all of them, participation in religious ceremonies was forbidden. When we asked the girls about other traditional taboos in connection with menstruation, for example, restrictions on entering the kitchen or cowshed, fetching water, and so on, many said that though such rules did exist, they could not be imposed strictly nowadays because of the scarcity of other working hands in their families. If they were barred from entering the kitchen, tending the cows, or fetching water, these chores would be left unattended. Girls who were married said that they and their husbands had to abstain from sex during this time.

Most of the households had no puberty rituals for the girls. A total of 41 families had such practices in their community; of these, only 21 families actually observed any. These were observed usually for girls who started menstruating after their marriage, at their in-laws' homes. They were given new clothes and a ceremony was held to celebrate their coming of age.

AWARENESS OF SEXUAL DIFFERENCES

The girl children were asked how and in what manner girls became aware of differences between boys and girls, and 38 percent were not able to answer, probably because the concept was unfamiliar to them. Almost 18 percent said that they were aware of sex differences, but were not certain of how they came to know about it or could give no specific reason for this knowledge. Most were made aware of the difference by others. Some came to know about it because of restrictions on socialization with boys. Some were told about it at the onset of puberty. Still others said that they knew boys were different from girls simply because they looked different and dressed differently.

QUALITIES DESIRED IN 'GOOD' BOY/ GIRL/ DAUGHTER-IN-LAW/ HUSBAND/ WIFE

We see that the quality valued most in boys is educational accomplishment. The other qualities considered important are good manners, non-abusive behaviour, honesty, modesty, a respectful attitude, obedience, and so on. Good looks and smartness are also considered desirable by a few. For boys, earning capacity or employment prospects are not rated as important qualities by most of the girls. This is possibly because when talking about good boys they are talking about boy children and as such their earning capacity has not entered their assessment significantly.

For girls too educational accomplishment appears to be the most desired quality. Good manners, non-abusive behaviour, respectful attitude, honesty, modesty, disciplined behaviour and obedience are also considered important in girls. Having good looks is, as expected, considered to be more important for girls, than boys. Employment prospects are considered important only by about 3 percent of the girls, the majority considering it to be a secondary quality, at the most, in combination with the other qualities mentioned before.

The most important quality in a good daughter-in-law is a good nature, combined with a willingness to share in household work, including cooking. Good manners, an adjustable nature and a willingness to share in family responsibilities, including looking after elders, are also expected. Good looks are important, but not overly so. Very few girl children considered educational accomplishment or earning capacity as specially desirable qualities in daughters-in-law.

This reflects the image the girl children expected to live up to when they became daughters-in-law themselves. It was clear that most of them felt that an expertise in household activities and docility were the qualities expected of them at their in-laws' homes. They would have little use for educational accomplishments there, they felt.

The most desirable quality in good husbands was a good job status or earning ability. Affectionate and protective husbands were also very much in demand. Educational accomplishment was not considered very important. A few girls had also said that they would like their husbands to be teetotallers, non-smokers and not addicted to drugs. These girls came mostly from the slum areas of Ward No.79 where drug addiction is rampant, and almost all families house alcoholics, country liquor being easily available, with local distilleries dotting the area.

More than 54 percent of the girl children, especially in rural areas and in urban slums where knowledge and opinions about the activities of good wives or about married life are considered precocious in young unmarried girls, did not respond to the question about 'good' wives. Many girls were of the opinion that wives should be fond of their husbands and be prepared to take care of and defend their husbands' interests. Qualities such as a good nature, the willingness to share in household work, honesty, modesty, obedience, and so on, were also considered important.

6
THE GIRL CHILD
PROFILES

MANJU : NOT CHERISHED BUT A CURSE TO BE RID OF

Manju is a young Hindu girl, eighteen years old. There are four members in her family: her parents, herself and her brother, who is two years younger. Her sister, who is two years older than her, has been married for almost four years now, and lives with her in-laws in a nearby village. Manju's family lives at one end of the village, close to the Santhal settlements and the village primary school. A large field lies adjacent to the house, cutting it off from most of the neighbouring houses. There is also a small pond right in front, which makes it rather difficult to walk up to her house. Their home has an impression of seclusion, which is somewhat unusual in such a small village. The neighbouring houses can be seen but they face the other way, heightening the feeling of isolation that surrounds the family.

The family is one of the poorest in the village. Manju's father is a sharecropper and is able to earn only about Rs. 700 per month, a substantial part of which goes towards repayment of the loan taken during his elder daughter's marriage. He does own some land, but fears that that too will have to be sold to provide for Manju's dowry when her marriage is arranged. It is for this reason that Manju's brother does not want to become a cultivator. His parents want him to learn tailoring, which may help him secure a job in the city, and provide the family with a steady income. The sixteen-year-old boy is studying in Class 8. As his mother says, boys must at least complete school to be counted as 'somebody'.

When asked about the levels up to which girls should study, Manju's mother said that it is enough for girls to be able to read their own letters and sign their own names. After all, what is the point of educating a girl further? Eventually she will have to be married off. At her parents-in-law's house, it is not how much you have studied that counts, but how hard you can work and how capable you are at housework.

Manju is very well versed in all domestic chores. Her day begins very early in the morning. Her first duty, after she wakes up, is to pack her father's lunch for he must go out to the fields before the sun gets too strong. She then sweeps the house and wipes the floor and the walls by smearing them with a mixture of cowdung and water. Next she gets breakfast for her brother and packs his tiffin for him since he has to go to school, which is in the next village. After this, she starts preparing the main meal of the day. Once the cooking is complete, she must go to fetch water. Later in the morning, she does the day's laundry: washing the clothes of the entire family.

After she and her mother have had lunch, Manju washes the utensils and fetches water once again. She puts aside some food for her brother, for he will soon be home from school, and will leave almost immediately, after a quick meal, for the tailor's shop where he is learning his trade.

The remainder of Manju's afternoon, is free. She spends her time knitting, or making and embroidering quilts (*kantha*). Sometimes she even plays carrom or ludo with the girls in the neighbouring houses. But she does not have too many friends, she said, so mostly she spends her time on her own.

In the evening, Manju must once again sweep the house and fetch water for the evening's cooking. Dinner must be ready before her father and brother come home. After they have eaten, she and her mother eat, and it is only after cleaning up everything that Manju's day is finally over. She goes to bed early, she said, for she must be up again at the crack of dawn the next day. And anyway, there is nothing very much to do in the village at night, is there?

Manju has studied up to Class 6. She used to go to school till about four years ago. But since her elder sister got married she has been staying at home to help her mother with the housework. Manju told us quite clearly that her mother would not let her go to school because she could not cope with all the work at home alone. It was all right for Manju to attend school as long as her sister was there to help out at home, but when she got married, it automatically became Manju's responsibility to stay at home to lighten her mother's workload. And didn't she mind not going to school, we asked her. Yes, of course, she did, she said. She used to like going to school, she liked studying. And besides, she knows that unless one is educated one will not make a good marriage. If you know how to read and write, you can teach your own children as well. Would she go back to school now if she had the chance, we asked her. 'No', she said, 'now it is too late.' She felt that she was too old to go back to a classroom. And, apart from that, neighbours and relatives would not speak well of her if she travelled to another village every day to go to school, for there was no high school in this village.

What hopes did Manju have for the future, we asked, 'Nothing. Nothing at all,' she said. 'I know that the only future for me is to get married and look after the household. That is what my parents want me to do as well. Anyway, I never really had any time to study at home even when I was at school. There was always too much to do at home. Besides, there wasn't any one to help me with my homework either.' So perhaps Manju would have had to drop out of school anyway, simply because she could no longer keep up with the work in class.

Manju's mother is quite unperturbed that Manju had to discontinue school. 'What could I have done?' she says. 'My health is no longer what it used to be. I need someone to help me with my work. Naturally, I would expect Manju to stay at home with me. After all, sons cannot be expected to do housework, can they? And besides, where does he have the time? He goes to school in the morning. And in the evening, he goes to a nearby tailor's shop to learn cutting and stitching. After all, he has to prepare himself to earn a living. Who else will look after us in our old age?'

'Can't a daughter look after you as well?' we asked. 'Oh, no. Why should we ask a daughter to look after us? Girls have to get married and make their own homes.' And when did she plan to get her daughter married, we enquired. 'As soon as possible,' she said. 'I think girls should be married by the time they are fifteen or sixteen years old. The younger they are, the lesser the dowry the groom's family demands.' And what about boys? When should they be married ? 'Oh, after they are twenty-five or thirty years old,' she said. What kind of a girl would she prefer as a daughter-in-law? She said that she would expect her son's wife to be hard-working. In families such as theirs, that was the most important quality in any girl. And what kind of a girl would be considered a 'good' girl? A good girl would be one who would conduct herself according to the wishes of her parents. She would be even-tempered, well mannered and adjustable. A good boy needed only to be well behaved and supportive of his parents in their old age.

Manju's ideas about a 'good' girl and a 'good' boy are exactly similar to those of her mother's. A good boy must be educated and well behaved; a good girl must be submissive and quiet. A good daughter-in-law would abide by whatever her mother-in-law wanted and would dutifully serve all her in-laws. Manju's only expectation from a husband is that he must treat his wife well.

There has been no change in perception from one generation to another. All her life, Manju has been told that her role in life is to be a wife and a mother. Her work is at home. This is the only kind of life she is familiar with.

Manju has always been told that men are superior to women. It is their right to have the best that can be obtained. That is why she has never resented letting her brother have the larger pieces of fish and extra helpings of sweets. She does not even mind that her brother is still in school while she has had to drop out. After all, boys have to study more than girls, she says. They have to interact with so many people, they have to earn a living. Girls do not have to do all this, do they? What she is unhappy about is not being married yet. Her sister was married at sixteen. Most of her classmates have got married and moved away. It seems as though this is a cause of major humiliation for her—on our second visit to the village, we found her emotionally upset to a degree which was telling on her health and her entire demeanour.

EPILOGUE

On our next visit, after about ten months, we found Manju a changed person. When we told the panchayat pradhan that we would like to meet her, he tried to dissuade us by saying that it was better not to, for she was an extremely ill-tempered girl, with a terribly evil tongue. She was, he said, the most quarrelsome girl in the whole village. Why did we want to see her at all? When we insisted on going, he took us to their house, and there we found Manju, her face drawn, her head bowed, clad in a dirty sari, leaning against a bamboo pillar in a corner of the house. She looked up and quickly lowered her head again.

This time Manju hardly spoke at all and was largely unresponsive when we tried to talk to her. After a while, neighbours revealed that a marriage had been fixed for her recently, but the groom's family backed out at the last moment. Manju told us that the match was broken because her father could not arrange for the huge amount of dowry they wanted. Her mother was about to say something more, when Manju looked at her warningly, plainly asking her to keep quiet. We suspected that there was more to the story. Perhaps her reputation as an ill-tempered, quarrelsome girl had put them off. Or may be it was something worse.

What had happened actually, we asked. 'What can we say?' replied her father, 'such things are best not spoken about at all.' It was clear, however, that the family blamed Manju for whatever had gone wrong. Manju seemed absolutely shattered at this turn of events. Gone was her spirit and her willingness to talk. And no wonder. We saw the continuous battering that she suffered in the form of whispered conversations around her, all discussing why the marriage negotiations had broken up. Added to this was that her parents and her near relatives were constantly berating her.

After all, as they said, it was no easy task to arrange a marriage of a grown-up girl these days. They were preparing to sell off or pawn almost all their assets to meet the dowry demands of the groom's family. But all to no avail. This ill-fated girl did not even have the good fortune to be accepted in marriage by any family. Negotiations broke down at the last moment. And now, not only was the family saddled with the responsibility of looking after the girl, but they also had to bear the indignity of people pointing fingers at them and discussing their plight. Incidents such as this scarred the family forever.

What were they going to do now, we asked them. They looked at us in surprise. Was there anything else to do but to begin the search for a bridegroom all over again? They would probably have to pay a dowry that was even higher—after all, everybody knew that their daughter's marriage had been broken off by the groom's family at the last moment. Besides, she wasn't getting any younger, was she? And a dark girl to boot. Yes, they certainly would have to pay dearly to get her married. But there was no help for it. They would have to find her a husband even if it meant selling off their last meagre belongings, even their last plot of land.

'Why did you discontinue her education?' we asked them. 'Couldn't you re-enrol her in school now?' 'Oh, no! In poor families such as ours, we cannot afford to spend hard-earned money on luxuries like a girl's education.' 'But you are willing to spend so much on her dowry. If you spend even a little of it on her education or arrange for her to attend some vocational training courses, then perhaps she could earn her own living and stand on her own feet even if she did not get married.' Manju's parents looked at us askance. 'This is not your Calcutta, Didi. In small villages like this there is nothing worse than having an unmarried daughter in your family. Even if a girl is educated, she will have to be married if she is to be socially accepted. There simply is no choice in this matter. Even if it means destitution, we have to get the girl married. This curse of a girl child must be got rid of, somehow!'

For Manju, therefore, the situation is quite unbearable. All day she hears that she is a curse, a burden on her family. Her parents are ready to get rid of her even at a very high cost. She knows that her father will become a pauper simply to put together her dowry. Her brother has already left school, and is working full time to provide additional money—part of which will go towards her wedding, if it can be arranged. She knows that her family will face financial ruin after her marriage. Her parents would rather be impoverished than keep an unmarried girl at home. A broken match is trauma enough for a girl in her condition. If, in addition, her closest relatives, instead of offering support and comfort, reject her out of hand as a curse and a burden, then where does she turn? The family has traditionally been viewed as a supportive institution particularly for the girl child and the woman. It is situations such as this which call out for a critical revaluation of this idea. Leaning against the bamboo pillar of her house, with her drawn face and untended hair tied anyhow, Manju resembled a cornered animal, caught in an inescapable trap. No wonder she has retreated into a deep shell from which she refuses to come out.

Unless a match is found for Manju, she will be a burden on her family all her life, forever listening to uncharitable words which say that it is a sin to have a daughter, it is a curse to have an unmarried girl at home. To her, even a lifetime of drudgery at her in-laws' would be better than this. Then, at least, she would no longer be different, a castaway among all the other girls of her age.

We asked her once again whether she would now consider going back to school. 'No,' she almost screamed at us. 'No, do you think I'm a fool? Would I want to go to school with my nieces, now?' Her fury at having all doors, all options closed on her, knew no bounds. On top of it all, she was being forced to talk about her humiliating and degrading circumstances to city-bred strangers who could never understand anything. We were shocked into silence. Truly, which way would this girl turn? What did the future hold for her?

MAYA: OPPORTUNITIES UTILIZED

Getting to know Maya, an eleven-year-old girl from a ST Santhal family in a village, was an encouraging experience. The youngest child of the family, Maya has four elder sisters and one elder brother. One of her sisters, the eldest, died, one and a half years ago, at childbirth. Two others are married. The remaining sister is now studying in a school, a short distance away from the village, and lives in the hostel there. Her brother, now twenty-four years old, is a graduate in Arts, and an employee of South-Eastern Railways. He lives in Calcutta. Thus Maya's family, living in the village, now consists of herself and her parents.

Maya's home is situated in the ST settlement, right on the main road of the village. It is a tiny one-room *jhopri*, made up of leaves covering a bamboo framework, and a roof thatched with straw and twigs. The walls are so thin, that if one strikes a match within the house, the flame is visible from outside. One has to almost bend double to enter the house. Maya and her parents spend most of their time on a folding charpoy spread outside the doorway. They go inside only for meals and at bedtime. Surprisingly, though, the family possesses quite a few pieces of modern furniture. We were offered wrought iron stools and cane chairs to sit on.

Our first glimpse of Maya revealed a small, dark and sturdy girl with a bucketful of freshly washed clothes in her hand. She hardly glanced at us. She spread out the clothes to dry and immediately hurried off to fetch water. Dressed in a frock which was too small for her, hair uncombed and unruly she looked sullen and uncommunicative. After much coaxing she agreed to talk to us. Once she started conversing, however, her manner thawed quickly, and soon we were rewarded with a dazzling smile that lit up her face.

She readily answered all our questions. She was a student of Class 3 in the village primary school, she told us. And did she enjoy going to school, we asked her. Yes, she said, for, if she stayed at home, she had to do a lot of work. She would like to study as far as possible—she felt that going to school saved one from hard labour in the fields. If one is educated, one does not have to become an agricultural labourer, at least. For her that is the best thing about education.

It is true that Maya has to work very hard at home. She has to fetch water, fuel and fodder. She has to cook for the entire family, because her mother goes out to work as an agricultural labourer. She has to sweep and mop the house, clean the utensils and wash the clothes. She also has to take the goats out to graze. All this has to be done in addition to going to school and getting her lessons done everyday. It is indeed no wonder that the child is prepared to do anything to escape this drudgery.

Maya works occasionally as an agricultural labourer as well. She earns about Rs.10 and 2 kg. of rice for a full day's work— from 7 a.m. to 3 p.m. However, she does not really need to work. Her family's economic standing does not make it necessary for her to earn in order to supplement her parents' income. She works because she likes the idea of earning something for herself, money which she can spend at fairs and during festivals. She keeps her money with her mother and asks for it when she needs it. That is why, in this matter, she is a free agent. She works when she wants to and for whom she likes.

For Maya, marriage is not a priority at all. According to her, a 'good boy' or a 'good girl' is one who is educated. A 'good wife,' too, has the same quality. A 'good husband', in addition, must also be able to earn a decent income. The generally accepted stereotypes of men being educated and women staying at home to learn the household skills seem, apparently, to have made no impression on her. This is perhaps because of her family environment and the manner in which she has been brought up. In her community, both men and women work shoulder to shoulder and share most family responsibilities. Women participate equally with men in celebrations and have the same rights of enjoyment as men do. She has not seen girls being treated in a different or discriminatory manner from boys. Moreover, her own family circumstances have taught her that in today's world perhaps the most important quality and qualification is a good education.

Both of Maya's parents are agricultural labourers and leave for work very early in the morning. Though they are both illiterate, they have a genuine interest in education. All their children are educated. Maya's brother has a bachelor's degree in Arts. All her sisters have been to school, and most of them have studied up to Class 8. The sister immediately older to Maya is now in Class 7. Maya, too, is doing quite well in school. It is no small achievement for Maya's parents to have brought up all their children to be educated and well-placed in life. Living as they do in that small hut, it is difficult to believe that even amidst such harsh economic circumstances they could have risen up to the level they have. Their son has obtained a good job and earns over Rs. 2000 per month. Their daughters are educated up to the elementary level and have been married to men who are qualified and well-placed in life. It is true that they have benefitted from the reservation policy for ST, but even so, the fact that they have utilized the opportunities to the best of their abilities, is, in itself, commendable. Not only have Maya's parents been able to instil in their children the desire to strive for excellence, but they have also been able to open their minds to the various possibilities that the world has to offer. They are conversant with current events and regularly tune into the Santhali news every evening. No sacrifice was too big for them to further the cause of their children's education. For years they have done with only the barest of necessities to finance their son and daughters' education. In fact, when their son was small, they moved from Purulia to Barddhaman because his education was becoming more and more difficult in their village, as he had to cross a river to reach school every day.

Maya's mother, herself, is rather unconventional. Though she would have dearly loved to have had another son, she does not neglect her daughters nor does it mean that her daughters were less cared for than her son. She has insisted on sending all of them to school. Though she got her three elder daughters married at a young age because of social pressure, she would not have objected if they had wanted to do something else. She believes that nowadays boys and girls should be equally educated. Her daughters will be allowed to study as much as they want to.

Should they decide to take up a job, she would be happy. A good boy or a good girl is one who studies hard and is well placed. She would seek an educated wife for her son. After all, her son was a graduate, wasn't he?

Maya's mother has tried to give her children the best of everything. She has an easy affection for all her children and believes in letting them strive for whatever they want in life. It is largely due to her encouragement and guidance that they have done so well in school and studied up to the levels that they have. Her greatest success, however, lies in the fact that she has been able to achieve all this and has still been able to preserve a strong family bond between all the members. None of them are ashamed of their background. They all try to help each other whenever required. As each one rises in economic and social status, the entire family benefits from this association: It is her son and son-in-law who have recently started to buy the few good pieces of furniture that we saw in their house.

Maya's brother is particularly fond of her. He comes home every weekend to coach her, so that she does well in school. She is a good student and a good athlete, as well. She, too, wants to go to the school where her sister is now studying.

Though Maya is not particularly fond of school, since she likes to study, she will continue going to school, simply because the other choice is not acceptable either to her or to her family. She has viewed, first hand, the lives of her parents as well as those of her sisters and brother, and she would much prefer to have the latter for herself. This, certainly, is very heartening. That a girl, from what is generally accepted as a backward tribe, should seek a life that is not all hard labour, a life that is interesting and varied in its choices, is perhaps one of the most happy set of circumstances that we have come across. Getting to know Maya is doubly rewarding because one can be optimistic about her future. Her family is supportive and will help her achieve her ambitions. She is not likely to be one who sinks deeper and deeper into the gloom of a life where there is nothing whatever to look forward to.

EPILOGUE

When we visited this village again, about a year after the completion of our survey, Maya was nowhere to be seen. Her sister and brother-in-law were there, however. They told us that she had been sent to live in her school hostel. She is now in high school and lives with her sister in the boarding that the school provides. 'She says that she wants to complete her school education,' said her mother.

This was good news, indeed! Maya's future seemed bright. With an education, she would be able to get a good job. With her motivation and capacity to work hard, she is sure to do well in school and will shine in whatever she wishes to do. May be sometime in the future, Maya, too, will be an officer in a government concern, just like the brother she idolizes!

MALINI: WORK, WORK, WORK — NO SCHOOL, NO PLAY

Malini is a twelve-year-old girl, from a SC family, who lives in a village of West Bengal. Her family has six members—father, mother and three siblings. Her two brothers are ten and two years old, and her sister is five years old. At twelve years, Malini is the eldest child in the family.

Malini's height is four feet two inches and weights 32 kg. She has no history of any serious illness. She and the brother immediately after her were not immunized because her parents were not aware of the importance of immunization at that time. The two younger children have, however, been immunized. Malini's minor illnesses such as a cold or a fever, go largely unnoticed, both by her and her parents. However, she said that her brothers are sometimes taken to the hospital for treatment.

Malini was enrolled in school when she was younger. But later, as the family grew larger, she had to drop out to look after her younger brothers and sister. She was then in Class 1. In fact, the birth of her youngest brother precipitated matters somewhat. Her mother, an agricultural labourer, had to leave home for work soon after childbirth, and Malini stepped in to take her place at home.

Even when she did go to school, Malini never had the time to study or to finish her homework. Nor were her parents able to afford a tutor for her, without whom it is almost impossible for rural children to learn anything because of the way schools are run. Malini said that she loved going to school. She had friends to talk to and play with. And, she was just learning to read—something that was very exciting for her. Being illiterate, she said, means not even being able to read your own letters.

The responsibility of the entire household rests on the shoulders of this young girl. She cleans the entire house, which is no small task, for mud houses have to be wiped and moistened every day by smearing with a dung and water mixture to prevent cracks from forming. She washes the utensils and the clothes for the entire family. She fetches water. She also has to take care of her younger brothers and sister. She has to get the two older children ready for school on time, and see that they are fed and washed and have everything that they might need in school. She has to take care of the two year old as well, which means cooking him soft rice, bathing him, feeding him, rocking him to sleep and keeping him out of trouble. She also bathes her other brother and sister when they come home from school and gives them their food. It is only after all this, that she can take a bath herself and have her lunch.

Her afternoons too, are not free. Directly after lunch she has to fetch water for the evening and start the preparations for dinner, for her mother feels too tired to cook after a whole day's hard labour. The only chore that she does not have to do is fetching fuel, for which her mother has taken responsibility.

Both of Malini's parents are illiterate, and her father has now begun attending literacy classes at night. The economic distress of the family is evident; both parents work as agricultural labourers to support the family. Her father also works as a non-agricultural labourer at times to supplement his income. The house that they live in is little more than a large jhopri. The house is kept more or less clean, which is quite a feat for Malini. The younger children look somewhat unkempt and untidy, often with runny noses and dirty hands and feet. Though they live in close proximity of relatives, the responsibilities of the entire household seem to be solely Malini's.

Malini's day begins very early in the morning. As soon as she has woken up and washed, she has to make the beds and sweep the house. Then she washes the utensils left over from the previous night. Soon after her parents have left, around 8 a.m., she has to give her two school-going siblings their breakfast and get them ready for school. When they have left for school she prepares soft rice for her youngest brother, bathes him, feeds him and lets him play for a while, all the time taking care that he does not hurt himself or come too near the fire, where she is cooking the lunch which her brother and sister will eat when they come home from school. When they have returned, she bathes them, gives them their food and then sends them off to school again, at the proper time. She then bathes and eats her lunch.

The afternoon is spent fetching water, washing the utensils left over from lunch, washing clothes and preparing dinner for the family. Her mother comes home around 6 or 7 p.m. in the evening. It is only after that, that Malini's day ends. She is so absolutely tired by then that she almost immediately falls asleep, sometimes even without eating. When her younger brothers and sister are busy getting the lanterns out, to sit down and study in preparation for the next day's school, Malini, hardly a few years older, is sleeping the sleep of an exhausted old woman.

When Malini was asked how she felt about having dropped out of school, she said stoically that she had to leave school once her younger brother was born, for her mother could no longer cope with all the household chores, looking after the two younger children and going out to work in the fields too. Malini dropped out of school, but her younger brother continued studying. About this, Malini said that looking after the house is after all a woman's job, men cannot be expected to do such work. Malini harbours no ill-feelings towards her family for depriving her of a chance to an education. In her society it is the accepted thing for the girl to stay at home to help look after the household and the younger children, more so, if the girl happens to be an older child. Education, school, books are all very well for boys, but for girls, interests of the house must come first. So Malini has quietly, and without protest, accepted her lot. She will grow up, she said, get married, and be a good wife and mother. That is all she expects from life.

In the meanwhile, she is to be a good girl. And what does a good girl do, she was asked. A good girl works hard, she replied. And a good wife cooks. She cannot imagine a life that might have different dimensions. Women are born to work hard at home, cook and clean for the family and look after the young. Men have to work outside. She said that if she is naughty, she will be scolded, beaten or not given food. The same holds true for her sister. Her brothers, however, go unpunished.

Malini's world is so limited within the confines of her house that she has no conception of the larger horizons that may exist beyond. She does not at all think it unnatural that she had to drop out of school to help her family. She does not even mind giving up her precious play hours, which are not many anyway, if her brothers need her attention. Though she feels that her parents love her brothers more than her, or her sister, she does not love them any less. Her parents are extremely strict with her, but can find no fault with their sons, especially the older one. Though she resents this, she accepts it as something natural.

Even at this age, Malini's face looks old with years of acceptance of unequal and discriminatory behaviour. She is used to doing all the work in the house, where her brother does nothing. She is used to staying at home to cook for her brother, while he goes to school. She is used to eating a little less, so her brother can have more; to being scolded for what her brother gets away with quite easily. Already, her little shoulders are bowed with overwork and responsibility beyond her years. Already, her face wears a perpetual look of worry. She nervously bites her nails all the time.

EPILOGUE

On our second visit to the village, about six months after our survey work, we went to see Malini. She had been informed a short while earlier that we had inquired about her, and were coming to meet her. So worried was she on hearing this, that she burst out crying the moment she saw us. Insecure and alone, in charge of the entire house and three younger siblings, she just did not know how to handle this intrusion into her life. Fear of authority and of being found guilty of some misdeed that she must have committed, if the people from the city wanted to see her, made her so apprehensive, that her tears would not stop even after we had reassured her in every possible way. Our experiences in many other places were quite different, where the little girls came running when they heard that the didis had returned.

There is really no kind of a future that Malini can look forward to. She will be married off early—for the earlier you find a match for a girl, the lesser you have to pay to get her off your hands, as her mother said. The quality of her life will essentially remain the same. She will do the same kind of work at her in-laws' house. There too, she will be quite thoroughly subjugated, and there too, she will do whatever is expected of her as unprotestingly as ever.

Malini's circumstances have induced in her a passive acceptance of her lot; of accepting all forms of deprivation and discrimination as natural. This has had an extremely crippling effect on her character and, therefore, on her life chances. There is no expectation, no striving to better her condition. She is shy, nervous and inhibited. Her potential is difficult to assess.

DEEPA : WHERE HAS HER CHILDHOOD GONE?

Deepa is the eldest of five children in a family which has seven members: her parents, her three younger sisters, her brother, who is the youngest of them all, and Deepa herself. The family is Hindu and lives in a village of West Bengal.

Slightly built, Deepa looks younger than her nine years. In fact, had we not known her age, we would never have believed that such a small, undernourished-looking child could be nine years old. However, her face bears a look of maturity that is rarely seen in a girl of her age. Pale and thin, in a blue frock, a size too large for her, hair falling over, her face looks careworn and weary in spite of the smile with which she greets us. She has a quality of stillness about her, a sad sort of acceptance in the eyes, that is born out of assuming responsibilities much too heavy to bear, much too early in life.

Neither of Deepa's parents have studied beyond Class 1, and are, in effect, illiterate. Extremely poor, the family has to struggle continuously to make both ends meet. Her parents own a small tea stall nearby. This means that they have to leave home very early in the morning, for the tea must be ready to be served to the customers before they leave for work. They also cut leaves for bidi-making for some shopowners, who pay them at piece rates. Deepa's father works as a hawker every evening, going from one railway station to another, selling his wares. Her mother attends to the tea stall alone at that time.

The family lives in a small, run down, *kutcha* house which used to belong to Deepa's maternal grandparents. Perhaps this is why Deepa's mother is the dominant personality in the family. Her behaviour towards her daughters borders on cruelty. According to her, daughters are the bane of one's life. And she, unfortunate as she is, has four of them. If the first child had been a son, then she would have had her tubes tied long ago, and the four daughters need not have been born at all.

Actually Deepa's mother had not been able to conceive for quite a few years after her marriage. Then she had two miscarriages in quick succession. Convinced that someone had cast an evil eye on her, she prayed for a baby—just a baby, who would remain alive and healthy, whatever its sex. Soon, she conceived again, but as her pregnancy advanced, she found herself wishing more and more for a son. After all, was that not what all women wanted? Only a son was worth the agony of childbirth.

As luck would have it, a daughter was born. Taking stock of her losses she decided to try again. Another daughter arrived. And, in this way, four daughters came one after another, much to the horror of Deepa's mother. The fifth child was the long awaited son, who is now about a year old.

So disgusted was she at the birth of her four daughters, that Deepa's mother was determined to get rid of them—to give them away, if possible. Fortunately for the little girls, however, their father refused to allow her to do that, and so, the children are still growing up under the shelter of their parents' home.

The girls are severely discriminated against. Not only are they denied all delicacies like milk or sweets, but they are also given too little to eat, which causes the undernourished look that all the children have. Deepa's mother very nonchalantly says that whenever her daughters ask for milk or a sweet, she tells them that the milk has turned sour or an insect has fallen in it; or that the sweet has got spoilt in the heat. And then, after they have fallen asleep, she puts the food away for her husband. According to her, men need nutritious food, for they have to work so much harder than women. By the same logic, she also believes that boys need to eat more than girls, for they must preserve their strength. And this, in spite of the fact that, in her own family, the women and even girls actually do as much, or even more work than men.

So biased is she against the girls, so callous about their state of health, that she has not even bothered to get them properly immunized. The first two daughters have had vaccines against smallpox, more due to the fact that the welfare workers used to call on each house themselves and provide this service free, rather than any initiative on the parents' part.

The two younger daughters have not even had these shots. No other form of immunization has been attempted. However, in her son's case, all possible medical attention has been provided.

Shortly before our survey, Deepa and her sisters had all suffered from a particularly severe and prolonged disease, which lasted for several months. Their mother said that it was some form of dysentery, but she was not really very convincing. This could have been connected with some kind of neglect, because, through the entire period, the little brother remained healthy and free from the disease.

The mother's prejudice is also reflected in her ideas about a 'good' girl and a 'good' boy. A good girl, according to her, is one who stays at home and helps with domestic chores and also tries to add to the family's earnings by going out to work herself. A good boy, on the other hand, needs only to be well behaved and good in studies. Her son is the most important person in her life. He is to go to school, he shall be looked after like a prince, he shall have the best of whatever the family can offer. When he is old enough to be married, she will look for a daughter-in-law who will always fall in with her wishes and who will never take her son away from her.

Deepa used to go to school till about a year before our survey. Then she dropped out. At that time, she was in Class 2. In one year, she forgot whatever little she had learnt. When asked why she stopped going to school, she said that it was because her brother was still so young that he needed a lot of looking after. Her mother went out to the tea stall very early in the morning and if she also went away to school, then who would do the housework? Her sisters were still too young to help effectively. In any case, after the arrival of her brother, her father could not afford to buy her books anymore. The school did not give anything for free, after all. Once, a very long time ago, they had given her a frock, and that was all. This is significant in the light of the fact that in West Bengal education is supposed to be free up to Class 12. Books are meant to be supplied free. Some time back a plan had been introduced to give two dresses every year to school-going girls. But the gap between plan and implementation comes up time and again.

Deepa has no regrets at having dropped out. The teachers never taught them much anyway. And she felt so sad to leave her little brother at home—he would cry and cry when she left.

So Deepa, old beyond her years, dropped out to take on the mantle of her mother herself. She is responsible now for all the domestic chores and for the care of all her younger sisters and brother. She cooks for the entire household both in the morning and in the evening. She brings water twice a day. She also has to fetch fuel, morning and afternoon. She does the cleaning, washing and sweeping as well.

Deepa's day begins at five in the morning, when her parents leave for the tea stall. The little girl cleans the house, sweeps it and smears the floor and walls with cowdung and water paste, if her mother has not had the time to finish this. She then wakes up her sisters and brother, washes them and gives them their breakfast. Her brother she feeds herself. Next, she prepares lunch for the family. The cooking done, she washes the dirty utensils and clothes of the entire family in a nearby pond. Then she sets off to fetch water. On returning, she waits for her parents to come home, serves them their lunch, feeds her sisters and then eats whatever is left over. Often, she has to make do with just a handful of rice. She quietens her hunger pangs by drinking a bellyful of water. The afternoon is spent fetching fuel and water. In the evening she must once again take up the reins of the household. She cooks dinner, washes up, makes the beds and plays with her sisters and brother. When the mother returns from the tea stall, she has dinner along with the four younger children and goes to bed with them. Deepa alone waits for her father to come home from hawking his wares. She will eat only after he has finished his meal and has gone to bed.

Before her brother was born, Deepa used to work at a doctor's dispensary everyday. She used to sweep the place and clean it up, earning about Rs. 20 per month. This money was handed over to her mother who would utilize it to meet family expenses. Even now, whenever anyone pays her for a job, Deepa immediately gives the money to her mother to use as she thinks fit.

Deepa does not have a single moment to herself. She has no time to play, no time to do anything but work. She has no friends. She also looks grave and serious most of the time. There are no girls of the same age around her. She loves her parents dearly and adores her brother and sisters. She is quite oblivious of the fact that her mother is not very fond of her. She thinks that it is perfectly natural that boys are given better things, more to eat, even more love, than girls. After all it is they who grow up to be husbands and heads of households. It is their birthright to claim and get priority in everything. There has never been any doubt in her mind that boys are far different from girls. They are a breed apart. 'They are like kings and princes,' she says. Girls are just girls.

Deepa's ideas about a good boy or a good husband are the traditional ones, where men go out to work and to earn so as to take good care of their womenfolk. Good girls and good wives are quiet, obedient and adjustable.

To Deepa, education, however, is unconditionally good. However much she says that she doesn't mind not going to school, the wistful expression in her eyes gives her away. More than anything else, she would like to be a schoolgirl again. She would like to learn to read. 'Illiterate persons are so easily duped,' she said. They cannot keep their household accounts. They can't even answer properly if someone asks them anything. People who are educated behave differently. They are so-o nice. How she would love to be like the didis (our investigators) who have come from Calcutta. When she grew up, she too would like to get a job. In this she had her father's support. But perhaps her mother would not let her do all this, she says ruefully. She just wants her to get married!

This case study reveals a rather tragic kind of son-preference and negligence towards daughters. The fact that the mother had wanted to give away her daughters and that it was the father who was instrumental in keeping them at home, may prompt many to repeat the old saying that women are their own worst enemies. The myth of this simplistic and erroneous interpretation has to be exploded. For this is not just an innocuous misconception. It helps to conceal and, thus perpetuate, one of the most potent mechanisms by which patriarchal exploitation of women is kept alive, generation after generation. This mechanism is the conditioning of the female psyche, which so internalizes the mores, traditions, values, of patriarchal domination of male over female; of male supremacy and power over the female, as being 'natural' and, therefore desirable; that it is they, the women, the victims, who apparently willingly and even gratefully, pull the noose of dependence and subservience to men over their own necks.

The idea that a woman who cannot give birth to a son is a failure is so deeply ingrained in women that they believe in this myth themselves. And because they are totally dependent on men for their social, economic and emotional security, they are willing to give up anything to live up to the male ideal and beget a son. Women believe that daughters are nothing but a perpetual source of misery to the family. It is thus quite understandable why Deepa's mother wanted to give her daughters away soon after their birth. There was the fear of not being able to bear any children, or losing them all, or of giving birth to one daughter after another, with no signs of a son on the way. Out of desperation, Deepa's mother started rejecting her own daughters. If they were not there, growing up in front of her eyes, she would be spared the constant reminder that she had failed in her role as a wife. What man would want a woman to give birth to daughters only? What kind of a woman would have her maternal urge satisfied by daughters alone? So, feeding the girls, clothing them, nurturing them, all became chores—a waste of time and money—for they were constant reminders of her failure as a woman.

And yet, it is her daughter who has made life easier for her by taking on many of the household chores; by looking after the younger children as a little mother; by helping in her work at the tea stall and by giving her whatever money she was able to earn on her own. And, all this in addition to a blind sort of adoration for her mother. But so ingrained is her son-preference that she fails to see the truth. Her daughters remain unwanted.

EPILOGUE

On our second visit to the village, in early 1992, when we went to Deepa's house, she was not at home. Four little children were sitting clustered together with their backs to a large haystack near the house. This somehow made them look even smaller. Dressed in dirty clothes, with hands and feet even dirtier, the three older children were eating berries and the eldest was feeding them to the youngest. On closer inspection, the three older children were revealed to be girls and the youngest, a boy. They were Deepa's sisters and brother.

Deepa, we were told, had gone to school. Since when had she been going to school, we asked. 'Since a month ago,' they said. 'Don't you go to school?' We asked the eldest girl among them. 'No,' she said, 'but my father will enrol me in school when my brother grows a little older.' Clearly, this child had now taken on Deepa's role in the family, while her parents were away at work.

We visited a neighbouring house and then passed by Deepa's house once again. Her mother was home by this time, but Deepa had not returned from school. 'Oh, please wait for a while. Deepa will be very disappointed when she hears that you were here and she could did not get to see you. She was always so happy in your company.' Yes, we could quite understand that. In the life of this woman-child burdened with work and responsibility far beyond her years, the experience of communicating with the didis from the city, who took so much interest in finding out about her thoughts, her life, her aspirations, and who also arranged the story-telling, reading, singing and reciting sessions, must have been like a breath of fresh air in a closed room.

We went and sat in Deepa's house to have a little talk with her mother. There were some changes now in the daily routine of the family. Deepa's mother no longer went out to her tea stall in the evenings. Deepa had taken her place there. She made tea, served it to the customers and kept accounts of whatever transactions took place. When she came home, she helped her mother to prepare dinner. Only if she was very late, did she come home to a prepared meal.

We left Deepa's house promising to look in again before return-ing to Calcutta. Towards late afternoon, when we inquired, Deepa was back from school. She did not come running to meet us, laughing and talking, as some of the other children had done. She came out in more grown-up fashion and walked up to us with a smile on her face. We asked her how she was and she nodded to indicate that she was well.

Though she has now been enrolled in school once again, Deepa's life has essentially remained the same in that her brother, her parents and her family must always come first. There is no thought spared for the little girl, whose body remains undernour-ished, yet whose mind is growing older and older every day. She has learnt her lesson so well that even the idea that this is not a very satisfactory state of affairs does not occur to her. She has no complaints, no resentments, no demands.

The good thing about Deepa's circumstances is that she is in school again and if she is able to acquire some 'education', her perceptions about her own potential and about her role in life may change. This will bring suffering, but of a kind different from that which she suffers now without knowing.

Our last view before we left that village was of little Deepa, pale and thin, in the same blue dress, a size too large for her, standing forlornly beside a lone handpump near her house. As we turned, she bent down, and drank great gulps of water. Perhaps she still quietens her hunger pangs with just a handful of rice and a bellyfull of water.

GOURI: UNDER THE FACADE OF A TOMBOY, SUBDUED AND INSECURE

At first glance Gouri could easily be mistaken for a boy. Thin and pale, with crooked teeth peeping out in a smile, her hair cropped as short as her brothers', she does not look a day older than five. She is actually seven years old. Dressed usually in her pants, she looks as though she is ready to take the world on single-handedly. Gouri will wear a dress only on special occasions—when she knows that visitors are coming, for instance. Perpetually hopping on one foot, then on the other, this child has an absolute inability to stand still. Her hyperactive behaviour notwithstanding, Gouri looks severely undernourished, weighing only 16 kg. at a height of 114 cm. In fact, she looks about as old as her younger brother, who is now four years old.

Gouri lives with her parents and two brothers in a West Bengal village. She belongs to a Hindu family and resides right in the heart of the Hindu settlement of the village. Gouri is the second born, and has an elder brother and a younger brother.

Gouri had been enrolled in the 'infant' section of a school when she was about six years old, but had dropped out soon after. When we asked her why, she told us that she could not keep up with the lessons done in class, and so, her teachers had told her to come back only when she had learnt enough to follow what was being taught. For Gouri, this feat was impossible to manage. We have often seen that children from backgrounds such as her's, with illiterate parents and severe economic distress, usually fail to pass school examinations without the help of private tutors. The type of teaching and the general approach in the schools, instead of discouraging this practice, actually fosters it. Gouri's parents could not afford private coaching for her. And, in any case, they would not have dreamt of spending so much money on a girl's education. So Gouri could not keep up in class. As a result, she was reprimanded and punished in school; her teachers did not take an interest in her; and she fared even more badly in her studies. Soon her parents began to feel that it was an altogether waste of money to keep her in school. After all, school did mean some expenses in the form of books, notebooks, pencils, and so on. Gouri was caught in this trap and could not escape from this vicious circle. She plaintively says that her teachers want her to learn more before going back to class. Her mother will not buy her books anymore. How can she learn without books? Indeed, how can she go back to school without knowing more about her lessons? And how can she achieve this with no one to help her? Besides, she would feel silly going to school without books, anyway.

In West Bengal, education is supposedly free up to the Higher Secondary level, but, even at the primary stage, the actual implementation of the available programmes leaves much to be desired. Even the textbooks are not distributed in many schools, not to speak of expenses incurred for private tuition and necessary teaching aids. The government schools do not charge any fee, of course, but the associated costs themselves being prohibitive, the really poor families cannot avail of this facility in most cases. This point is additionally relevant for girls because whatever resources the family can manage to spend on the children's education at the cost of hardship to the entire family naturally goes to educate the boy children, given our socio-cultural perceptions. Proper implementation of even the available schemes, which include free supply of textbooks, would go a long way towards making elementary level education available to our girl children in a more meaningful way. The 'private-tutor culture' is another very serious stumbling block in this sphere.

Gouri, therefore, remains illiterate, with no foreseeable chance of acquiring even a minimum level education at school. Her only hope now is the informal literacy classes which are being held as part of the districtwise literacy drives. But, whereas such efforts may be of some relevance for adult members, they are hardly likely to be of any significance for little children, unless they are followed up with proper schooling up to at least the primary level. And this seems to be beyond the reach of our Gouris.

Having dropped out of school, Gouri has had to take up housework in earnest. For a child of her age, she does a surprising amount of work. She collects fuel, fetches water, sweeps the house, looks after her younger brother, runs errands for her mother, helps her with the cooking, and at times, even does the day's marketing for the family.

A typical day in her life begins around six in the morning. She wakes up, washes and has her morning tea. She then makes the beds, sweeps the house and smears the floors and the walls with a cowdung-and-water paste to prevent them from drying up and cracking. Then she sets out to fetch water. After coming home, she is sometimes sent out to the market to buy vegetables for the day's cooking. Otherwise, she helps her mother with the cooking and cleaning. Looking after the younger brother, feeding him, bathing him and playing with him is her responsibility. Only after her mother is free from domestic chores can Gouri take her own bath and go out to play with her friends. Gouri has her lunch late, after her father and brothers have eaten and she has cleaned their utensils. Never is she allowed to eat before them, not even with them, for, according to her mother, a girl has no right to eat before the men in the family have eaten. Even when she is very hungry, her mother refuses to let her have her meal earlier. 'Do not forget you were born a girl,' she says, 'girls have no business to feel hunger pangs.'

The afternoon is spent fetching fuel. And then, she must go out to fetch water once again. Gouri's evenings, however, are her own. She is free to play, or to do whatever she wants. During the period of our survey, she usually chose to come to our investigators to listen to stories and to learn to read. At night again, she would eat only after the menfolk had eaten. And then, finally, she could go to sleep.

Gouri's family is extremely poor. Both her parents are illiterate. Her father works as an agricultural labourer, but with the money that he earns he can hardly make both ends meet. In addition, her father is a chronic alcoholic and spends almost all that he earns on drinks and on women. An incorrigible womanizer, he often disappears for days on end, going off on a binge with some woman or the other and getting drunk till he passes out. When he returns, the month's earnings have gone. Often, he borrows money to support his habits, and the family currently has an outstanding debt of Rs. 2000.

The family's economic condition is further worsened by the fact that Gouri's father fritters away the money obtained from government loans as well on women and liquor. Twice, the family has been granted loans for income-generating purposes and both times her father has poured the money down the drain. The first loan granted to make paper bags went to pay back previous debts incurred from private sources and *mahajans*. The second loan, granted for the purchase of a van-richshaw, never saw the light of day. Gouri's father disappeared with it, and when he came back, there was no money left.

The family now runs on the largesse of Gouri's uncle, her father's elder brother. Gouri's mother is full of praise for her brother-in-law. He holds their family together, she says. It is because of him that the children have food to eat. Their father is a good-for-nothing who spends all his money on drinks. Besides he keeps other women as well. Her chief complaint seemed to be his indiscriminate spending of money rather than the fact that he refuses to take responsibility for his family. She did not even seem to especially mind the fact that he had other women in his life. It seemed as if he was free to take himself off wherever he wanted, do whatever took his fancy, as long as he gave his wife enough money to run the household.

The fact that Gouri's mother seems unperturbed by her husband's lack of interest in her is perhaps the result of years of living with the pain of the situation. Perhaps she has stopped caring about him to the extent that what he does or does not do has ceased to matter to her totally. At the same time, her effusive praise of her brother-in-law seems a little unusual, for one does not normally come across such a free and easy relationship between a woman and her older brother-in-law who does not live with them and has his own family to support.

The situation certainly hints at something strange in the circumstances. More so, because Gouri made it amply clear that she hated her uncle. He had killed her younger sister when she was two and a half years old, she said. That horrible man had burnt her to death. She was the twin of her younger brother, and would have been just as old as him today, had she lived. We noted that although Gouri's mother mentioned that her younger daughter had died a year and a half ago, she did not mention the fact that the child had died of burns. There was no mention of any accident. As to where Gouri got her facts from, or what the basis of her allegations were, we have no idea, for she did not take us into her confidence to that extent. As it is, she would talk about her family only in the relative safety and seclusion of the investigators' house. At home she would not open her mouth at all. It was clear that at home she was under some kind of repression and was therefore afraid to talk to us.

It seems that there is something mysterious and unhealthy about the relationships in this family. To be caught in a situation of this sort must be extremely traumatic for the children and, especially so for Gouri, because apart from the other problems that she shares with her brothers she is also a victim of discrimination because she is a girl.

Her mother, she says, does not love her. She is never given enough to eat, and so she always goes hungry. She has never been allowed to eat with her brothers, for it is considered a girl's place to wait till the men have finished. Her father and brothers are given milk every day, but her share is put aside to make tea. The boys always get the lion's share of food—rice, milk, eggs, fish, everything. Gouri has to make do with leftovers, if there is anything left over at all. She told us that she had never even tasted that lovely yellow part of an egg, the yolk. Her elder brother always snatched it away from her when they had eggs to eat at home. We asked her why she also did not playfully snatch away a piece of food from him one day. Maybe, he was only teasing her? Gouri emphatically shook her head. She had, she said, once grabbed a piece of meat from his plate, but her mother had immediately slapped her hard and told her that it was not for women and girls to be so greedy. She ought to have given up her food willingly. Girls should learn early that their lives were meant for hardship. They had no right to the good things in life. There was no point in hungering for tastier things. Gouri would never get them, she must remember that she was born a girl.

Though Gouri has had to drop out of school, her elder brother is now in Class 2. He is twelve years old and is expected to continue studying at least up to a level which would enable him to get a job. His mother's fondest wish is to send him to Bombay to learn the trade of a goldsmith, so he can set up his own shop some day. Gouri's younger brother, too, will be enrolled in school soon. However, Gouri does not know whether she will ever be sent back to school. She will go, if her mother wishes it. After all, girls do need some education these days to get married, don't they? If she is illiterate, no one is going to marry her. Her father-in-law may even beat up her father for trying to marry off an illiterate girl. If she is able to go to school, then she can get a job when she is older. Then she and her husband would both go off to work together. That would be a lot of fun, wouldn't it? However, her dreams of going to school are not likely to materialize, for her mother feels that it is sufficient for girls to be able to sign their names. What is the point of educating them, since they have to be married off as soon as they reach puberty? She herself plans to get Gouri married when she is about fifteen years old. 'A girl child after all—the sooner I get rid of this burden, the better. It is an unfortunate day when a girl in born, but they have their uses too. Who else would help with the household chores if not your own daughter?' says her mother. Gouri has at least lightened the load of housework that she has to do.

Gouri's brothers too share the same attitude with their mother. A girl must be kept in her place. Her elder brother beats her mercilessly, but if she complains to her mother, or hits him back, her mother always takes his side and unleashes her wrath on the little girl with beatings and scoldings. Her older brother never plays with her and, emulating him, the younger one doesn't either, though Gouri is almost a little mother to him. Boys, after all, are far superior to girls. They cannot stoop to a girl's level to the extent of playing with her.

When asked what the qualities of a good boy were, Gouri said that a good boy was one who never used swear words and never beat his sister. A good husband, according to her, was one who worked hard and stayed at home with his wife. This quality particularly impresses her because her father she said is not a 'good' man. 'He no longer has any character,' she intoned, exactly as a grown-up would. It is obvious that the desirability of this trait in men has been deeply embedded in her psyche. Her mother too, feels that a good man should not run after other women, when he has a wife of his own. It is clear that little Gouri is only repeating what she has heard her mother say a thousand times.

A good girl, according to Gouri, will stay at home, cook, clean and look after the house. So will a good wife. Additionally, a good wife will eat only after the rest of the family has eaten. Evidently, her mother's constant litany of what a girl's place should be, has rubbed off on her. For a little village girl of seven, this sort of role stereotyping must seem like a divine law!

Interestingly, though, the first quality that a good girl or a good wife must have, according to Gouri, is education. This shows how much Gouri sets store by education. Though she has only been to school for a few months, the impression that books, printed words and their world have had on her has been indelible. She realizes that nowadays, one cannot get by without being literate. Not only does it offer a glimpse of a world as yet unsampled, a world now brought closer by the didis from Calcutta through the stories that they tell her; it also offers a way of escaping the sameness of her everyday life. What fun it would be to be like these didis. How lovely it would be to go to school. Though there is not the slightest doubt in her mind that a woman's chief duty is to get married and look after her husband, her enchantment with education is such, that she is easily able to reconcile a job with marriage. It is all very simple, according to her. She and her husband could both go to work after she has cooked for him and given him his food, she dreams.

When we asked her what she wanted to be when she grew up, she told us in no uncertain terms, that, of course, when she grew older she would get married. And then, life would be so exciting! She would cook rice for her husband. She would make tea for him. After all, her parents' home was not her real home, was it? A girl's real home is her in-laws' house. That is where all girls must go one day. But, much to her sorrow, she feels that her mother does not want her to get married. If she went away who would do her work? Marriage means a lot of dowry, more so because she is illiterate. Her mother would never spend so much money on her.

Gouri is starving for affection. She once mentioned an aunt who loved children. All women should be like her, she said. She sorely misses her mother's love. Resentful, on the one hand, of the fact that her mother cares more about her brothers than about her, she also in a sense accepts it without question. To her mind, boys are meant to be loved more than girls.

Gouri's mother's attitude is also a typical one. Deprived of even the basic necessities of a normal life; forced to live with the indignity of the fact that her husband has relations with other women; constantly frustrated in her attempts to set the family back on its feet with the help of income-generating loans; she vents all the anger of her unfulfilled needs and desires on Gouri. After all, who else would bear the burden of your sorrow and your anger except your daughter? Who else would still do your bidding without question and offer you all the love and trust that her little heart can hold? Sons are a breed apart. They are to be treated as higher beings. They cannot be a part of your unhappiness. Your sadness cannot be allowed to cast a shadow on their lives .

Like many others who have lost their husband to other women, Gouri's mother feels that she herself is to blame for not being able to hold her husband. She must have done something wrong, or not done something right, or else why would a man take resort to drink? Why would he even look at other women? Whatever the reason, the fault must somehow be hers.

Because of her husband's total disregard for family welfare, she has to fend for the entire family, which traditionally was never a woman's job. She too must have had dreams of her own. Not only are those dreams shattered, but it is again she who must pick herself up and take care of the home. For, never can a mother desert her children. Gouri must bear the brunt of her pent up anger and frustration. In this way, the mother perhaps tries to release some of the impossible pressures building up within her. On the other hand, by punishing Gouri—a female child—she is punishing herself for not being woman enough to keep her husband with her. Somehow mixed up with all this is a warped logic that Gouri should learn early in life that this is a woman's lot. In a sense, the mother is preparing Gouri for a life of hardship and deprivation, which she feels is the inevitable destiny of women. It is possible that Gouri, as she grows older, will totally take on her mother's characteristics, perhaps even adopt her personality, as her own. She too may begin to believe that life cannot hold anything better for her. Her role model being her mother, she too, may be equally unloving towards her girl children.

Brought up in such harsh conditions, deprived of love, affection and security, Gouri's personality and her psyche are likely to be severely damaged. This, combined with the fact that she is not being given any education, may make her future prospects rather bleak. Without acquiring any education she cannot hope to learn a trade, or become economically independent. She must, thus, perforce be married at an early age, and marriage, under such circumstances is hardly likely to be the bed of roses she thinks it will be.

EPILOGUE

We visited this village once again, about a year after we had completed our survey. Gouri was, as usual, running around the place, barefoot, in a shirt and shorts about a size too small for her. She happily posed for all pictures we cared to take, utterly unselfconscious. At the prodding of her mother, however, she suddenly disappeared, to emerge minutes later, dressed in her best frock. She was so thin that the dress seemed to engulf her little body. Dressed thus she now looked small and vulnerable and cowed down.

When we tried to talk to her, she would answer only in monosyllables, saying yes or no to our questions. Was she happy? Yes, she was, she said. Did her brother still beat her? No, of course not. He never had. Did she have enough to eat? Oh, Always. Nothing, it would appear was wrong with her life!

This was only to be expected. For, Gouri opened up only when she felt secure in the exclusive company of the didis, who encouraged her to talk about herself, to think of herself as a person, to give her enough confidence to be able to voice her dreams and sorrows. In the presence of her family, she was totally unresponsive, or gave answers acceptable to her mother and her brothers.

And so, Gouri grows up with her schizophrenic personality. Under the facade of a carefree tomboy lives a repressed and increasingly insecure little girl. Gouri still does not go to school. There seems no possibility of her starting school in the near future, either. Her life chances remain bleak. The pity of it is that Gouri is, by nature, lively, energetic and bright. Given half a chance, this little girl has the potential to lead a happy and productive life.

SAKINA: A YOUNG BRIDE POSSESSED BY AN EVIL SPIRIT?

Sakina is a Muslim girl who lives in a village of West Bengal. She is seventeen years old and has been married for the last two years. She lives in a large joint-family which has a total of twelve members: Sakina herself, her father-in-law, mother-in-law, husband, three unmarried sisters-in-law, one unmarried brother-in-law, one older brother-in-law, his wife and two daughters.

Sakina's paternal family was rather poor. The eldest of six children with three younger brothers and two younger sisters, Sakina often had to go without food at home. By comparison, her life is easier now. Her mother-in-law is actually her aunt, her father's sister, and is quite fond of Sakina. Whatever other problems she has now, at least she does not have to go hungry anymore.

Sakina is illiterate. In her childhood, she had once been enrolled in school, but she dropped out very soon, in Class 1 itself, because of the harsh behaviour of the teachers. 'They used to beat us at the slightest mistake, and that put me off school forever.' Though she feels that education is necessary, because that is what helps one to create a decent atmosphere at home, she herself is not keen to go back to school. The question does not arise now, she told us. Once you have left your parental home and come to your in-laws, you cannot expect these things anymore. She is a respectable married woman now, and is expected to behave accordingly. She realizes that had she been educated, she would have been able to do a lot of things apart from housework. She would have even been able to teach her own children to read. But there is not much she can do about it now. Anyway, she feels the chief advantage of education for girls is that it helps to make a good marriage. Since she has successfully crossed that hurdle, she does not have too many regrets about not going to school.

Sakina has to do all the work that a rural housewife is expected to perform. Her day begins around 6 a.m. She and her sister-in-law (her brother-in-law's wife) together manage all the housework, for their mother-in-law no longer shares the domestic chores. Early in the morning, Sakina first sweeps the whole house. Then she and her sister-in-law start making preparations for cooking. They light the *chulha*, fetch water and prepare breakfast for the entire family. Once the men have left for work, cooking for lunch begins in earnest. There are a million other things to do as well —washing clothes, cleaning utensils and mopping the floors of the house—before the menfolk come home for lunch. Food is served first to the male members of the family and the children, while Sakina and her sister-in-law wait on them. By the time these women have eaten, it is almost evening. Fetching water in the evening and fetching fuel are Sakina's job exclusively, for her sister-in-law has two small children to look after. Looking after the cattle too is Sakina's responsibility. The evening is once again spent in cooking. And at night, as usual, the women eat last after the men have finished.

Sakina is a friendly, cheerful and healthy young girl, with the capacity for very hard work throughout the day. Dressed in a sari, with one end drawn over the head in the fashion of traditional Indian housewives, she looks somewhat older than her years. When we asked her whether she had any major illnesses she said that she did not remember anything major before marriage. However, after marriage, she had been possessed by evil spirits, and she still suffered under their influence. We asked her what happened to her exactly. She told us that during the day she was fine but she started feeling unwell from early evening. As night approached, she felt more and more afraid and started weeping and crying for her mother. The fear reached its peak when it was time for her to go to bed with her husband and her screaming and crying got worse progressively. 'All men are beasts,' she said, suddenly. 'Can't you do something, Didi, so that I don't have to sleep with him anymore?' From the symptoms she described and from her remarks we surmised that she was perhaps suffering from a form of hysteria brought on by severe sexual trauma.

Our belief was confirmed later, when she told us that she needed to speak to us alone, away from the presence of her in-laws. Sakina told us that she hated going to bed with her husband. She felt afraid of him. Afraid of the advances he made on her. 'He doesn't understand my pain, Didi. He just has to have his way. "That's how men are supposed to behave," he says. Everything he does fills me with revulsion. I spend all day dreading the night.'

Sakina's experience is perhaps not very unusual. After marriage girls first and foremost need to become familiar with their new families. They need to feel comfortable in a new atmosphere. The separation from friends and family is traumatic even for older girls. For a child of fifteen, the wrench is far greater. In fact, Sakina herself told us that she missed her family very much. Her heart was still in her parents' home. Whenever she thought of them, she felt tears coming to her eyes.

At a time, when she most needed comforting, when her primary need was for understanding, her husband's insistence on leading a conjugal life right away shocked and traumatized her. The fear psychosis that Sakina suffered was, however, a rather extreme reaction. More so, because she found nothing else objectionable about her husband and in-laws. She even quite liked the fact that her husband was exclusively hers, and would take care of her forever. The intensity of her fear thus indicates something more than just emotional trauma. There must have been quite a bit of physical pain involved in her sexual relations with her husband. A young virgin is likely to suffer some amount of pain but it is possible that Sakina had additional physical problems which intensified the pain. The situation was probably worsened by the inexperience of her husband who was a young boy himself, only seventeen years old, to her fifteen years.

What was needed in this situation was counselling by someone older, who would have been able to comfort Sakina, to explain things to her and to her husband, and who would have taken her to a doctor, if need be. However, no one at home, even Sakina, connected her sexual trauma to her hysteric behaviour. Her weeping and crying were explained away as 'possession by evil spirits' and nothing was done to help her with her real problem.

Sakina's mother-in-law, in fact, insisted that Sakina had been possessed by an impure 'Hindu' spirit. These spirits abounded all around, she said, because the Hindu rites of cremation were not pure. In spite of her affection for Sakina, it never occurred to her to ask the girl exactly what her problem was. She even failed to make the connection that Sakina's hysteric behaviour worsened at night when she had to be alone with her husband. The abnormal behaviour of the girl, the frightened tears, the calling out for 'mother' were all interpreted as the work of an evil spirit.

Considering the kind of family that Sakina had been married into, this reaction was not unusual. Her father-in-law, husband and both brothers-in-law were agricultural labourers. All members of the family were illiterate. Her father-in-law, in particular, was extremely short-tempered and very conservative. Under such circumstances, it could hardly be expected that Sakina's predicament would be understood in the right perspective or that it would receive too much attention or sympathy. Though her mother-in-law was otherwise kind, she too was unable to diagnose Sakina's real problem.

Sakina's life otherwise seemed to be quite happy. She was fond of her in-laws and respectful of her husband. Apart from the fact that she was terrified of sleeping with him, being married suited her very well. After all, girls had to get married. That was their life. Even her ideas about a good girl or a good wife reflected this attitude. They must give their unquestioned obedience and must be willing to please everyone at home. A good boy will never use bad language and never look covetously at girls. The ideal husband, according to her, will not beat his wife and will always take care of her needs. All her reactions and opinions were stereotyped, and typical of a girl of her background and circumstances.

The only unusual feature about her was her vehement dislike of spending nights with her husband. That she was able to speak out about her source of trouble to sympathetic strangers from the city was a mark of the intensity of her fear and desperation. Not even the thought that her in-laws might resent her candour, or punish her in any way, could deter her.

EPILOGUE

On our second visit to the village, about a year after our survey we found the circumstances somewhat changed. When we first knocked at the door, Sakina's mother-in-law gestured to us to go away. As we retreated, Sakina herself came out and told us that her father-in-law was at home for the afternoon *namaz* and that he absolutely refused to let us into the house. Sakina herself was very pleased to see us, however, and entreated us to come back a little later so that she could talk to us. We agreed and went on to visit a few other people. After a time we returned, but before we could look in to inquire about Sakina, we heard a male voice raised in anger and Sakina's mother-in-law trying to smoothen things out. As the sound of the altercation got more vicious, we began to fear for Sakina's safety. The girl would perhaps be beaten up for daring to speak to us! We could not even leave under such conditions, for we felt responsible for the trouble that our presence had caused. As we were waiting nonplussed and embarrassed, one of our investigators ventured close to the house to tell Sakina that we were leaving so she need not be worried anymore. But Sakina came out and asked us if we could not wait just a little longer, till her father-in-law left, for she had a lot to tell us. A little later, we saw him leave, obviously still in a temper.

As we put our heads round the door of their house, Sakina's mother-in-law smiled and gestured to us to come in and sit down. Very apologetically she said, 'Did you see him leave? Didn't he look like a wild beast?' Apparently, he has always had a foul temper. 'Just like a ferocious tiger's. As long as he is home, I do not have a moment's peace.' Illiterate, always angry and ready to beat her up at the slightest discomfort or disagreement, her husband has been the bane of her life. 'He is a good-for-nothing,' she said. 'He can't even hold on to a steady job.' All through her youth she had to work in other people's houses to support him and their family. Even if she managed to get him a job, he was sure to lose it within a few days because of his stubbornness and foul temper. If it had not been for her, the children would have starved to death long ago. They would not even have had a roof over their heads. She pointed to the house that we were sitting in and said that she, with years of hard labour, had built this house for her children. Her husband would have let them live on the streets without turning a hair, if things had been left to him. Why, even when he himself fell ill she had to go to the doctor, feign his symptoms as her own, and get medicine for him. Could anyone else have lived with such a man?

Even if she discounted these, she would never forgive him for not letting her children go to school. To him, education has no value whatsoever. The boys will ultimately have to work as agricultural labourers, just like him, so what is the point of sending them to school, he said. And as for girls, for them it was out of the question, because decent Muslim girls do not step out of the house. She had tried, on more than one occasion, to smuggle her children out to school, but her efforts had not been successful, because of his eagle eye and evil temper.

Sometimes, unable to take the hard work and the constant abuse, she had contemplated suicide, in a desperate attempt to escape the life that she was forced to live. But she had never been able to take that final step, for then, who would take care of the children? Who would protect them from their father? There was no peace as long as he was around. Coming from a Muslim matron of a traditional family these were desperate words indeed!

Years of painful abuse, hard work and frustration had taught this woman that men and women had to have the rudiments of some sort of an education to be able to live in the modern world. Driven to desperation by life with an 'animal' of a husband, she had learnt in some vague way about the value of education, the one doorway to a better kind of life.

During this year, Sakina had changed quite a bit. For one, she had grown up. No longer was she afraid of sleeping with her husband. She had now come to accept as natural what had once terrified her. In fact, now she was very worried because she had not been able to conceive so far. All her friends had children, what then, was wrong with her that she did not? We asked her whether her in-laws were pressurizing her to have children. 'No,' she complained. Her mother-in-law, in fact, did not even want her to have a baby so soon. It was interesting to note that Sakina was the one who was anxious to have a child right away. Her mother-in-law was quite against it. She felt that Sakina could afford to wait a little longer, an attitude that is rare in most mothers-in-law, especially in rural households. This woman, having experienced the problems connected with the birth of too many children too soon in a poor family, realized that this brought only hardship and misery. She wanted a better life for her son and his wife.

Sakina's life will take the predictable course. She will, in time, become a mother, possibly the mother of several children, since family planning is frowned upon by conservative Muslims. She will spend her days cleaning and cooking and looking after her husband and children, and, in all probability, she will be quite happy doing so. Her perception regarding marriage and conjugal relations will remain the same as that of her mother-in-law and other matrons like her. And if, her daughter-in-law or daughter faces problems of sexual trauma like her, she will replicate her mother-in-law's behaviour in explaining away the entire matter as the responsibility of an evil spirit!

DURGA: THE MYTH OF BEING SHELTERED INSIDE AND OUTSIDE THE HOME

Durga is a fifteen-year-old girl from a scheduled caste family. She is the third among six children with an elder brother, an elder sister, two younger sisters and a younger brother. Her elder sister was married some years ago. Now Durga's family has seven members—her parents, her four brothers and sisters, and herself.

A reasonably healthy-looking child, Dugra has no remembrance of any serious illness in her life. Though she is somewhat underweight for her height and age, weighing only 35 kg. at a height of 135 cm., her appearance and demeanour give the impression of a sturdy, hard-working young girl.

Durga comes from a reasonably affluent family in her village. Her father owns a substantial amount of land (about 25) and several heads of cattle. He is considered a large farmer in the area and spends practically all his time out in the fields. Besides, they also have a small business making puffed rice (*muri*).

Making puffed rice is chiefly a woman's job. Durga, her mother, and her sisters have to boil the paddy, steam and dry it, husk the rice, and then puff it by dry-frying in the oven, to produce muri. All this takes an immense amount of time and labour. This is not all. The women do a lot of work in the fields as well. As a matter of fact, Durga's brother told us that except for actually ploughing the land, the womenfolk had to lend a hand in all other activities of farming. As for domestic chores, who else would take the responsibility for them but the women?

Under the circumstances, it has not been possible to send any of the daughters to school. After all, daughters are sent into this world to look after home and hearth and to lighten the mother's load of work. Going to school or learning to read cannot be a priority in a girl's life. A girl has to learn to keep house, to cook and clean and look after the family. School is a luxury in her life.

The situation is, however, entirely different for boys. They, after all, have to get a job. Speaking of her own sons, Durga's mother said that they would be encouraged to study as long as they could. It is true that they will inherit a lot of land. But getting a job is additionally desirable. That will help provide for a few 'extras' in life. Besides, farming is very hard work. The produce is often dependent on the weather. The boys are young. They are not used to such hard labour. How are they going to take care of all the work? Moreover, a steady job brings security, regular income and a better status in society. The farm will be looked after for them by their father for some time.

And so, the sons are being groomed to grow up to be educated enough to get a good job. The older son is now a student of Class 9 in a good school. He lives in the school hostel, away from the village. The family does not mind spending over Rs. 300 per month to meet his expenses at school. After all, a good education for the boy is worth everything it costs.

The same rule does not hold for the daughters, however. All four of them are illiterate. As their mother says, 'Of what good is an education to a girl in a farmer's house? The only problem these days is that it is very difficult to marry off an illiterate girl. One has to pay a lot of dowry.' Now she feels that she should perhaps have sent them to school for some time. If they had studied even up to Classes 4 and 5, she would not have to pay such a high price to get them married.

It is significant that there is a thirteen-year difference between the eldest and the youngest sons. Five daughters were born in between, of whom three survived. Among the two who have not survived, one is Durga's twin, who was stillborn and the other, younger than Durga, died in infancy. Her mother emphatically said that she would not have had so many children if she had had two sons right in the beginning. A woman needed two sons at least, she confided. It was foolish to tempt providence to the extent of resting content with only one son. Suppose something happened to your only son? Where would you be then? Who would look after you in your old age? It is only in the hope of a second son that she had so many daughters. Would anyone in their right mind take on so much liability otherwise? True to her words, she had had her tubes tied right after the birth of her second son.

There is discrimination between the boys and girls in this household, not only in the field of education, but also in the type of food given to the children. Specially nutritious food or delicacies are put aside for the boys. After all, boys must be given a little extra, mustn't they?

Though Durga's mother realizes that educating a girl is a good thing in itself, she also accepts that her daughters should not go to school. There is simply too much work at home to permit luxuries like studying. Even when her sons marry, she would prefer daughters-in-law who are fair and hard-working. 'Of what use is an educated girl in households such as ours?' she asks. 'The women of this house have never been to school.' She herself is illiterate and that has never hampered her life in any way. Her daughters,too, would grow up to be good wives and mothers like her. And that should be enough for any girl.

Durga, however, is unhappy that her parents did not think fit to educate her. She told us that when she was young, she used to constantly nag her parents about putting her in school. Now, of course, she realizes that there is no point in asking for something that she will never get. Besides, she said, she is now too old to go to school, anyway. She certainly cannot start learning the alphabet at this age. She has more or less accepted the situation now. She and her sisters were brought up with the expectation that they would help with the domestic chores, work in the fields with the family, and participate in any household enterprise, till such time as their parents decided to get them married. Going to school did not enter into this scheme of things at all.

Durga realizes that it will be difficult to find her a husband, because she is illiterate. Moreover, even after marriage, her in-laws' family will constantly belittle her. Even now, people ridicule her. 'But what can you do,' she said, 'if your own parents do not want you to study? How can one overcome that handicap?' After all, it was not as if they could not afford it. Durga will not be able to teach her own children to read. 'And will they ever respect a mother who is illiterate?'

Already, Durga suffers from a sense of inferiority that will remain with her for the rest of her life, perhaps even increase as she grows older. This is where Durga is different from her mother. Her mother cannot perceive how education could have changed her life in any way. For Durga, being illiterate is a severe handicap. Both of them have accepted the same life style. Whereas for Durga's mother, this is the one and only kind of life that is possible; for Durga, glimpses of the other kind of life have changed her perceptions. She is now awake to some of the possibilities that life can offer. The fact that she will have to settle for exactly the same sort of life as her mother fills her with sorrow. Whereas her mother accepts her life without question, Durga accepts it because she has been forced to.

Durga's gender-based conditioning, however, remains largely unaffected. Though unhappy that she has been denied an education, Durga thinks that it is perfectly natural for boys to have a better deal in life. Of course, they have to eat better. Certainly they should be given more food. It is necessary for them to preserve their strength. Natually, her brothers will go to school. There is no question of their staying back at home to help. After all, they have to study, get a job, and look after the family. She does not mind having her meals after her father and brothers, for this is what she has seen her mother do all her life. She feels that there is nothing unusual in the fact that her brothers' mistakes go unnoticed, whereas her's and those of her sisters' bring on punishment.

The ideal that girls must be quiet, obedient and adjustable, and must try to get along with everyone's wishes is very deeply ingrained in her. The one quality that she wants her husband to have, is kindness—so that he will forgive her faults and not scold her all the time.

Durga's day begins at 5 a.m. and ends after sundown. 'Is there any end to our work?' she says. Early in the morning, she first sweeps the three rooms of her house. Next she feeds the cattle and cleans their stalls before they are taken out to the fields. She then helps her mother with the cooking. Once this is done, she wipes the floors and the walls of the house with a paste of cowdung and water. Next, she must go out to fetch water, the nearest source being at least a kilometre away. This she does three times a day, each time traversing a narrow strip of land which serves as a bridge over a canal, which separates her house from the main road. It takes her about an hour to travel back and forth every time. After fetching water in the morning, Durga has to take her father's lunch to the fields where he is working. When she comes home she supervises her younger siblings' baths and lunches. After everyone has eaten, she and her mother have their lunch.

There is no period of rest, whatsoever. Immediately after the noon meal, Durga and her mother start preparing the day's lot of puffed rice. Next, Durga has to fetch fodder for the cattle and also fetch drinking water once again. By the time she is home, the sun has set.

Evenings are spent looking after her brother and sisters, and it is only after her father and younger brother and sisters have eaten, that Durga can have her meal and go to bed.

Durga has also to work in the fields. She helps with harvesting paddy, reaping it, and boiling the rice before it is husked. The pressure of work on Durga is tremendous. But so was it for her mother and for her elder sister before she got married. Life is expected to take the same course for her two younger sisters, as well, who are as yet too young, at 8 and 6 years respectively, to be able to help her effectively. In Durga's family, and in many others such as her's, this is the natural thing. They know no other way of life.

Durga has resigned herself to her lot. The odds stacked against her are far too many to be able to beat single-handedly. Though she resents her lack of education, it is a passive sort of resentment. She does not protest, knowing that it would be futile to do so. She will get married, have children and work from morning to night. She has nothing else to look forward to.

This lack of something interesting in life, something that will brighten her day, give her something different to think of apart from her endless chores, is what makes Durga appear older than her age. Though she was dressed in a bright yellow dress when we met her, her eyes looked tired and resigned.

The pity of it all is that even when economic conditions are not a constraint, girls like Durga still have all the windows to a different world closed for them.

One cannot even blame the parents entirely. They too, like Durga, are trapped in a world which runs according to rules and laws built up over hundreds of years. They are not particularly unkind to the girls. Whatever they do is, in their perception, the 'natural' course to follow. Quite clearly, attitudinal problems, not economic distress, is the cause of the deprivation of this girl child.

This is also one more of those cases which, time and again, cry out in protest against the age old myth that women are fragile and delicate; that they are capable of doing only the lighter kinds of work; that they are soft and ornamental, cared for and protected by their men. The stark reality is that it is the women, especially of the lower and middle socioeconomic-status who carry the major burden of work on their shoulders, saddled as they are with a dual burden of work, outside and within the home. Coupled with this is the deprivation, mostly self-imposed because of psychological conditioning, from education, from sufficient and nourishing food and also from proper health care.

EPILOGUE

We went back about a year after our survey was completed. Durga's life had not changed. Her mother did say that she would enrol Durga in literacy classes (a district-wise literacy drive was on at that time) but Durga was sceptical. Who will do all the housework? Grown-up girls don't go to school.

Besides, she will soon be married—who had ever heard of a girl going to school after marriage? Her life will consist only of unmitigated toil for as long as she lives.

As we were talking to Durga, her mother came out to meet us. Though barely thirty-six years old, she looked twenty years older. Thin to the point of emaciation, her eyes sunk deep in her face, toting her youngest son on her hip, she looked like a walking skeleton draped in a sari. Her eyes are dull to the extent of being lifeless. Suddenly it was as if we had a glimpse of what Durga would look like in another twenty years' time. Overworked, and worn out by years of successive childbirth, Durga too would become an old woman long before her time. The saddest part of the story is that Durga realizes this. To live with such an image of the future—to be actually resigned to it—speaks more volubly of her helpessness than a thousand words of protest could have done.

RUPA: THE GIRL CHILD FINANCES THE BOY CHILD'S EDUCATION

In a village that we surveyed we came across a Christian tribal family, which had nine children. Rupa, who is twelve years old, is the youngest daughter.She has four sisters, all older than her, and four brothers, one of them older and the other three younger than her. Her two eldest sisters are already married. The other two now live in Calcutta and work as full time domestic servants for two families. Her older brother also lives away from home. He is a student of Don Bosco School in Calcutta, and lives in the school hostel.

Rupa's family in the village, therefore, now consists of six members: her parents, her three younger brothers and Rupa herself. The family is more or less affluent. However, the comfortable financial situation is a recent phenomenon. They are new settlers in this village. When they first came here, they were extremely poor. Her father worked as an agricultural labourer and her mother as a domestic servant to make a living. Gradually, Rupa's father was able to buy some land for cultivation. He also started growing vegetables for sale. Now, the family owns about thirteen bighas of agricultural land, a sizeable vegetable farm, some cattle as well as some poultry.

None of the girls of this family have ever been to school. Rupa's mother said that when they had first settled in this village, they had been so poor that sometimes they had not even had enough to eat. Sending all the children to school was out of the question. Only the eldest son was enrolled in school. After all, boys have to have an education to get on in life. The two older girls were sent to Calcutta to work as live-in maidservants in two households. The money that they earned was sent home and that helped pay for some of the necessary household expenses.

As the family gradually became a little better off, the eldest son was sent to Calcutta and enrolled in one of the best missionary schools of the city as a boarder. The girls, however, continued working. Their income now went towards supporting their brother's education. Though this education is subsidised to a large extent because he is a Christian, the cost of education in an elite school is nevertheless substantial. Uniforms have to be bought, pocket money has to be provided for and coaching fees have to be paid. The family has thus to incur all these expenses to meet his needs.

Soon it was time for the eldest daughter to get married. She was brought back home, and the third daughter went to Calcutta to take her place. The second daughter too got married soon after. Hers was a love marriage and she married a Hindu boy of her choice in Calcutta itself. She has not come home since then. In any case, their community would not accept her any more. The fourth daughter thus had to be sent off to take her place.

By this time, Rupa's younger brothers had been enrolled in school. Rupa was still illiterate. When we questioned her mother about this, she told us that they had made a very big mistake. They should have enrolled all their children in school, irrespective of whether they were boys or girls. Nowadays it was impossible to get by without an education. Though it was too late for her four older daughters, she apparently told Rupa to go to school. She had even bought her books. But Rupa seemed uninterested. She did not even want to go to school. Why was it too late for her daughters, we asked her. 'Well, the older ones are already married —and the other two are working,' she replied. 'How can they start school now?' It is inconceivable for her even to contemplate the idea of pulling the two girls out of work and getting them enrolled in school. How then would they meet the heavy expenses of her son's schooling? Without their income, the boy's education would become a major burden on the family.

Rupa's mother readily admits that today the definition of a 'good girl' has changed. An illiterate girl has a very difficult time. Girls should be sent to school. But she seems indifferent about her own daughters' education. Whatever she professes, it is obvious from her manner and behaviour that she really does not care very much about her daughters' education. She has no qualms about the fact that her daughters work as maidservants to keep their brother in a style that is difficult for even the more affluent to maintain. Though she has enrolled her three younger sons in school, she thinks it is sufficient to talk about enrolling Rupa in school, with no actual steps being taken in that direction. She uses Rupa's lack of interest in school as her excuse. And for Rupa, being uninterested in studying is quite natural. She has never seen her sisters go to school. She sees nothing out of the ordinary in a life spent as an illiterate person, working most of her adolescent years as a maidservant, and then getting married when her parents so decide. However, contrary to what her mother says, Rupa categorically states that she was not encouraged to go to school because the family could not afford to send the girls, as well as the boys, to school. Though she says that she would like to go to school if given a chance, the answer seems to be merely lip-service to an accepted current convention.

Rupa's horizons are severely limited. Studying or working does not enter at all in her ideas about her own future. In answer to our query about what she wanted to do when she grew up, she said that she wanted to get married and look after the household. After all, girls are expected to stay at home and work. Boys must study and get a job. She does not even have a clear idea of what a good girl or a good boy means. She has totally internalized the conventional and traditional ideas about the roles of men and women in society. She does not even know that a different kind of life is possible, let alone desire it. She is just passing time till the day she gets married. And then, after marriage, her life will resume, more or less, the same pattern, only in a different family.

Rupa is adept at all kinds of household work. Since all her sisters live away from home, it is Rupa's responsibility to help her mother with the domestic chores. Her day begins early in the morning. She first fetches water for the day's work. Then she washes the utensils required for cooking. After sweeping the house, she helps her mother with the cooking. When this is done, she washes the clothes for the entire family. Taking care of her brothers is also her responsibility. She plays with them, keeps them occupied, feeds them, bathes them, and sends them off to school every day on time. After lunch, Rupa must set out once again to fetch fuel and fodder. When she gets home, she has to wipe the floors and the walls of the house with a paste of cowdung and water, to keep them moist and prevent cracking. Her evenings are spent playing with her friends. At night, again, she has to help her mother prepare the evening meal for the family. And then, after a dinner that they all have together, Rupa's day is finally over, and she can go to sleep.

For Rupa's mother, her sons are far more important than her daughters. Boys are treasured children. Girls are tolerated because one cannot really be expected to be so lucky as to give birth only to boys. And once girls are born, what else can one do, but put them to the best use possible—use them to earn money for the family, to help with the domestic chores, and so on. Though Rupa's mother has four sons, she was disappointed at the birth of each of her five daughters. If she had had nine sons instead of four, she would have been happier. Her attitude is neither strange, nor unusual. Society conditions most women to cherish sons and reject daughters; to believe that sons are the salvation of one's life and daughters, a mere burden. The degree of son-preference that Rupa's mother has is revealed by the fact that she would feel happier to have no daughters at all, in spite of the fact that it is her daughters who make her work at home lighter and additionally bring in extra money to run the household. It is not as if Rupa's mother has no feelings for her daughters at all. But, naturally, daughters can in no way compare with sons. She does not go to the extreme of discriminating in the matter of food or living conditions. But there is a great difference in affection and attitude, in treatment and behaviour.

EPILOGUE

A year after the completion of our survey, we went back to this village for a visit. Rupa was not there. She had been sent to Calcutta to work as a domestic servant.

Girls like Rupa and her sisters have nothing in life to look forward to. They are exploited, overburdened with work, expected to give up their time and their lives for their families, which, in return, give them nothing but indifference and ill-treatment. These girls accept it as they know no better. Unless something is done to enlarge their horizons, to change their way of thinking and their work prospects, there is nothing but bleakness in store for them. It is very necessary to motivate them to think of themselves as equal with boys, for otherwise, in such cases, the gap between boys and girls in the same family will widen over time.

Rupa's brother is growing up in a very different, privileged environment. He is likely to be alienated from his family. His family circumstances are so far removed from that which he has at school, that there is no question of his ever going home to settle down. It is highly probable that he may end up being ashamed of his illiterate parents and of his illiterate sisters as well. The same sisters who gave up some of the best years of their lives to finance his education. Not that this will make any material differences to Rupa's life, however. She will have performed her role in her father's home by then. Her life will have taken the usual turn in that she will be married, with a husband and a family. But, there too, her role in life will be fixed. She will continue to be a beast of burden. For girls like Rupa, life just continues. Only the form and content of the burden they carry changes over the years.

PRABHA: IS THIS EDUCATION?

Prabha comes from a Hindu middle class family household in Calcutta. She is thirteen years old and is the only child of her parents. She lives in a large joint family, with her parents, her grandparents, her two uncles, their wives and their two sons. A cousin of her father's has also made his home with them. Prabha's family, thus, has twelve members including herself.

Prabha is a tall, slim girl, with her hair cut short. Dressed in a skirt and a blouse, she looks fragile and delicate and comes across as someone who is quiet and reserved. She speaks very softly and enunciates in a precise manner, which makes her appear far more mature than her years. She is extremely pale though, and looks somewhat anaemic. She has no history of any serious illness except certain types of allergic disorders.

Prabha is a student of Class 7 in one of the better English-medium schools of the city. Not only is she a good student, but she also actively participates in several extracurricular activities. She cannot take part in any of the sports events, she told us, because her skin is particularly susceptible to any sort of injury, but she paints, sings and dances and has also jointed the Girl Guides recently.

Prabha likes going to school. She gets to meet her friends there. Her teachers like her. And generally, the school atmosphere is one in which she thrives. Even though there is considerable pressure of work at school, Prabha has no private tutors. Her father is able to coach her in all her school subjects, except Sanskrit, which she learns from her mother.

When she grows up, she would like to be a scientist, she told us—because she is particularly interested in physics and chemistry and her grandfather has also set his heart on it. To Prabha, the chief advantage of being educated lies in the fact that education enables one to achieve one's ambition. If she is educated, she feels, she will be able to do all the things that she has ever wanted to. Why, she could even travel around the world on her own, and no one would stop her. She feels that girls should be given the opportunity to study up to whatever level they want, even more than boys, for boys are already privileged in society. For instance, they have the licence to come home as late as they like, to go out as often as they want to, whereas, if a girl did so, the whole family would get together to stop her.

Prabha is a very talented young girl. She is learning to paint in a nearby art school, and shows definite promise as an artist. She sings well, and is at present training under a renowned vocalist. She is also a good dancer and takes lessons from a well-known dancer in the city. After all this, she still finds time to do her school work and is among the top students of her class.

Prabha, however, does not have to do any work at all at home. At the most, she spends about ten minutes every day dusting, and that too, not out of her own volition. Her mother insists on it. Prabha feels that since there is no need to do such work around the house, why should she waste her time doing them? She would much rather spend that time reading a story book. She would like to learn cooking though, but both her parents object to this. There is time enough to learn to cook, they tell her. Now she should make the best of all the opportunities she has been given, to explore and develop her talents.

All the members of Prabha's family are highly educated. Her grandfather, father and eldest uncle are technically qualified professionals and are highly regarded in their chosen fields. Prabha's mother has a master's degree in Arts and is a trained teacher, with a bachelor's degree in education. Under such circumstances, it is natural for Prabha, too, to strive for excellence in academics. That is what the family expects from her. This has been ingrained in her so that Prabha takes failure of any kind very hard. She is serious about her extra-curricular activities as well. There too, she must be the best. Here, however, her mother's encouragement and enthusiasm is far greater than that of any other member of the family, including her father. Prabha's mother had at one time learnt to play the guitar. Marriage, childbirth and family responsibilities did not permit her to continue with her musical aspirations. She has now transferred her own desires and ambitions to her daughter, seeking satisfaction and glory from her daughter's achievements.

Considering the kind of family that Prabha comes from, with all the family members highly educated, and socially and economically well established, one would have expected them to be rational and liberal in their attitudes. The reality, however, is very different. Prabha's mother has cause for unhappiness and bitterness. Her husband is quite highly placed in his profession. So was her father-in-law. However, despite having brought a highly educated and professionally qualified daughter-in-law into the family, they flatly refused to let her pursue any career. Since the family was quite well-off, her mother-in-law categorically told her that she would not be allowed to take up any job because there was no pressing economic need for her to do so. In fact, she considered it a major crime for a woman to hold on to a job unless she was really needy, for otherwise she would be depriving some man of a job that should rightfully have gone to him. Since she had been married to someone who was able to earn more than enough to support her, there was no reason why she should even think of taking up a job. Prabha's mother bitterly complains that no one, not even her husband and father-in-law, supported her in her desire to pursue a suitable career.

Prabha's mother has even more serious allegations against her in-laws. She openly accused her in-laws of negligence during her pregnancy. They had not even taken her for regular check-ups, she told us. Even the mandatory shots of ATS had not been given. Only after her father had taken her away to her parental home had she had her first check-up. As a result of not having taken the ATS injections in time, she suffered severe post-delivery infections—so much so that she became incapable of having any other children. We were shocked to hear of such negligence in an apparently highly educated, socially established family. Incidents such as these are common in the rural areas of our country or the slum areas of the cities, where the people are largely illiterate and ignorant of the procedures which make childbirth safer for both mothers and children. Their negligence may be excused. But that this kind of an incident could possibly occur in this day and age, particularly in a family which professes to be educated, modern and cultured, was almost beyond our comprehension.

'Why, they even took money from my father as dowry,' said Prabha's mother. 'Though, to be fair to them, they did not demand anything during the marriages of my two brothers-in-law.' All this was narrated to us quite openly, in the presence of her father-in-law. Even though he glared furiously at her, she did not stop. Prabha's mother has developed a devil-may-care attitude over the years about what she says and about what her in-laws might think about her—as if she believes that whatever she says or does, she will be damned anyway.

For years, she said, she has been cooking and cleaning and doing everything that a good housewife should do, and watching her mind slowly turn inert and her intellect become sluggish. As the years went by, her husband started looking down on her. She was, after all, only his wife, and a housewife to boot. Why, she could not even hold her own against anybody. If she had really been serious about a career, she would have found a way of pursuing one.

Men, like Prabha's father, will marry educated and qualified women. Yet the moment such women become their wives, they turn into mere possessions—they will cook and clean for them, make their homes comfortable, bear their children and provide them with company when they so wish. They expect women to be around to cater to their needs, and yet look down upon them as being physically, emotionally and intellectually their inferior. Such men behave as though it is a man's birthright to obtain the 'services' of a woman without question, and that it is a woman's duty to perform the functions of a wife like an automaton. When a man looks for a wife, he will accept only someone who has qualifications to match his own, but as soon as he is married, he completely ignores her intellectual capacity. He does not object to colleagues who are women, and hold similar posts as he does. He appreciates working wives of friends and acquaintances. But his own wife has her duties fixed for her. She is to be nothing more than a glorified housekeeper and nanny, waiting to make his wish her command. Then, as the woman lets her mind get rusty from disuse, her husband starts getting tired of her. After all, she can discuss nothing more intellectually stimulating than the affairs of the household. Soon he begins to wish that his wife were socially and professionally more accomplished. Why, look at all the women who worked nowadays! Contempt and condescension for his wife are but a step away.

Prabha's mother feels that her opinions and wishes do not matter at all to the rest of the family. Once, she had arranged for a TV performance of her daughter's dance recital, but her husband had cancelled the show without even informing her or asking her about it. To this day, she says, she has not forgiven him, not just because he had so summarily dismissed her desires, but more because of the insufferably high-handed manner in which he had dealt with the issue.

As a direct result of this condescending attitude that Prabha's father has towards her mother, Prabha, too, has started believing that her mother's ideas and opinions do not matter very much. 'What does mother know?' is Prabha's attitude. Both she and her father, whom she idolizes, have a sort of an indulgent attitude towards her mother, as though she were an extremely unreasonable and ignorant person, whom they were honour-bound to humour. Prabha interrupts her mother all the time, shutting her up with a terse, 'You don't understand!' She deliberately refutes her mother's statements and if her mother has a suggestion to offer, she, more often than not, pretends not to have heard it. Though she does all this in front of her father and grandparents, none of them ever reprimand her. Far from it, their demeanour actively encourages such rude and downright callous behaviour towards her mother.

Even the fact that her mother teaches her Sanskrit is not a matter of pride for Prabha. After all, it is only Sanskrit, a language that is almost extinct, quite like her mother in fact. The 'important' subjects like science and mathematics are her father's sole domain and entirely beyond her mother's reach.

The most pathetic part of the situation is that Prabha's mother genuinely wants her daughter to be friends with her. She shame-facedly laughs at all the jokes made against her and accepts Prabha's rebukes in a docile fashion. While talking to us, she kept seeking Prabha's opinions about everything she said.

Prabha's mother's unhappy situation can be easily perceived. In answer to our question about whether she had any special skills, she blurted out in self-sarcasm, 'Yes, cooking. That is what I do best now!' Years of repression and condescension aimed at her by her family members has made her somewhat desperate. She is, however, quite conventional in her ideas about a 'good girl' or a 'good boy'. Anyone is a good boy or a good girl if he or she obeys the elders and does well in school. She also believes that girls should be married when they are about twenty-three or twenty-four years old, for by then they will already have obtained their master's degree, and beyond that age it really becomes very difficult to find good husbands for them.

Prabha, too, like her mother, believes that a 'good' boy or girl will listen to his or her parents and do the best he or she can do at school. After all, fulfilling one's parents' hopes and wishes is a child's duty. A 'good husband' should necessarily have a good job and a 'good wife' must be friendly and adjustable. Her ideas, too, are set in the conventional mould.

Not only Prabha's ideas, but also her entire demeanour speaks of a traditionally attuned mentality. She is totally dominated by the male point of view. She blindly idolizes her father and her grandfather. Everything that her mother says is wrong according to her. Without even realizing it, she is emulating the age-old attitude that men have had towards women.

The tragedy of the situation is that many children, like Prabha, imbibe all the attitudes and values of their fathers and other male relatives, and look down upon their mothers. With the opportunities that she has been given, Prabha will probably do well in whatever career she chooses for herself. One hopes, however, that society will have changed vastly within the span of the twenty-five odd years which separate her generation from her mother's. Otherwise, she too, may well end up exactly as her mother has—with an excellent degree, a sharp mind, and a craving to pursue a meaningful career, and yet be forced to spend all her time in the kitchen, simply because her in-laws will not permit another kind of life.

Prabha's case, or more important, the attitude she and the members of her family have towards her mother, brings to the fore several important issues that need to be addressed. Prabha's family is one that would be called 'educated' by general standards. All the members of the family are highly qualified and the men hold responsible jobs. Yet, it is this family that selected a highly qualified and educated bride for their son and then refused to let her make a career for herself. They practically forced her to live the life of a mere 'housewife' and now look down upon her for that very reason. Is this education?

It is unthinkable in modern times that a pregnant woman should have to do without the minimum of health care. Such incidents might occur in families that are illiterate and uninformed. Prabha's mother had no proper medical check-ups for the first six months of her pregnancy. She was not given the compulsory anti-tetanus injections, either. That this should have happened in a family which boasts of highly qualified, educated, well-placed and cultured family members came as a shock to us. Is this education?

This case also brings to the fore the long discussed need in our society to focus attention on the value and the worth of women's work at home. Perceptions have become so oriented that we cannot attach any worth to work which is not seen to be commercially productive. Unless wives and mothers are seen as doing work which is indispensable by virtue of being 'productive' in this sense, husbands and children do not perceive any worth in it. Simply fixing a price for housework, however, is not necessarily a solution. For what, then, would be the wages of love, for all that a woman does for her husband and children? Why do they have no appreciation for these values? Is this education?

The time has come to take a look at what exactly we are teaching our children. Unless something is done to reorient our education system, not just with regard to technique, but, more important, with regard to content, we may well end up with a generation of skilled doctors, engineers, accountants and scientists who have lost human values somewhere along the way.

PINKY : THE RIGHT TO WORK OR THE RIGHT TO LEISURE?

This story is about Pinky, an eighteen-year-old Hindu girl from Calcutta. Pinky's family has five members: her parents, her two younger brothers and Pinky herself, She lives in one of the colonies which house resettled refugees from East Bengal (now Bangladesh). Pinky's family, too, had migrated to Calcutta from Dhaka more than forty years ago, right after the partitioning of India.

Pinky's father used to be factory worker. However, some years ago, his company declared a lock-out, and subsequently he lost his job. At present he is unemployed. He finds it even more difficult to find alternative work, because he has studied only up to Class 8 and has no other skills. Pinky's mother, however, has studied up to Class 10. She has another skill: sewing. She is now the sole earning member of the family. With the help of her husband, she obtains orders for making aprons and overalls from various factories, and stitches them at home. She is able to earn about Rs. 1000 per month, which she said was just enough to make both ends meet.

Pinky's mother seems extremely upset, however, by this role reversal. She had always dreamt of having a successful husband and a home where she would reign like a queen. She had always wanted to be an exemplary housewife. Working for a living, leave alone working to support a husband and 3 children, had not figured in her plans for the future. She bitterly says that no woman should have to work after marriage. If your husband is an able-bodied man, he should be able to support his family.

Pinky's mother has totally fixed ideas about the roles of men and women in life. She believes that women should stay at home and look after the family. Unless absolutely necessary, they should not venture out of the house at all. This is the kind of life she would want for her daughter. Education is another matter. Girls should at least have a B.A. degree, she feels. Less than that is not acceptable in today's society. However, no girl should marry later than 20-22 years, she said. After that, they lose the freshness and beauty of youth.

Though Pinky's mother professes to have an interest in Pinky's education she probably does not pay as much attention as required. Pinky at eighteen years is only in Class 10, whereas other girls of her age have already finished Class 12, and are in their first year of college. Her younger brother who is now fifteen years old is already in Class 9, which is as it should be. Her other brother at thirteen years is in Class 7. It seems rather surprising that Pinky should have fallen so far behind as compared to her brothers, for she seems no less intelligent than them. It is possible that Pinky often has to stay at home to help her mother with the housework when there is heavy pressure of work from the factories which give her mother orders, for which reason she cannot spare much time for her studies, This might have affected her school attendance and her performance in class. Pinky is quite adept at all forms of sewing and knitting. she can make beautiful doormats of different kinds as well. She also coaches small children privately at home. Sometimes the parents of the children she teaches are extremely callous about payment.They do not pay her on time and sometimes even create problems about the amount to be paid. This kind of behaviour is extremely insulting, she says. However, she loves teaching so much, that she would like to take that up as her profession later on. That is why, she said, she was so keen on doing well in school. Not only did education help one to know the world better, but it also gave one the opportunity to meet new people and to make friends. Besides, studying would give her the necessary qualification to take up a teaching job in future.

Though Pinky wants to work when she is older, she would not do so at the cost of her family life, she says. When she gets married, she will pay equal attention to both, so that neither is neglected. Working is necessary to help supplement the family income and that is why she has decided that she will take up a job. It remains to be seen how far Pinky's ambitions about the future will be realized. She faces two problems. One is her mother's attitude towards women in general and towards her in particular. And the second is her own ambivalence about what a woman's role should really be.

Her mother, quite clearly, is far more fond of her two sons than she is of her daughter. She makes no bones about saying that if needed at home, she would naturally ask her daughter to stay back. It was out of the question to keep any of the sons to help at home. She had all her hopes pinned on them. She certainly would not allow anything to interfere with their education or their chances in life. They are everything to her. She is living in the hope of their obtaining secure and good jobs one day. Why should they waste time doing anything else just now? After all, one day they would have to take care of their parents, wouldn't they? When we suggested that Pinky too might grow up to get a job and look after her parents, her mother grew quite angry. Why should she have to work, she asked. She would get married and live happily with her husband. And besides, who would want to be looked after by a daughter when there were two sons present?

Although Pinky's mother feels that girls should not have to work at all, under the force of circumstances, she seems to accept without protest the fact that her daughter works as a private tutor and helps earn money by sewing. In fact, Pinky told us, that her parents encouraged her to earn some money, for it made things easier at home.

Pinky's mother wants her daughter married and happy. However, she flatly refuses to spend a penny on any form of dowry. This is not because she objects to it on principle, but because she is not able to afford it: 'We will never be able to pay any dowry,' she says. 'I would rather my daughter remained unmarried.' Pinky's mother is not prepared to pay dowry, but perhaps for the wrong reasons.

Pinky has adopted the modern-day image of the working girl for herself. She likes school, she likes teaching, she knows exactly what she would like to do when she grows up. She has had a taste of an independent income and identity as well. She also wants to get married and have a family. When asked about her future aspirations, she said that she wanted to be a teacher. When asked aboout her ideas of a good girl or a good boy, a good husband or a good wife, she replied that a good girl would stay at home, be obedient and do well at school. A good wife would look after her husband's family. Though a good boy has qualities almost the same as a good girl, a good husband is one who behaves well with his wife. The age-old gender-based role stereotyping is back with a vengeance.

Pinky's mother's attitude towards working may perhaps be because she is doing something so totally against her wishes that she hates it. Besides, the pressures of supporting a family and the tension that goes with it does not make it an easy job. Moreover, she has to shoulder the responsibility of being both the sole earning member of the family as well as a housewife. Added to it all is the stigma and the loss of prestige in having to live with a husband who is unemployed, and lives on his wife's earnings. All this together has possibly made her totally bitter about working. Saddled with dual responsibility, her cry is not for the right to work, but rather for the right to leisure.

What is not so easily explained, however, is her attitude towards her daughter, her one helpmate. Her affection towards her sons is so much greater, that she virtually neglects the girl. There is no reason why this should be so. One would have expected her to be more affectionate towards the girl who was giving up so much to help the family out in its time of difficulty. Except for the traditionally imbibed culture of son-preference there really seems no other explanation. Pinky's mother makes life as disagreeable as possible for her daughter. As if she wants Pinky to realize early in life that she cannot have what she wants. As though she is teaching Pinky that women cannot expect a better deal in life than this.

What Pinky's life holds for her is difficult to assess just now. The demand for the right to work, even paid work, is not a meaningful slogan for many women and girls coming from families who belong to the low and middle socioeconomic status families, both rural and urban. Stark economic reality forces most of them to work, anyway. But in our present socio-cultural environment, the gender-specificity of domestic work remains fixed, resulting in serious problems of overwork for working women. Also, social propriety, specially in middle class localities, cries shame on a family where the man is unemployed and the woman the bread-earner. So the woman works and feels ashamed that she has a good-for-nothing husband. Hence, women condition themselves to the expectation of the 'ease, comfort and luxury' of a married life where her man earns and she keeps home for him. For girls like Pinky, such perceptions, imbibed from their mothers and other female relatives, coupled with the modern-day image of the educated working women results in the kind of ambivalence, contradictions and confusions with regard to their rights, responsibilities and roles that is often observed.

MADHURI: THE POOR LITTLE RICH GIRL:

Madhuri's material circumstances are not adverse. In fact they are somewhat on the affluent side. Along with her brother, she also has had access to good food, good clothes, good education. Yet, there is deprivation. Of what kind? Her story reveals this aspect of the girl child's condition in our society.

She is a seventeen-year-old Oriya, Hindu girl, who lives in a large apartment complex in one of the more affluent parts of a ward which we had surveyed in Calcutta. There are four members in her family—her parents, her brother and herself. Madhuri is the first born and is two years older than her brother. He has just completed Class 10 at school, and is awaiting admission into Class 11. He is a rather pampered young boy, and his demeanour shows it.

Madhuri's father has a successful business that is based in Calcutta and Cuttack. Though her father is a Commerce graduate, her mother has studied only up to the Matric-level. On acquaintance, Madhuri's mother seems to be a rather warm person, but she is somewhat timid and conservative. Whereas the rest of the family converses fluently in English, Madhuri's mother finds it difficult to speak in any language other than Oriya. Even Hindi or Bengali does not come easily to her. She is happiest in the kitchen, cooking for her family. She also does most of the housework herself.

The apartment in which Madhuri lives with her parents is quite a large one. She has her own room, as does her brother. The family has its own car and also owns gadgets such as a colour TV, a VCR, a large music system, and a plethora of modern kitchen and household equipment. Brought up in an atmosphere of affluence and luxury, Madhuri takes all this quite for granted, and considers these as part of normal living conditions.

Madhuri has recently entered college. She has always studied in the English-medium and is fluent in this language. She can also read, write and speak Hindi. Additionally, she can speak both Bengali and Oriya quite fluently. Apart from lessons in school, Madhuri used to participate regularly in debates and quiz programmes.

A bright and healthy young girl, Madhuri does not remember ever being seriously ill. She is tall (five feet three inches), athletically built and extremely attractive. She has short hair, sharp features and looks sleek and well-groomed. Though she is somewhat lean, weighing only 43 kg, she says that this is so by choice, for today, one has to be slim to be considered good-looking.

Madhuri loves sports, and has won a number of cups and medals in school . She has a distinct flair for painting and sewing and enjoyed these classes in school, as well. In fact, she is seriously considering a career in dress designing in the future. Madhuri has also attended cooking classes at school, more at her mother's insistence, however, than any knack or desire of her own. She is also taking computer courses at one of the best institutions of the kind in the city.

A full-time student, Madhuri is occupied all day with her classes at college, her computer courses and her studies at home. Whatever free time is available is spent in sketching and painting or reading story books. Her day follows a routine that is typical of any teenager's in her social milieu.

She wakes up around seven o'clock in the morning, reads the newspaper, looks up her day's routine, and finishes whatever work is required to attend classes on any particular day. She then gets ready, has a heavy meal, and leaves for college. After college she attends her computer classes and comes home quite late in the evening. Evenings are usually spent reading, listening to music, or watching television. Sometimes, when she has time, she paints, or embroiders. Occasionally, they have guests to entertain. Since she has been in college only a few months, the workload is still quite light, and she can get by with the minimum amount of studying needed to follow classes. However, since she is expected to do well in her examinations, she soon plans to start attending a coaching class. Though Madhuri does not spend too much time studying for her lessons at college, her computer classes take up a lot of her time and attention.

Madhuri does not need to do much around the house. She occasionally does small jobs such as cleaning or dusting. It never takes on the character of a compulsory chore, however, which is just as well, for she is not too fond of housework anyway. All that is expected of her is keeping her own room clean, and little things like setting the table, serving the food, or helping her mother in the kitchen when they have guests. Madhuri's mother would have dearly loved it if her daughter had occasionally cooked a dish or two, but Madhuri professes to have no inclination towards cooking at all.

Madhuri has all the material comforts in life that any young girl could ask for. She has been given an excellent education. Her talent for painting has been encouraged. She has been enrolled in the best computer course available. Her hobbies of reading and music have been indulged in. In fact, in a sense, she lacks for nothing in life. In spite of this, she suffers from a sense of deprivation; of being denied some of her most basic rights and needs. She feels that she is always second best. Her brother comes first with her parents. According to her, her brother takes the first place in their parents' affection. They are more concerned about his needs, his necessities and his claims. His opinions are always given greater credence. His feelings are always considered more important than hers. When she and her brother have an argument, her parents always take his side. She is supposed to back down every time, ostensibly because she is older, but really, she feels, because she is a girl. Otherwise, why doesn't anyone ask him to shut up sometimes because he is younger? He is conceited, opinionated and egotistical but manages to get away with it all, simply because he is male. After all, boys will be boys, according to her parents.

It is taken for granted that the boy will take over the family business—Madhuri has no claim on it whatsoever. Her mother believes that girls are brought up to become good wives, good mothers and good hostesses. They should be married off as soon as they attain maturity. They are not supposed to be entrusted with the responsibility of something as important as the family business. A good education is a different matter. Nowadays, it is a necessity if the girl is to make a good marriage. But business? That certainly is not ladylike. Girls should essentially be soft-spoken, compromising and accommodative, and well-versed in domestic activities. When her son gets married, this is the kind of daughter-in-law she would want. She must be educated enough to qualify as his wife, but she must, more important, adjust to his personality, be alert to his needs and be able to satisfy his requirements. Since her son is rather headstrong and short-tempered, his wife must be the obedient kind. In addition, she must be able to cook and clean for him. In fact, Madhuri's mother had insisted that Madhuri take cooking classes at school so as to be able to prepare special dishes for her brother, who is not too fond of the traditional food his mother cooks. But much to her chagrin, Madhuri does not even step into the kitchen.

Madhuri feels deprived of the trust of her parents. It is as if they are making her an alien, a stranger in her own home. She feels that they are just waiting for the opportune moment so that they can get rid of her by getting her married. They do not have enough faith in her to trust her with participation in the family business, though she is older and better educated than her brother. Madhuri is certain, that she will never ever be given a chance to prove her worth. Her father does not deny her a career. He is quite willing to let her take up something lady-like, such as dress designing. He is even prepared to put up the finances for a boutique, if that is what she wants. But, he expects that whatever she does, it will be in keeping with their status, bearing in mind that she is the daughter of a prominent businessman. And, of course, when the time comes, she is to get married to the 'right' man. On no account is she to embarrass him by taking up something so blatantly masculine as the family business. The role stereotyping is rigid. There are some things in life that women are just not meant to do. How can a girl take the extensive travelling that a business of this kind requires? Who would permit her to travel alone anyway? Madhuri is certain that her father would never even have allowed her to take up a career in the hard sciences, such as engineering or mediciene. She is expected to grow up to be a 'lady', get married, be an excellent housewife, and, as a concession to the twentieth century, have some kind of a feminine occupation, such as running a boutique or some such essentially cosmetic activity. She is merely an ornamental showpiece at home. She feels as though she exists as just another decoration among many others and will soon decorate another home in a similar manner. Her decisions, her opinions, are all quite superfluous. The worst part of it is that not only do her parents feel this way, but her brother too has picked up this attitude and behaves condescendingly with her. This indeed is a bitter pill to swallow, for all things apart, he is after all, her younger brother and his lack of respect for her and her abilities really rankles.

Under the circumstances, Madhuri feels discriminated against. She resents the fact that she is considered to have lesser worth than her brother, simply because she is a girl. She is upset that her parents are always taking her brother's side during an argument. All her activities are considered mere pastimes to amuse herself with till she gets married. She feels that she is being deprived of her birthright which means equal affection from her parents, equal worth in their eyes, equal responsibilities to shoulder, and equal pride in achievement. Aptitudes and abilities notwithstanding, she is being made a victim of social conditioning simply because she is a girl child.

The discriminatory behaviour of Madhuri's parents has affected the psyche of this young girl. She harbours a resentment towards her parents as well as her brother. She views him as someone who will always get a better deal, even if he does not deserve it. She looks upon him as someone who is usurping her rightful inheritance, not just in terms of the business or property, but also in terms of the legacy of love due to her from her parents; the right to exploit her talents to their fullest extent; the power and responsibilities of functioning as a person, and not merely a girl.

Her self-worth suffers blows at every step. In spite of her abilities and her training, she is considered good enough only to take up something cosmetic and undemanding and feminine, like running a boutique. Here too, it has been made amply clear to her that she is graciously and indulgently being granted a wish. A whim of hers is being satisfied, because her parents can afford it. It is not necessary to run the boutique at a profit. It will be there, expressly to amuse her, when she wants to play at being a working woman. Her role in life has been pre-determined by her gender— and she has to submit to it, willy nilly.

Madhuri is not fighting a discrimination that can be defined in material terms. She comes from a family which knows no material scarcity. She has not been discriminated against as far as food, clothing, education or pocket money goes. The form of deprivation she suffers is more subtle and, hence, more difficult to address. Madhuri is fighting for her rights to equality, to responsibility. It is true that she and her brother have received an equally good education. But, whereas her brother will have the opportunity to put his training to use, Madhuri's training, as well as her innate ability, will all be wasted—sacrificed, as it were, at the alter of social rigidity. She is fighting to assume responsibility for her future; to prove her worth to her parents; to show the world, that she is no less a person because she was born a girl. Women are born with the same abilities as men. In households such as Madhuri's, much is invested in bringing up a girl. And then with a single sweep of stakes, all her rights, her dreams and ambitions are dashed to the ground, simply because society decrees that a girl's place is at home. In this sense, the chips are always stacked overwhelmingly on the man's side.

Apparently a bright and cheerful girl, Madhuri's resentment against her family does not surface unless deeply probed. Perhaps she will perforce fit herself into the mould cast for her. But the sense of discrimination which she suffers from may leave her scarred. Constantly being induced to accept standards lower than her abilities and being forced to live by values that she considers false, may eventually stunt her spirits. She will perhaps make an apparent success of whatever life she is allowed to lead. But this will be a facade, which hides from all but the most perceptive the turmoil beneath. The fact that as an individual, she is living at a level lower than she could have achieved; the perception that she will always be judged according to these standards; will be a constant source of pain. What is most upsetting is the usual attitude that this kind of a life should suit a woman perfectly well as long as her material needs are satisfied, and she has a husband and home to care for. After all, what more could any woman ask for? Yet, given half a chance, Madhuri, and hundreds of her kind, would have been able to live a life that could have been mentally and emotionally stimulating, and one which would have satisfied their need for an identity as an individual, rather than the gender-stereotyped one of a wife and a mother.

Is Madhuri over-reacting? Is it a discrimination-complex that Madhuri suffers from? Or is it simply inter-sibling jealousy? Even if one discounts some part of her problems and complaints, the core point remains. She is not complaining about not having food or clothes or gadgets. She is complaining about not being taken seriously as a responsible individual in her own right. She has no role in the decision-making process of her family, although her younger brother does. The serious matter of the family business is not for her. If she wants a 'career' as a businesswoman she can have one since her father can afford it. He does not refuse or deny her any financial commitment—she could also have asked for, and been given, ornaments or some other consumer durable instead. There is no difference in perspective with regard to the expense incurred, whether it is for her 'career' or for some ornaments. Her business would not be taken seriously anyway, otherwise why is her opinion not even asked for, or given fair consideration, regarding matters of family business?

Madhuri's case begs the question of defining what gender equality really means. In the midst of reasonable affluence, her situation is not one of genuine equality of opportunity with her brother. Even when a girl apparently has equal rights and access to opportunities that parents can afford for their children, differentiation is often present in the way parents react to the utilization of these opportunities by their male and female offspring. The girl's achievements or failure may not be appreciated unless it lowers her worth in the marriage market.

The silver lining in this picture is that Madhuri has acquired a good education and training in certain skills, and also that she is sensitized to the fact that equality means much more than being given material comforts. If she can translate her feelings into positive action directed towards utilizing her training and abilities in some serious occupation of her choice, then she may yet be able to achieve something worthwhile in women's fight for the right to genuine equality with men as individuals.

MAJIDA : A TWELVE - YEAR - OLD BUSINESSWOMAN'S

In a Calcutta slum we came across a twelve-year-old Muslim girl called Majida. Right from the beginning, Majida struck us as a very special person. We first met her sitting in front of a tiny shop, selling toffees to some small children. In fact, it was the sight of this shop, tucked into a corner of a house, that initially caught our attention. We went closer, and found this little girl selling sweets. She professed to be the 'proprietor' of the shop. In an area where Muslim girls still have a lot of restrictions imposed on their movement, this was indeed unusual. 'Will you talk with us for a while?' we asked her. Majida enthusiastically agreed.

By this time, quite a large crowd had gathered around us. It consisted mostly of curious young children. From the midst of them peeped an old lady, Majida's grandmother. 'What are you asking the child, Didi? She will not get into any trouble, will she?' Once we had reassured her on this count, we were welcomed into the house. We entered a long, corridor-like verandah with several rooms built in a row along one side of it. All the rooms opened out into the same verandah. These rooms housed the families of Majida and her two paternal aunts. All the three families had separate cooking arrangements. Majida's grandmother lived with her eldest daughter.

Majida's family has seven members—her parents, her three younger sisters, her brother, who is the youngest of them all, and Majida. Majida is the only literate member of her family. No one else has ever been to school. When we asked her mother why this was so, she told us that when she herself had been young, girls did not go to school. For men, too, education was not very important. Besides, there were no free schools at that time. As for her children, she said, they could not afford to send anyone to school, except the eldest, Majida. Even she had had to drop out about a year ago, after her father lost his job.

Majida's father works in the docks. He sails for about six months a year and works as a labourer for the remaining six months. However, about a year ago, he was retrenched from service and could not secure any other job. This was a period of immense hardship for Majida's family. Her father tried to make a living by selling vegetables at the market, but he did not earn enough even to be able to provide food for the entire family. Luxuries like school were therefore out of the question. Even if one did not have to pay any fees, or buy school books, one had to give the child some tiffin every day. Moreover, Majida had outgrown her uniform and a new one could not be bought for her at that time. Also, the child had had to discontinue her private coaching classes, and it was impossible to keep up in class without that help.

So, Majida dropped out of school. She was then in Class 4. She dropped out without any question or resentment. She was needed at home, she said, and her first priority was naturally her family. The little girl started accompanying her father to the market every morning, to help him sell vegetables. Often, when he came home for lunch, Majida would mind the shop herself. In the evenings when she came home, she would try to help her mother, either by taking over the evening's cooking or by taking charge of her brother and sisters, so that her mother could get her work done quickly.

Soon Majida started feeling that she was not doing enough to help her family during this difficult time. She decided to open a shop. She would keep sweets and toffees and sell them to the children in the locality. She spoke to her aunts and her grandmother, and they agreed to provide the capital for this venture.

With the money given by them, Majida got herself a large, portable wooden rack, some glass jars and things like lollipops, which she could sell easily. She set the rack up adjacent to an outer wall of her house, placed the jars with the sweets on it, and then she was in business!

Majida had chosen her place well. Her shop was in the corner of a large open space, which all the slum-children used as a playground. She never lacked customers, for the little children were always stopping by her shop to buy something or the other. Majida was able to earn about Rs. 50 every month. She gave all her earnings to her mother, keeping nothing for herself.

Majida was extremely caring and protective about her younger siblings. She would play with them, see that they got their meals on time, and would also try to teach the two older girls how to read so that when their financial condition improved, they could accompany her to school. For nine months, the situation remained unchanged. Majida would go to the market in the mornings with her father, come home in the evenings and look after her shop, and later, when it had grown dark and she had closed her shop, she would take over from her mother at home.

Nine months later, her father got his job back. The family's economic condition improved immediately. Once her father had sailed away, Majida no longer needed to run the shop. But she refused to give it up. Already, in these few months, she had realized that an individual earning capacity gave her a power which she would never have had as merely a daughter of the house. Her shop and her business were the result of her own toil and initiative. It gave her a sense of identity which she had never had before. And besides, she pointed out, school sessions would begin only after three months. In the meanwhile, what would she do at home all day?

Majida now started running her shop full time. She would be there from nine in the morning to about four in the afternoon. Since her house was right next door, she could, if she needed something, just go in for a moment and be back before anyone had missed her. At lunch time, she would get one of her sisters to stand in for her. She was now able to earn a lot more—about Rs.100 to Rs.150 per month. All of this, too, she gave to her mother. After all, if she needed anything, she could always ask her mother. And whatever she asked for she got.

We asked Majida what she wanted to be when she grew up. 'I want to be like you, I want to teach other people,' she said. That is why she wants to go to school. In her mind, there is no doubt that she will go back to school. She is sure she will be enrolled again. And what is more, this time she will take at least one of her sisters with her. 'You do not get a good job without an education,' she said.

Majida seemed to have a well-adjusted and strong personality. Small and thin, dressed always in salwar and kurta, with the chunni dropped over her head and shoulders, she looks surprisingly mature for a twelve- year-old child. For such a young girl to have so much conviction about what she is doing, is indeed very rare. She know her mind exactly—and believes that she will get what she wants, if she works for it. And she is prepared to work very hard for something she believes in. The most remarkable thing about her is that she does whatever she has to do with a minimum of fuss. When she dropped out of school, she did so quietly, without protest, anger or reluctance. It was her duty to help her family and she was quite willing to give up school for that. When she started her shop, she started it out of necessity. But later, when the need was not there anymore, she was quite certain that she did not want to close shop, and she did not, though it meant sacrificing her leisure. She has no hesitation about surrendering her entire evenings to her family, either. She does so happily, for she believes that this is the natural thing to do. She asks her mother for money when she needs some, just as any other twelve-year-old would. Majida is equally convinced that she will go back to school at the beginning of the new season. It never occurs to her that some mothers, having got used to having a helping hand at home, and to the extra money brought in by the girl, may not want the child to go back to school.

To be fair to Majida's mother, one must say, that she too is quite a remarkable person. Majida is her first surviving child. Before that she had lost four children—two sons and two daughters, in infancy, right after their birth. She stoically accepts that they had come to her as gifts from God, and he had taken them away when he decided so. She then had Majida and three more daughters, one after another. Unlike other women in her position, she was genuinely happy at the birth of each child, and loves all of them dearly. Certainly, she wanted a son, but never did she penalize her daughters for not having been born male. When her son was born, she was very happy. It is true that she believes that boys should have more amenities in life than girls, but, she makes it clear that to her both her sons and her daughters are equally dear. We asked her what she wanted her sons and daughters to be when they grew up. How far did she want them to study? She refused to answer, saying only that she did not want to talk about this at all. All that she wanted, was for them to grow up—to live and to be happy. She would not be able to bear it if these children died too. She just wanted them to stay alive and healthy.

We asked her whether there were any special restrictions imposed on her daughters. With a smile she said that in Muslim households, girls are supposed to stay at home, observe purdah and not speak to strangers at all. But she did not want to confine her daughters that way. Why should they be bound to the house? She believed that the more they were able to mix with other people, the more they got to know the world, the happier they would be.

This attitude is certainly extremely rare even today. Perhaps, losing four children has made her aware of the fact that there is nothing more important in life than for the children to live happily. She has given all of them equal love and affection. She has encouraged them to pursue their own interests. As a result, her children have responded with an overwhelming love for her, and for each other. They are bound to each other with strong ties of love and affection, not merely those of blood. It is perhaps from her mother that Majida has inherited her quiet strength, her firm resolve and her unconventional attitude.

Unusual as Majida is, there are some areas, of course, where she retains traditional ideas of what is done or not done. For instance, when we asked her what qualities she would expect a good husband or a good wife to have, she said she did not know. How could she? She was not married yet, and unmarried girls are not ever supposed to think of such things. About the qualities of a good boy or a good girl, however, she was characteristically unequivocal. They must be well-mannered, that is all.

Majida also naturally accepts the fact that her brother has a more important place in the household than she and her sisters have. It is true that their parents love all of them very much, but she realizes that her brother is special. Their aunts are happy that there is someone to carry on the family name. Their grandmother will not let him out of her sight. Majida, too, thinks that all this is very normal. A male-child is, after all, the most coveted offspring everywhere. She finds no reason to be upset about the fact that people are always more concerned about his welfare than that of hers or her sisters'. She too, is very protective about him. After all she has only one brother and he too was born to the family after the thousands of prayers offered to Allah by her mother.

Majida's life has a comfortable pattern. She is not compulsorily burdened with any kind of work anymore. As a rule, she does not even have to help her mother at home. She cooks if she feels like it—sometimes when she wants to prepare a particular dish, or at times, when she feels her mother is tired. She does take care of her younger brother and sisters, but only because she enjoys doing so. Her only full-time activity is looking after her shop. That too, is a lot of fun for her, for she loves talking to all the children who come to buy candy from her. She makes new friends every day. The older boys tease her sometimes, and threaten to break her jars, but that she dismisses with a shrug of her shoulders. She can always complain to their parents if they get out of hand.

She is determined to go back to school in the summer. She says this, not in the manner of one fighting for her rights, but as though it were an already settled fact. She had dropped out during a crisis in the family, and had done all she could do to help. Now that there is no longer any crisis, she expects life to resume its normal course, which means that she will go back to school again to study. When we asked her whether she had ever had to go hungry, she replied in an absolutely matter-of-fact manner, 'Not anymore.' Dismissing with one phrase those months when she had had to work hard to help supplement the family income, often going without food, simply because there was not enough for everyone. Never once, in all the days that we met her did she ever utter a word of complaint.

The brightest facet of Majida's character is her ability to face calmly all the ups and downs in life, and to carry on living the best she can. This quality will stand her in good stead, whatever direction her life may take. And if there is ever any major upheaval in her life, it is this characteristic feature of her nature that will help her to face the situation without getting unduly excited or upset. This will help to pull her out of the deepest of quagmires, should she ever happen to fall into one.

EPILOGUE

When we met Majida once again, about a year later, we found her appearance and her manner quite unchanged. She was taller— but still dressed in a salwar kurta, with the chunni draped over her head. Her shop was no longer in sight. What was she doing now, we asked her. She went to school, she said. And was her younger sister in school, as well? Yes, of course, she too went with her, we were told. What about the shop then? Oh, that's only opened on holidays now. There was no one to look after it on school days when Majida was away. Did she have any regrets, we asked her. None at all, she replied. She did miss being an independent income earner sometimes, but as she saw it, a good school education was an investment for a future job that would be far more satisfying than running a small shop. There was no time anymore for her shop every day. She had to go to school, then to a private coaching class and also had to prepare her lessons at home. Besides, she was learning to sew in a sewing school now. Some housework also had to be done, for her mother had not been keeping well lately. Her time was all accounted for. On Sundays, she still opened her shop, but more because it was so much fun, rather than anything else, she said. Majida was perfectly happy with the turn that life had taken. She had gone back to being a young thirteen-year-old school girl, and life for her was just wonderful at present.

Majida's character has a lot of determination and confidence. This may be due partly to her innate characteristics and partly to her home environment where all the children are loved and cherished; are given almost equally whatever facilities, amenities and opportunities the family can afford; and where their efforts, and initiatives are encouraged and appreciated, irrespective of their sex. This must have helped Majida's personality formation and permitted the realization of her own potential. Even during the days and months of acute economic distress, the morale of the family, including that of the children, did not break. The maturity with which the twelve-year-old Majida absorbed and reacted to the shock of retrenchment of the sole earning member in her family; her concern and positive approach to the problems her family was facing; and finally, the easy grace with which she adjusted to the improved financial family situation by going back to her studies, while retaining her 'business venture' as a part-time activity, out of personal interest rather than necessity were heartening to observe. These qualities of maturity, confidence and strength are not to be found among many older people of either gender. It reflects what the much derided girl child is capable of, given a healthy family environment.

SHANTI: IN A HAVEN OF PEACE OR A FOOL'S PARADISE?

Shanti is eighteen years old and very recently married. She now lives with her husband, his parents, his three younger brothers and a younger sister. Before her marriage Shanti had no family, no home. She was born into a migrant Hindu family, originally from Bihar. There were three children—two older boys, and Shanti, the youngest. Circumstances forced Shanti to leave home when she was only twelve years old, and she has been on her own ever since.

Shanti looks young for her age. Dressed in a salwar-kurta, she could easily pass for a thirteen- or fourteen-year-old girl. Her height is four feet six inches and her weight 36.5 kg. Thin, undernourished and small for her age, her face and eyes, however, bear a look of grit and determination. Though she does not like to admit it, she often had to go hungry, for as she says, after all, a servant girl can't ask her employer for a second helping, can she? Even now, as the bahu, she eats after all the other family members have eaten, and more often than not, she makes do with whatever little is left over. She said that she does not remember being seriously ill. Minor ailments such as a fever or a stomach ache went largely unnoticed, for there was no one to take care of her. She used to have severe menstrual cramps and often went to the local chemist for 'tablets' that would kill the pain.

Shanti never had a chance of a proper education. She was enrolled in school a very long time ago and studied for a few months in Class 1. For all practical purposes she is illiterate. Nor is she very interested in enrolling in school now for she feels that luxuries such as school are not for her. Until recently, Shanti used to work as a part-time maidservant in a neighbouring house. She was able to earn about Rs.100 a month. She had to work every day, seven days a week, from 8 a.m. to 12 p.m. and again from 3 p.m. to 9 p.m. in the evening. Though she was given both meals, lunch and dinner, at her place of service, it was never adequate. Moreover, she never had any holidays, or actual periods of rest, even on working days, except at mealtimes. She practically never had the opportunity to watch television, because that is when her employers would demand tea or snacks. Moreover, she would have to prepare dinner for them before she left. Absenteeism or late-coming would unleash a stream of abuse or result in a pay-cut. Previously, she had worked for about two years as a full time, live-in-maid, but this had its own problems which finally led her to quit. From her experience she felt that living in someone else's house at night was not safe for her. At present Shanti is not doing any outside work, but may have to resume doing so in a short while due to economic necessity. She now spends her entire day doing household chores and looking after her in-laws.

Shanti was born in a Calcutta slum. The family, consisting of father, mother and their three children lived in a tiny one-roomed tenement. Soon after Shanti's birth her mother fell ill and died. Shanti was then about two and a half years old. Her father, unable to look after three small children, took then to their native village in Bihar, with the intention of leaving them there under the care of his family. His family agreed to keep the boys with them, but refused to take the responsibility for a girl child. So, Shanti came back to Calcutta to the old slum with her father.

In a short while her father remarried, and moved to another slum. Shanti went with him. Life with her father and step-mother, however, proved to be unbearable. She lived with them till she was twelve years old and then decided to leave to make a life of her own. Her father did not object. He did not even ask her where she would go or how she would make a livelihood.

Shanti sought refuge in her old slum locality, with her old neighbours. They found her a job as a full-time domestic servant in a house where she would stay. She worked as a live-in-maid for about two years. She then decided to quit the full time maid's job because the people she worked for were not 'good.' She would not elaborate about her experiences, but said that she realized that for young girls, stay-in jobs involved hazards. It takes little imagination to understand that she must have gone through some form of sexual harassment which forced her to seek other accommodation at night.

Before she got married, Shanti lived with one of her neighbours. She was a kindly matron, whose own house was already over-crowded with sons, daughters and grandchildren. This lady had known Shanti since she was a child and had agreed to let her sleep in her house at night when Shanti decided that spending nights at her employer's house was unsafe for her. But her neighbour's shelter too was essentially a very temporary one for Shanti. She knew that she would have to move out as soon as her neighbour's son got married, for then, her sleeping space would be given to the son's young bride.

It was perhaps this need for shelter that induced Shanti to marry a young man from a neighbouring house in the slum. This man had initially wanted to marry her three years ago. But, at that time, Shanti, fiercely independent and idealistic as she was, refused to marry anyone who demanded a dowry. Besides, who would provide a dowry for her anyway? At that time, she was still working as a live-in maidservant in a nearby house. Now, with the imminent possibility of being turned out on the streets, as the date of marriage of her neighbour's son drew close, she needed to think about her future. She decided to accept the boy's proposal when it came the second time.

Other circumstances had also changed. Meanwhile, this boy had been married off to a young girl from a village in Chhapra, Bihar. The bride developed some sort of an illness soon after marriage, and was sent off to her parents' home, as her husband found it impossible to live with her. Now, in the position of a married man, he proposed to Shanti and told her that he wanted no dowry whatsoever, knowing that Shanti's predicament might well make her capitulate and give in to his offer this time. And that is exactly what happened.

Shanti was married quickly to this young man and moved to his house. Her in-law's household consists of her father-in-law, her mother-in-law, her husband, three brothers-in-law and a sister-in-law. None of them are educated beyond the level of Class 2, except her husband, who has studied up to Class 4. Shanti's father-in-law tries to run a small business, working with cut pieces and whatever tailoring jobs may come his way. He is able to earn Rs.200 in some months, but usually earns even less. Her mother-in-law works as a part-time maidservant, earning about Rs.250 per month, the only source of regular income in the household. Her husband remains unemployed most of the year, securing part-time jobs now and then, as a peon, which pays him Rs.150 or less per month.

Her husband's first wife now lives away from the household in her native village. But she may come back some day. In fact, her family has been threating her in-laws with court action and police intervention if they do not take her back. Thus, Shanti realizes, that even though she may not work now, so soon after her marriage, so that no one thinks that her husband married her to lay his hands on her income, she may soon have to take up a job as a domestic servant once again to help support her new family.

Shanti's life has undergone a radical change after her marriage. Before that, her day would begin early and consist of working in the house where she was employed. She would have to be at work by 8 a.m. in the morning, clean the previous night's soiled utensils, wash the clothes, clean the rooms and sweep them, and help with the preparation of lunch. The same routine would be repeated in the evening. And this was what her life consisted of—every day, every year.

Now, after her marriage, her day is spent doing domestic chores. Since her mother-in-law leaves home early and is out most of the day, the entire responsibility of cooking, cleaning, fetching water, and so on, rests on her. She does all the work happily, for she feels that after all she is working for her own family and not for someone else, where she is only a paid employee. Moreover, now she has her sister-in-law to help her sometimes.

At present, Shanti is very much the happy young bride. She is fond of her in-laws and feels that they genuinely care for her. Though marriage means added responsibility, and perhaps a greater workload, she feels the security that she has achieved now, after marriage, is worth all that. The price of a secure shelter far outweighs the problems resulting out of marrying into an economically distressed household, and even the trials of being a second wife in a Hindu family. She feels that she has not done anything that is grossly wrong by marrying this man, because his first wife was seriously ill, and did not live with her husband, offering him no conjugal satisfaction. Despite that, to make up, she is willing to relinquish her claim on her husband and to work to help support them and the rest of her in-laws. In the eventuality that the first wife recovers, comes back, and claims her husband, Shanti has decided to go out to work to support both her husband and his first wife, because she feels that is her duty. After all, her right to her husband comes second to the first wife's claim.

When asked about the nature of the work that she used to do, she said, that what upset her was not the workload or the long work-hours, or the lack of rest, but the feeling of being perpetually at the mistress's beck and call. But, most of all, she disliked the nature of her work. She hated washing up after others. She was tired of cleaning other people's 'jhutha', she said. If it were up to her, she wouldn't do this sort of a lowly thing—in fact, she would give anything to get out of the 'domestic-servant job market.' But, she also realizes that she has no skills to speak of, nor is she educated, even up to the primary level. So, finding a job of any other kind is impossible for her.

Her most important aim in life at present, is to help her husband get a reasonably well-paid job, something that will pay him Rs.600-Rs.700. Marriage, she says, is not only security. It also means taking on the responsibility for all of them. Earlier, when she had only herself to worry about, she was much more independent, and willing to take on a lot more things. But now, she not only has to worry about all the members of the family, but also has to take care that nothing she does jeopardizes their honour or prestige. All in all, she is happy because now she is secure in the folds of a real family, from which she believes that no one can turn her out summarily, and above all she has been able to stick to her principles in getting married without a dowry.

Actually, her expectations from life were minor. To her a good husband means someone who will not beat his wife up or be addicted to drugs or alcohol. In fact, all a good boy needs is a good job and decent habits. Also, conditioned by living in a society where girls are treated as little more than possessions, her ideas of what a good girl should be like are very conventional. A good girl is one who can protect herself and her honour from being violated. A good wife means someone who will look after and obey her husband. Her independence of spirit, and unconventional attitude towards other issues, somehow makes these ideas sound more tragic, coming from her.

Shanti is an odd mix of the innocent and the cynical, of the conventional and the unconventional. She is a very sincere person, with deep emotions and strong commitments. Some of her ideas show remarkable modernity, yet, some are steeped in conventionalism. The chief impression one gets, is one of strength and courage, a willingness to take on the world for the sake of her family, and a lasting sense of open and outgoing friendliness. In fact, when almost everyone in the cluster where she lives was openly sceptical and apprehensive about our survey, Shanti was the first person to come to us and say that she was willing to answer any questions we cared to ask her. Even though she entreated with us to get her a 'good' job, her manner did not change a bit after she realized that we probably would not be able to find her one.

Shanti is one of the examples of the most crippling kind of discrimination that we have come across. Right from her childhood, she has been deprived of a home, chiefly because she was born a girl. Had she been a boy, she would have been accepted into her father's family in her native village and would have had the security of a home, and may be rudiments of an education. It is because no one wants to take on the responsibility of looking after a girl child, specially with the added burden of providing a dowry for her, that she was pushed out from one place to another throughout her childhood. Apart from being unwanted by her step-mother merely because she was a step-child, the degree of deprivation was greater because she was a girl child. A male child is dear to the father not only because he carries the family name, but also because he is a security for the future. A girl child is not perceived as anything but a burden. Hence, Shanti was not given an education, nor taught any skills whatsoever. And when she left home, her father never enquired after her.

With no education or job-skills, and moreover, being female, Shanti had no option but to become a domestic servant, where the pay was a mere pittance. Because she had nowhere to live, she chose to become a live-in maid. But that option too, was fraught with problems because she was a girl. Shanti was unable to continue living in her employer's house at night for fear of being sexually molested. She thus had to sleep elsewhere in a neighbour's house, but, of course, this arrangement was at best a temporary one.

Her need for a permanent roof over her head pushed her into a marriage with an already married man. This man too, married her without a dowry only because he already had a first wife who was living. Before his first marriage, the marriage with Shanti had not been settled because of Shant's insistence that she could not marry someone who asked for a dowry. Presumably an 'eligible' boy does not get married under such circumstances. It is only after the circumstances became a little unfavourable for him and the situation for Shanti became acutely distressed that this marriage finally took place.

Even now, though this young girl of eighteen has a roof over her head, she is not free from worry. Her mother-in-law is the sole earning member with a regular salary, and she too, is a domestic servant with no job security. Her husband and father-in-law are largely unemployed. There are, in addition, three young brothers-in-law and a fourteen-year-old sister-in-law who has to be married off soon. Moreover, the first wife of her husband may be sent to live with them any time. The meagre income of the family can hardly feed so many mouths. So, Shanti will perhaps once again be forced to take up work as a domestic servant . Lacking any other skill, this is the only option open for her.

The only asset that Shanti had been able to retain, is her spirit, which gives her the strength to remain hopeful even in the face of such severe adversities. What is most tragic about Shanti's circumstances, is her naive belief that now at last she has a roof over her head—a secure shelter from which she cannot be summarily thrown out. What she does not realize is that with the first wife living, a second wife in a Hindu family is no wife at all and has absolutely no legal rights. This case once again focuses attention on the serious need for legal literacy among women.

EPILOGUE

A year later we went back to the slum. Shanti came running out to greet us. She had a baby in her arms. 'Bless my daughter, Didi,' she said. She took us by our hands and led us to her home. We were surprised to see her living at her foster mother's house. For a moment we were afraid that her husband had abandoned her. 'Don't you live with your in-laws Shanti?' we asked. " No, Didi, my husband and I live here now,' she said. Her husband's first wife had come back. Her in-laws had had to take her in, because, after all, she was their daughter-in-law. Their son had married her first. Besides, her own family refused to take responsibility for her anymore—and they had threatened to take legal action if she was not accepted by her in-laws. 'A man cannot live in the same house with two wives, can he? There would be bickering all the time. I do not like to quarrel with anyone, Didi. And so, I have moved here. At least now I shall have peace at home.'

What Shanti called 'home', was really only a very small room, constructed of tin, canvas, cardboard and straw, in one corner of the open verandah of her foster mother's house. She could not even stand up inside the room without bending. It was unthinkable, almost, that a family of three was residing in that tiny living space. But Shanti did not mind. In fact, she was almost abjectly grateful to her foster mother for letting her live in one corner of her house. 'Who else would do me such a great favour?' she asks. Shanti's husband apparently refuses to live with his first wife. This, in itself, was a source of pride and gratification for her. Her haven of peace was unthreatened, she felt.

Our worst fears had been realized. Shanti, innocent as she was, did not even realize that she was living in a fool's paradise. She really had no secure future to look forward to . Her husband, whom she considers her strength and support, might decide to desert her any day. Or, worse, if anything happened to him, Shanti and her daughter would have no claim whatsoever on his home or on his belongings. Her in-laws had been forced to accept their son's first wife simply because she had a legal identity as a married spouse. What was Shanti's identity? No one, not even the state or the law could protect her for being the second wife of a married man! Shanti would then be forced to fend for herself once again. She would also have to provide for her daughter. And once again, she would be plunged into a situation where there was no protection from unwanted attention and sexual molestation—the very set of circumstances she had hoped to escape with her marriage.

Even now, Shanti's husband has no permanent job. He occasionally obtains work in a part-time capacity. Already it had become difficult to run the household. Perhaps 'I will have to go back to my old job as a maidservant,' Shanti told us.' I have to take care of my daughter, after all.' It was ironic that marriage and family responsibilities were forcing her to take up once again, the job she hated. Time and again she would tell us how much she disliked working as a maidservant. She would entreat us every time she saw us to find her some kind of a decent job somewhere. She was willing to acquire any skill, she would say. With her indomitable spirit and her determination to learn, Shanti would have benefitted greatly from a training programme which would have given her the opportunity to learn a trade which might have helped her to eke out a living for herself and her family while retaining some sense of dignity. But, for the likes of Shanti, such opportunities are non-existent.

We asked Shanti the standard question: was she happy? Shanti smiled. Yes, she said, she was quite happy. She had a husband, a home, a child. Only, she wished her child had been born a son. 'How can you say such a thing, Shanti, a brave and courageous girl like you? You always used to say that girls were no less than boys.' 'No, Didi,' she said. 'Life is not easy for a girl. I only hope I can give my daughter a life in which she will not have to face as much pain and adversity as I have.' For a small moment she looked ineffably sad and vulnerable. But only for a fleeting instant. And then that unbeatable, dazzling smile was back on her face with optimism shining through.

Shanti's spirit was yet unbroken. But how much more strain would it have to bear? With so much character and resolve, will this girl ever get the opportunity to realize even a part of her potential? The chance to live a life of dignity and worth even at the minimum level of subsistence?

CONCLUSION

These questions loom large as we prepare to enter the twenty-first century with pomp and fanfare, with computers and high technology. Industrialization of the sort which will permit India to compete 'freely' in the world market has been identified as the magic wand which will transform us into a prosperous country. But when we plan and also when we assess our performance, we must take care that averages can be misleading. Sectorwise and groupwise planning and evaluation is of critical importance, otherwise it may take too long for the effects of this 'growth' to 'trickle down' to the really underprivileged. What will be the impact of our policies on employment? If negative, so much the worse. If some jobs are created, who will get these skilled jobs? Those with previous or on-the-job training. And will our Shantis get the opportunity to take such training? It is hardly likely, handicapped as they are by both class and gender. Employers do not want illiterate workers. nor do they want women, unless it is for some specific types of jobs which are monotonous, painstaking and particularly hazardous for health. Will even Shanti's daughter be able to get out of this vicious circle of poverty, ill health, low or no education and skill, unemployment and poverty?

This underlines the need for questions of discriminatory behaviour, of differential opportunity by gender, class, ethnicity or whatever, to be focussed and addressed as specific and special issues requiring specific and special policies and programmes for their solution. Nominal equal opportunities in a basically unequally structured society is no justice. It only helps to perpetuate the inequalities—sometimes even to accentuate them. Hence the need and demand for special programmes for training and employment of women and other underprivileged groups. This is not a demand for special status or special privileges, but rather a demand for effective similar opportunities for all. For this, steps need to be taken to counter-balance the initial systematic handicaps which certain groups, including women, are subject to. Unless some genuine breakthrough can be made in these directions, our Shantis, generation after generation, may continue to live battered lives at the edge of subsistence and in perpetual fear of going over the edge.

7
ACTION PROGRAMMES

TEACHING-CUM-LEARNING EXPERIENCE : KUSHTIA VILLAGE

What shall we call this programme? A literacy class? An informal education centre? Story-telling and poetry-reciting sessions? The setting up of a library? Maybe it shares the complex nature of all these functions to some degree. Maybe that is how it should be because these functions are never as effective and meaningful in isolation as they are in combination. It all started when a few children asked one of our investigators,'Didi, will you please help us with our studies?' The idea seemed a good one. It would also help our investigators to establish a rapport with the people in the village. A time was fixed in the evening. The panchayat pradhan was kind enough to let us use a room for this purpose; and the action programme was on.

The response from the children and parents was, in general, very encouraging. Within seven days the classroom was full. The majority of the children were in the age group 5-12 years. Older children were relatively few. Most of the children were from the scheduled castes and other castes. Initially there were no Muslim children. Later, our investigators, all young women, were able to persuade four Muslim girls to come to our 'school'. Once they joined, they continued to come as long as the young women were there.

The requirements of the children were varied. There were some who were attending school regularly and wanted help with their homework. There were other small children and some older girls, who were not going to school and wanted to learn the basics. Our investigators catered to these varied needs as best as they could within the limitations of the time at their disposal. It must have been useful because the number of children increased steadily.

A second dimension to the programme was initiated by the children themselves. After lessons one day the children said, 'Didi, please tell us a story.' The city-bred 'instructors' were, initially, quite at a loss as to what stories to tell, but they succumbed to their pleadings. Starting hesitantly with some fairy tales they had read and heard as children, very soon they themselves caught the infective enthusiasm of the children and found that they were enjoying the story-telling as much as the listeners were.

On their next visit to Calcutta, the young women took back with them, on their own initiative, children's books which they owned or had collected from friends and relatives for the little children. The eager appreciation and glow in the little faces when they saw these books, old and faded as some of them were, was enough recompense for whatever trouble had been taken in collecting and taking the books to Kushtia.

From then on, after lessons, there were regular sessions of recitation, story-telling, reading, singing—by the children as well as their teachers. It was a wholly participatory session with interjections, questions, comments and, of course, laughter.

This was an entirely different experience from reading by oneself. These group-reading sessions had a very significant impact on socialization. There was a sharing of experiences, emotions, thoughts and concerns, yielding a feeling of involvement and joy in the face of severe distress, economic or otherwise. It was like a breath of fresh air in their lives and, come hail or sunshine, they would flock to the 'classroom' in eager anticipation. If the investigators were tired out after the day's survey work or were slightly indisposed and told the children that there would be no class that day, the disappointment in their forlorn faces was so touching that they would have to relent.

As the days passed, the young women realized that it was a pity that along with the lessons, the general reading as well as the group-reading sessions would come to a halt as soon as the survey was over. So they decided to try lending a few books to see how the children would handle them. This led to the third dimension of the programme: the formation of the rudiments of a library. They found that the books which were lent out came back without any damage. In fact it was found that some books which were torn had been pasted together with loving care.

There were some children who could not read the books themselves but came to the 'school' to listen to these being read out. This was true for many older girls as well. Besides, everyone enjoyed the group-reading sessions so! Couldn't some elders be persuaded to arrange such sessions in their locality?

One family in Dhalipara (a scheduled caste settlement) had been taking an active interest in these activities all along in spite of their acutely distressed economic condition. The mother of the children, Aparna Dhali, had studied up to Class 5 and she agreed to let the children meet at her house, where she would read out to them from our books. And so, a beginning was made in this direction as well.

Soon the survey in Kushtia was over. It was time for the investigators to return. They decided to leave the books with someone from whom others could borrow and read. Perhaps the group-reading sessions could continue from time to time. We could visit Kushtia sometimes, give them more books and see how things were shaping. Perhaps this could be the beginning of an interactive process between our friends in Kushtia and ourselves, which would be of mutual benefit in fostering understanding and concern.

The books were left with Aparna Dhali. If the books were left with an upper caste Hindu family, the access of the scheduled caste children to them would be severely limited, not to speak of what the plight of the Muslim children would be. As it was, some children said that they would not be allowed to go to the Dhali house to borrow books because they were scheduled caste. The investigators explained that such behaviour was undesirable and intentionally left the books with the Dhalis to encourage and induce other children and their families to overcome their caste-based prejudices.

This programme was not gender-specific in the mechanical sense, since both boys and girls were participating in it. It could not have been done for girls alone. Besides, the problems involved and their solution, as we saw it, lay not in educating girls separately, for this would serve, in a way, to preserve the gender-based discrimination; but in treating girls and boys in a similar fashion so as to inculcate a feeling of equality in both. We wished to orient the children and elders towards treating boys and girls as children rather than in a gender-specific fashion; to focus on the need for the same facilities, attention, choices and opportunities for boys and girls, rather than on segregated courses and programmes.

From this angle, the programme was effective. The girl children were quite moved that the young women from the city were giving them equal importance and care as their brothers. Many of those girls who were initially somewhat inhibited and shy soon became free and confident and took part in the different activities.

The boys, whose sisters had not come to the 'school' to start with, were encouraged to bring their sisters with them. And in their eagerness to please the teachers many boys did actually do so. Later the mothers themselves showed eagerness in sending their daughters.

Our investigators found out that it was quite common for some boys to beat their sisters, and so they brought this matter up in 'class' and explained that this was not how good children behaved. Soon the children themselves started pointing out which boy had been seen ill-treating his sisters and the boy concerned felt ashamed of his behaviour, perhaps for the first time in his life,

and promised not to do so again. Other forms of social discrimination were also addressed. Initially, children from the Hindu
families (except the scheduled caste) refused to sit next to the
Muslim children. Force and persuasion had to be used to make
the children sit together. The children would not address the
Muslim girls by name—they insisted on referring to them as
'Mullah's daughters'. It took a lot of effort to get them to call the
girls by their names.

One day a child's slippers were found to be missing. The
children said they knew who had taken them. The investigator
announced in class that unless the slippers were returned no
more classes would be held. The slippers were returned the next
day. There are many such examples of incidents that reveal the
genuinely educative impact of such activities. And the good thing
was that the children complied with these changed behavioural
norms, not out of fear but because of the joyous experience which
they cherished.

Another very positive aspect of the entire programme was that
it was genuinely interactive. The young women from the city
received much more joy perhaps than they gave. A bond was
created which, for some young women, lived on even after the
survey was over and they were no longer working for our project.
They would visit Kushtia on their own initiative, and the people
would come over to visit them. The proximity to Calcutta has been
an enabling factor, of course, but the interest and involvement
had to be created.

EPILOGUE

In February 1992 we visited Kushtia again and took some new
books for the children. The enthusiasm with which many of our
little respondents came running to meet us, as soon as they heard
of our arrival, was a joy to see. The books, which we had left with
them earlier, were in the same good condition that they had been
when given to them. The new books were received with a lot of
interest and would liven things up, one would expect.

AWARENESS-GENERATION IN PHULMALANCHA

AN IMMUNIZATION CAMP

Phulmalancha is spread out over a large area. The different *paras*
or localities are situated at substantial distances from one another. It is also a very poor region, with a generally low standard
of living and inadequate infrastructural facilities. During our
survey it was observed that among other things, the health care

situation was bad with regard to both awareness and facilities. In particular, for example, the immunization rates left much to be desired. Many mothers did not know about this basic health care requirement. Others complained that immunization camps which were held in the area were often quite a distance away from their areas and information about these camps did not reach them till it was too late. Hence the immunization drive had not really caught on in this area.

Taking their cue from this need the investigators arranged with the health centre nearby to organize an immunization camp in Phulmalancha while our survey was on and took care to see that prior information about this camp reached the far-off paras as well. Efforts to generate awareness about the critical need for immunization were also made. The investigators received enthusiastic and active help from the panchayat pradhan and his entire staff. The camp was a success. But the more important and lasting effect that was expected was that the problem of the information gap had been identified and it was hoped that future camps would no longer be crippled because of it.

THE KRISHAK SABHA OR FARMERS' MEETING

The investigators were surprised when the panchayat pradhan asked them to address a meeting of the Krishak Sabha. 'What would we talk about?' they asked. 'About your survey and about your experience in our village,' he replied. 'But our survey is about girl children and women. Will the men be willing to listen at all?' 'Yes, Didi. We want to know more about our womenfolk. We want to learn about their condition and their problems. There is so little understanding about these matters,' he said.

This was indeed a surprise. Phulmalancha was the least developed of all the villages that we had surveyed: not only in terms of the physical assets that it held but also with respect to the status of women. In a village with a large Muslim population, as well as a relatively high proportion of scheduled caste and scheduled tribe households, the women were backward and downtrodden and suffered a multitude of indignities that were the consequence of poverty, lack of education and awareness, and years of social conditioning biased against the women. That is why we were a little sceptical about our reception at the Krishak Sabha which would be attended chiefly by men.

Our fears were reinforced when we reached the venue. It was a large gathering of farmers and there was not a single woman in sight. We were sure that the men would not be very pleased with whatever we had to say. After all, we would be talking about issues such as discrimination against the girl child, the preferential treatment of boys, and the men's lack of concern about the condition that their women lived in. These were serious allegations and concerned issues which many considered personal. There was every possibility that the men would take offence at our interference. Besides, we were city-bred strangers. The men might very well feel that we could comprehend little, if at all, of the magnitude of their problems.

The men, however, greeted us with enthusiasm. What had we found in our survery? The discussion began informally. We first explained to them the purpose of our survey and then talked about our findings. In Phulmalancha we had found that girls were looked upon as inferior to boys. In fact, a man who had only daughters was considered to be childless and his wife sterile. Why did they think so? The men, fathers and grandfathers, most of them, seemed taken aback. 'Of course, daughters are inferior. They bring nothing to the family but additional expenditure. Not only in the form of their food and clothing but also in the form of the dowry that had to be provided when they reached a marriageable age. After all, a daughter would never look after her parents in their old age. But a son? Why, a son was the only asset that they had!' When we pointed out that girls, too, did a lot of important work, and in fact, looked after their parents as much as boys did, the men were at first slow to grasp the concept. They had never, so far, considered women's work to be important at all. What would they do without wives and daughters to run their households? Who would cook their meals? Who would fetch water? Whom would they call upon when they needed additional help in their fields? Who, indeed, would give them their sons? These were questions that they had never asked themselves.

Though the women in Phulmalancha did a lot of useful productive work, such as preparing *muri* (puffed rice), husking paddy, weaving and knitting, their work was never accorded its due value because it was the men who sold the products made at home by the women and the money came directly to them and they considered it to be part of their own income. The women's role was, therefore, quickly forgotten.

We told them that the women could endeavour to sell their own products through voluntary agencies or by forming co-operatives for this purpose. If their worth was recognized in terms of the money they were able to earn, they would seem to be much less of a burden on their husbands and fathers. In fact, they might even be trained to do skilled work such as machine knitting or sewing which would give them an avenue for earning or a substantial income for themselves. The first step towards this was education.

This suggestion was greeted with a lot of enthusiasm. They had never quite thought about this matter in this way, they told us. The panchayat pradhan, in fact, admitted that a lot of the state grant earmarked for women often had to be returned unspent because they could never think of a way in which to spend it usefully. He made a commitment then and there that he would henceforth put that money to use in training women and in evolving ways and means to market products that they made at home.

Another important issue that was addressed was in connection with women's health. The men agreed that they had never really given serious thought to the health of their wives and daughters at home. They accepted as natural the accordance of higher status to themselves, men and boys, that is, within the household and so found nothing unusual in the fact that they were given better or more food than the women and the girls. After all, they did hard labour in the fields all day. Women did not have to go out at all. It had never occurred to them that women had to work as hard within the house as the men had to work outside. Also, women's work was never confined to the house exclusively. They had to spend a lot of time outside, in activities such as fetching water, collecting fuel and fodder. Moreover, women too often had to work in the fields with the men. And at the end of the day the men usually had time to rest, which the women almost never did. Some men, who worked as agricultural labourers, and so were assured of one square meal, at least, during the day, confessed that they were aware that their wives often went without a full meal day after day; but they said they often did not admit this even to themselves. After all, they had no means of solving the problem. However, the majority said that they now realized that their inconsiderate behaviour was taking its toll on the health of the women and the girls at home. They promised to be more vigilant about this in the future.

Another factor that greatly influenced the health of these women was the burden of frequent childbirth. Since there was great social pressure to produce sons, and many of them, women often had a child every year, and this affected their health adversely. The lack of information about family planning measures and religious-cum-social prejudice against birth control in most of the families further compounded the problem. The men, too, admitted the seriousness of the problem. No one, they said, had ever talked to them openly about these issues, and so, they had not been able to take their queries to anyone who might offer a solution. The Muslims admitted that their religion forbade birth control altogether. The mullahs had told them that if they resorted to such heathen practices they would be barred from entering paradise after death. In fact, no one would even agree to bury them. The investigators talked to them about natural birth control measures and explained the basic ideas of the rhythm method of contraception. So interested were they that they even wrote down much of what was said. Moreover, during the rest of our survey in the village, men and women alike would come to seek information and advice in this regard. Interest and motivation had been generated. The people of Phulmalancha would now be more receptive to the ideas and suggestions coming from health-care workers, doctors and nurses who were competent to give them proper advice on these matters.

EPILOGUE: A DOCTOR IN THE VILLAGE

We went back to Phulmalancha nearly a year after our survey had been completed with a well-known woman gynaecologist, Dr. Arati Basu Sengupta. We had told the panchayat pradhan ahead that she would be accompanying us and had requested him to arrange a meeting of women, girls and paramedical personnel in the village. Consequently there was a large gathering of women and girls in the panchayat office when we arrived. Dr. Basu Sengupta talked to the women about practical methods of health care in the absence of trained medical personnel or necessary medical provisions such as antiseptics and sterile instruments for childbirth. She told the women that they could boil neem (margosa) leaves in water and use this as antiseptic solution during childbirth. The women were invited and encouraged to ask questions, and soon they overcame their shyness and asked many relevant questions about menstruation, contraception, childbirth and menopause. Dr. Basu Sengupta took great care to explain in simple language the precautions and remedies that they could avail of, and also advised them as to situations when a doctor's advice was needed immediately. Traditional *dais* (midwives) were also present in the gathering and they said that they had benefitted greatly from their discussion with Dr. Basu Sengupta.

Dr. Basu Sengupta also impressed upon the men the need to be aware about women's health problems. For instance, she spelt out clearly what a woman should or should not be allowed to do during her pregnancy, and immediately after childbirth. A woman should not be permitted to lift heavy things, fetch water or do strenuous work like mopping the floor when she was pregnant.

Not only would this be bad for her health but it would also harm the foetus. This was news to the men present. The pradhan himself admitted that they were under the impression that such strenuous activities were actually beneficial to a pregnant woman because these helped to ensure an easy delivery. When we were leaving, the women and the men entreated that we return soon. They had a lot more questions to ask; they had a great many things to learn.

Work in Phulmalancha continues. Shibani Barik, one of the women in the village who had become a constant companion to the investigators, came to Calcutta on our advice and enrolled in an auxiliary nursing course, 'Artasangee', organized by the School of Women's Studies, Jadavpur University. Shibani completed the course and returned to the village where her work is indispensable.

CONCLUSION

We would like to draw attention to some of the interesting findings from our survey, which are:

- No case of amniocentesis was found in our sample. Sex-determination methods had been practised only in a few tribal households (45 in number), and these were traditional techniques, which were not really practised seriously.
- About 43 percent of the mothers were not given ATS and 44 percent did not have any check-ups during pregnancy.
- More than 40 percent of the respondent girl children had not received any kind of immunization.
- Inadequate breastfeeding is not a problem. The problem, rather, is that of nutritional deficiency of lactating mothers.

Significant discrimination in the matter of food distribution within the family has not been revealed through our survey. Some discrimination with respect to the quality and the kind of food has been observed. It has been our experience, however, that when there was a rapport with the girl child, casual conversation with her away from her family members, revealed in many cases that she did suffer from additional deprivation, sometimes quite severe, as compared to her brothers. When a direct question was posed, however, or when she was in her family environment, the large majority of girl children denied any deprivation, discriminatory or otherwise. The reason was that she had been taught to believe that such circumstances were 'natural' and 'normal'—and that complaints in such matters were frowned upon. She had also learnt effectively what the 'right' answers to these questions would be. A similar situation prevailed in the matters of disease and treatment. No discrimination was admitted, but relative neglect of the girl child and greater concern for the son came out clearly in conversation with the mother and other family members.

In our sample of 600 girls, 32 percent were illiterate. Around 18 percent had never been enrolled in school while 17 percent had dropped out. The maximum proportion of drop-outs was from Class 1.

The major reasons responsible for non-enrolment were :

(i) Poverty and the need to do income-earning work: 32.8 percent (36 girls out of 110);

(ii) Housework and care of siblings: 21.8 percent (24 girls out of 110);

(iii) Traditional belief about girls' role and consequent lack of interest in girls education: 1·0 percent (11 girls out of 110);

(iv) Girl child's lack of motivation and low self-image: 6.4 percent (7 girls out of 110);

(v) Parents' addiction to liquour, gambling, and so on: 16 percent (18 girls out of 110).

The major reasons for drop-out were :

(i) Poverty and need to do income earning work: 30.3 percent (30 girls out of 99);

(ii) Housework and care of siblings: 24.2 percent (24 girls out of 99);

(iii) Traditional belief about girls' role in life and consequent lack of interest in girls' education: 6.1 percent (6 girls out of 99);

(iv) Early marriage: 5.1 percent (5 girls out of 99);

(v) Girl child's lack of motivation and low self-image: 8.1 percent (8 girls out of 99);

(vi) Fear of examinations and failure in examination 7.1 percent (7 girls out of 99);

(vii) Teachers too harsh: 9.1 percent (9 girls out of 99).

The availability of schools does not emerge as any significant problem. But their usefulness is seriously jeopardized by:

(i) The official programme for free distribution of books, and so on, is largely ineffective, as these books do not reach the children. Among those who attended or have ever attended school, 70 percent said that books and other learning material were provided by their parents. Only 24 percent said that the schools or the panchayats gave them some books.

(ii) Around 44 percent of the girls who ever attended school said that they had tutors at home to help them with their studies, and this is from a sample of low- and middle-income group households, two-thirds of which are from the rural sector. This is a matter for concern, for our school system and the quality and nature of teaching must be linked to this phenomenon.

(iii) Infrastructure, such as a library, is lacking to an extremely severe degree.

About 25 percent of those currently enrolled wanted a graduate level education; 19 percent wanted a school-leaving or Higher Secondary level education; 17 percent aimed at postgraduation or a professional degree and 19 percent said that they would like to study up to the level that they will be permitted. It is heartening to know that even among girls in this socioeconomic group, a good many of those who are in school wish to complete school education and a large number wish to acquire a graduate or even postgraduate level of education. Only 3 percent would be content with literacy alone.

With regard to the advantage of being literate, 49 percent spoke about its help in personal development, acquiring self-confidence, better communication ability and good manners. Only 18 percent connected literacy with career advancement and better job prospects. On the disadvantages of being illiterate also, 52 percent referred to low self-image, personal frustration and problems in coping with day to day work. As compared to this, only 8 percent connected illiteracy with lesser job opportunities and lower level of employment. It is a healthy sign that education is being seen here in its broader, personality-forming aspect, not as a technical skill improving earning potential. Unfortunately, as we move up to the more affluent, elite and so-called educated sections of society, the mechanical approach becomes the more common. Another aspect, however, must be borne in mind when we observe that the girl children did not connect education with job opportunities. Such a linkage was not understood because it did not exist in their lives. Unless we are able to give the girls who do acquire education some job openings and not let marriage remain as the only option open to them, the chances of education for the girl child are not likely to improve.

Forty percent of the girl children would choose an income-earning career if they had a choice in the matter; but only about 20 percent felt that their parents would encourage them to do so.

Out of 600 girl children there were 72, or 12 percent, who were working girls, of whom 28 were agricultural labourers and 17 were workers in home-based industries. Out of these 72 working girls, 12 received no individual payment for their work in cash or in kind—the elders in their families got the payment for the work done by all family members. No working girl earned more than Rs.500 per month, and 43 percent (25 girls out of 60) earned less than Rs.200 per month.

Out of the 600 girls, 290 had acquired no skills. The others were skilled in typical feminine activities like stitching, embroidery, knitting (the majority); some in music, dance and painting (urban areas mostly); and about 6 percent in food processing and allied activities (rural areas). This is in conformity with parental expectations. Only 9 percent, however, used their skills for economic benefit, mostly in the rural areas.

Gender-based role stereotyping is almost complete: cooking, cleaning, washing and care of children were all exclusively done by women and girls; fetching fuel and water were done by girls to a much greater extent than boys; while running errands and going to the market were done by boys.

There were birth rituals for boys alone in only 2 percent cases, and more elaborate rituals for boys in about 9 percent cases.

About 35 percent girls listened to the radio regularly and 22 percent sometimes, which gave a total of 57 percent. Television viewership also was quite substantial, with 33 percent watching television regularly and 15 percent sometimes, a total of 48 percent. The audio-visual media, therefore, is likely to have a significant influence on the perceptions, thinking and personality of the girl child. But what did she hear and see? Favourite radio programmes were film songs, plays or serials and musical programmes. Around 4 percent listened to news-oriented programmes. Only 1 out of 600 listened to children's programmes and not even one to educational or women's programmes. On television, film songs topped the list. Then came plays, serials and films. There was almost no viewership of children's or educational programmes. This clearly indicates the need for changes in programme format and orientation to capture the interest of target groups.

From the responses of the mothers it appeared that their ambitions for their daughters followed traditional norms: the majority wanted them to be housewives. Most mothers also wanted their daughters to be married early.

These are some of the features of the life of the girl child which emerge from our survey. We get a picture of the girl child pre-conditioned to see herself as a 'sojouner' in her parents' home. She is told from childhood that her husband's house is her true home and that she will be married as soon as she grows up. As a result, she is never given a chance to consider herself a member of her parental home and is in turn regarded as a liability by her parents. Denied a sense of belonging to the family in which she is born and reared, she is treated and learns to think of herself, as the lesser child. Her needs are dispensable and in a scarcity situation, the first to be sacrificed.

In later life she is to adopt her husband's family as her own, simply as his wife; usually, this will be the only identity permitted her. In preparation for this role, her individuality is stunted from childhood. She is taught to be submissive, docile and adjustable. Her education is not considered important. She is not encouraged to develop her individual potentials.

And yet, given half a chance, she is capable of the best that any individual can achieve. Many of our case studies reflect this potential. Others show how the family, and through it society, guillotines this potential from early childhood in the name of conforming to accepted norms and traditions regarding gender roles. The girl child of our study is located in West Bengal and interesting comparisons may be possible with the girl child in other parts of India and also in other countries. There will be some regional specificities in her circumstances side by side with significant common traits. To facilitate such comparisons, and also to get a better understanding of the life of the girl child in our region, more detailed study is needed of the regional survey results.

The data collected in our survey have not been adequately utilized as yet. The analysis is fully aggregative. Even variations which may exist between different groups within the sample, such as those based on income, occupation, religion, caste, and so on, have not been worked out. A study of the girl child-to-household link, with a view to identifying the progressive and retrogressive factors that operate on the life of the girl child, has not been carried out. Many questions remain unaddressed. All these questions cannot be analysed on the basis of the present survey, but many can. The data have been collected and provide us with material for future research in relevant areas.

SURVEY TEAM

JOINT COORDINATORS   Jasodhara Bagchi and Jaba Guha

TRANSLATION OF THE QUESTIONNAIRE   Chandreyee Niyogi

THE SURVEY RESEARCH INVESTIGATORS
Grade 1 Baby Das
Grade 2 Piyali Sengupta, Chandreyee Niyogi, Sarmistha Deb,
         Ishita Chakraborty, Sarmita Chatterjee, Sarmistha De

CODING   Piyali Sengupta, Sarmistha Deb, Ishita Chakraborty,
         Sarmita Chatterjee, Sarmistha De, Damayanti Sen,
         Debjani Dasgupta, Sudeshna Pal, Runa Sinha, Subroto
         Sarkar, Paramita Chattopadhyay, Mousumi Ghosh
         Dastidar, Ruma Adhikari, Suparna De, Indrila Guha,
         Baidarbhi Chatterjee, Rachel Weber, Shibani Banerjee
         Chakravarty, Sarbani Goswami, Abhijit Sen

PREPARATION OF TABLES   Piyali Sengupta, Debjani Dasgupta,
                        Nandini Mukherjee

INDEX